"Mathewson gifts us with a gold mine of insights into Old Testament narrative. He expertly guides pastors on how to approach a text, prepare a message, and deliver a sermon. There are resources for going as deep as one wants or can, from biblical examples and sample sermons to an introduction to Hebrew discourse and select bibliographies for many Old Testament books. Let's bring the Old Testament to life and into lives! Here is an able guide."

—**M. Daniel Carroll R. (Rodas)**, Wheaton College

"Just about twenty years ago, Baker Academic wisely published Mathewson's fine book *The Art of Preaching Old Testament Narrative*. It has helped to instruct, inspire, and guide at least two generations of preachers on how to handle some of the most engaging portions of God's Word as they speak to God's people. Now we're blessed to have the newly minted second edition, and it's even better than the first. Mathewson has gone the extra mile to skillfully incorporate much of the exegetical and homiletical work that has been done on this biblical genre over the past two decades. The result is a book that is fuller, richer, and even more valuable than the original. I can't recommend it enough to pastors, professors, and preachers who seek to communicate these narratives in an accurate, clear, and compelling way!"

—**Scott Wenig**, Denver Seminary

"Mathewson brilliantly delivers the wealth of his experience preaching Old Testament narrative. It's quickly clear you're learning from a master of preaching who loves the biblical text and the hearers of God's Word. Mathewson writes in the same engaging manner in which he preaches, showing and not just telling. He interacts meaningfully with scholarly and literary works on Old Testament narrative literature. Whether you're a novice or highly experienced preacher, Mathewson offers valuable insights, resources, and examples to enhance your effectiveness and invigorate your desire and ability to preach narrative from the Old Testament. A must-read for students, pastors, preachers, and teachers of preaching."

—**Ingrid Faro**, Northern Seminary

"The same passion to communicate that eventually led to the incarnation, first drove God to dress up vast amounts of his self-revelation in the narratives of the Old Testament. This updated edition from Mathewson is a wonderful gift to every preacher: a guide to getting below the surface of these narratives along with coaching on how to preach them engagingly. This book combines exegetical skill, helping us to grasp the meaning of the text, with the wisdom of a seasoned preacher, encouraging us to communicate these texts effectively to others. God is a great communicator. God's heart is for you and your hearers. May this book guide you and those to whom you preach into the rich world of Old Testament narrative—a place where we can know ourselves better, but more importantly, a place where God reveals himself and points us forward toward Christ."

—**Peter Mead**, pastor of Trinity Chippenham (UK); director of Cor Deo

"Mathewson has written the go-to book on interpreting and preaching Old Testament narrative. Clear, insightful, and practical, it deserves a place on every preacher's bookshelf."

—**Darryl Dash**, pastor of Liberty Grace Church, Toronto, Ontario; author of *8 Habits for Growth*

The Art of Preaching
Old Testament Narrative

Second Edition

The Art of Preaching Old Testament Narrative

Steven D. Mathewson

Foreword by Haddon W. Robinson

a division of Baker Publishing Group
Grand Rapids, Michigan

© 2002, 2021 by Steven D. Mathewson

Published by Baker Academic
a division of Baker Publishing Group
PO Box 6287, Grand Rapids, MI 49516-6287
www.bakeracademic.com

Printed in the United States of America

All rights reserved. No part of this publication may be reproduced, stored in a retrieval system, or transmitted in any form or by any means—for example, electronic, photocopy, recording—without the prior written permission of the publisher. The only exception is brief quotations in printed reviews.

Library of Congress Cataloging-in-Publication Data
Names: Mathewson, Steven D. (Steven Dale), 1961– author.
Title: The art of preaching Old Testament narrative / Steven D. Mathewson.
Description: Second edition. | Grand Rapids, Michigan : Baker Academic, a division of Baker Publishing Group, [2021] | Includes bibliographical references and index.
Identifiers: LCCN 2021004454 | ISBN 9781540962027 (paperback) | ISBN 9781540964311 (casebound) | ISBN 9781493430871 (ebook)
Subjects: LCSH: Bible. Old Testament—Homiletical use. | Bible. Old Testament—Sermons.
Classification: LCC BS1191.5 .M38 2021 | DDC 221—dc23
LC record available at https://lccn.loc.gov/2021004454

Unless otherwise indicated, Scripture quotations are from THE HOLY BIBLE, NEW INTERNATIONAL VERSION®, NIV® Copyright © 1973, 1978, 1984, 2011 by Biblica, Inc.® Used by permission. All rights reserved worldwide.

Scripture quotations labeled ESV are from The Holy Bible, English Standard Version® (ESV®), copyright © 2001 by Crossway, a publishing ministry of Good News Publishers. Used by permission. All rights reserved. ESV Text Edition: 2016

Scripture quotations labeled KJV are from the King James Version of the Bible.

Scripture quotations labeled NASB are from the New American Standard Bible® (NASB), copyright © 1960, 1962, 1963, 1968, 1971, 1972, 1973, 1975, 1977, 1995 by The Lockman Foundation. Used by permission. www.Lockman.org

In keeping with biblical principles of creation stewardship, Baker Publishing Group advocates the responsible use of our natural resources. As a member of the Green Press Initiative, our company uses recycled paper when possible. The text paper of this book is composed in part of post-consumer waste.

21 22 23 24 25 26 27   7 6 5 4 3 2 1

To my wife,
Priscilla,
whose love for Jesus has stirred my own devotion
to him and whose love for me still fills up my senses

And to my parents,
Maynard† and Ruth Mathewson,
whose insistence that "God is still good"
during their respective struggles with cancer
has strengthened my trust in him

Contents

Illustrations xi
Foreword to the First Edition *by Haddon W. Robinson* xiii
Preface xv
Acknowledgments xix

Part 1 Preparing to Preach

1. The Challenge of Preaching Old Testament Narratives 3
2. The Christ-Centered Preaching Debate 15

Part 2 From Text to Concept

3. The Journey Begins 29
4. *A* is for Action 41
5. *C* is for Characters 65
6. *T* is for Talking 75
7. *S* is for Setting 81
8. Drawing Conclusions 87

Part 3 From Concept to Sermon

9. Starting the Second Half of the Adventure 107
10. Adding the Finishing Touches 121

11. Shaping the Sermon   127
12. Outlining the Sermon   137
13. Mastering the Storyteller's Craft   147
14. Entering and Exiting   165
15. Delivering the Goods   171

Appendix A: Sample Sermon on Judges 17–18   179
Appendix B: Using Hebrew in Narrative Exegesis   193
Appendix C: Commentaries for Narrative Exegesis   221
Bibliography   229
Scripture Index   243
Subject Index   246

Illustrations

Discourse Layouts
 B.1 Genesis 38 (Hebrew)   208
 B.2 Genesis 38 (ESV)   211
 B.3 Joshua 1 (Hebrew)   215
 B.4 Joshua 1 (ESV)   216

Figures
 9.1 The Process of Application   116
 11.1 Types of Reasoning   129

Tables
 1.1 Robinson's Stages of Sermon Preparation   13
 4.1 Elements in the Plot   43
 4.2 Ryken's List of Plot Motifs   47
 4.3 Culley's List of Action Sequences   49
 4.4 Narrated (Actual) Time vs. Narration Time   53
 4.5 Points of View   56
 4.6 Indicators of Shifts in Focalization   57
 4.7 Three Types of Irony   58

4.8 Dorsey's Chiastic Structure of Judges 3–16   61

4.9 Fokkelman's Chiastic Structure of Genesis 11:1–9   62

5.1 Types of Characters in Old Testament Stories   66

5.2 Character Classification in Genesis 38   67

8.1 A Summary of Features to Examine in Old Testament Narratives   88

8.2 Works on Old Testament Narrative Literature   89

8.3 Components of a Big Idea   91

8.4 Expressions of the Big Idea   94

8.5 Range of Possibilities for Making an Element Timeless (2 Sam. 11–12)   98

10.1 Big Idea Development in Genesis 13   124

12.1 Tips for Effective Outlines   138

14.1 Marks of an Effective Introduction   166

15.1 Preparing to Preach without Notes   172

B.1 Notations Used in Discourse Analysis   196

B.2 A Clause Taxonomy for Biblical Hebrew Narrative   197

B.3 A Color Scheme for Verb Identification   206

Foreword to the First Edition

My grandmother lived in Northern Ireland, and I visited her once when I was a lad about eight years old. When I met her, she was wrinkled, had snowy white hair, and stooped a bit under the weight of her years. I felt I knew my grandmother. She was that thin old lady who gave me cookies and told me how much I resembled my grandfather who had died many years ago. Recently, I visited Ireland again and talked with cousins who knew my grandmother far better than I. They pulled out faded yellow photographs of grandma when she was a girl and later when she was first married. They shared their memories based on knowing her much longer than I did. I came away from that second visit wondering if I ever really knew my grandmother at all.

For many modern readers, the Old Testament narratives resemble my memories of my grandmother. We know them, but then again we hardly know them at all. Some of us grew up hearing these stories, and they form part of our memory bank. We listened to them at home curled up in a parent's lap, or we saw them pasted on flannelgraph boards in Sunday school, our short legs dangling from the big chairs. We identified with David, the brash teenager with slingshot in hand, taking on Goliath, who resembled the bully at our grade school. We smirked at the neighbors who mocked Noah and his boys for building a boat miles from the nearest lake because we knew how the story came out, and we decided the moral was not to laugh at someone doing something strange because you might need them later on if you were drowning in a flood. We pictured Moses and Aaron battling Pharaoh much like the Lone Ranger and Tonto standing up against the bad guys, or we admired Daniel taming the lions in their den at the zoo. We knew these stories well, but we may not have known them at all! Because we thought of them as simple little stories, we missed how thick they were with meaning.

In recent years, many literary critics, both Christian and Jewish, have also read the stories again for the first time. Instead of regarding the narratives as cadavers to be dissected and "demythologized," they began to approach them for what they are—sophisticated literature of great significance and splendid power.

Because narrative makes up the dominant genre of the Old Testament, biblical preachers need to revisit those narratives. As adults, we can look at the stories with fresh eyes, and we can develop an appreciation for the skill of the authors who composed them. They were not only corking good storytellers, but they were also brilliant theologians who taught their readers about God through stories. We can read these old, old stories in a new way and sense how much they speak to the condition of modern hearers. More than that, we can see God through them.

One of the strongest reasons for a serious and fresh study of Old Testament narratives is reflected in the sad history of what happens when we misread them, read them poorly, or read them to prove a point outside the purpose of the biblical storyteller. In fact, the more committed we are to the authority of Scripture, the more dangerous it is to read the narratives incorrectly. There is no greater abuse of the Bible than to proclaim in God's name what God is not saying. God commands us not to bear false witness.

In this book, Steve Mathewson helps us to read Old Testament narratives perceptively. As you study them, you will realize they are not quaint tales crafted to teach children simple moral lessons. They are great literature, every bit as powerful as Homer, Milton, Shakespeare, or Hemingway. And as God-breathed literature, they speak to the entire person. I commend Steve Mathewson as a thoughtful guide to help us get a handle on the great stories of the Bible. I also commend him as a preacher who provides some very workable leads on how to effectively communicate these stories to modern listeners.

Haddon W. Robinson

Preface

I remember my fledgling attempt to preach through an Old Testament narrative book. In 1988, my second year of pastoral ministry, I decided to take my congregation (read: victims) through 1 and 2 Samuel. Coincidentally, I was reading John Steinbeck's novel *East of Eden*. A scene in *East of Eden* forced me to admit my ineptness at preaching the stories of the Old Testament. Three men are sitting at a table and discussing the Cain-Abel story in Genesis 4. Lee, Adam Trask's pig-tailed Chinese cook, pinpoints the genius of Hebrew narrative during the exchange with Adam and a neighbor, Samuel Hamilton. Lee argues, "No story has power, nor will it last, unless we feel in ourselves that it is true and true of us."[1] He concludes, "A great and lasting story is about everyone or it will not last. The strange and foreign is not interesting—only the deeply personal and familiar."[2]

I thought about the sermon I preached the previous Sunday from 1 Samuel 7. Did people leave with a sense that the story was about them? I had to admit they probably did not. After the worship service, a parishioner had approached and asked me to repeat point number three. I had presented the point too quickly for those taking notes. "Uh, point number three was 'The Resulting Prosperity of God's People' from verses twelve through seventeen," I said.

1. Steinbeck, *East of Eden*, 268.
2. Steinbeck, *East of Eden*, 270.

I had preached a sermon chock-full of exegetical insights and laced with historical-cultural data. I even pressed it into a neat analytical outline. But my sermon did not do justice to the purpose of Old Testament stories: to lure people into real-life dramas where they run smack into God's agenda and his assessment of their lives. Instead, I had created more interest in acquiring an outline of the story.

This experience, along with the conversation in Steinbeck's novel, prompted a quest to raise my level of preaching in Old Testament narrative texts. I invite you to join me in learning how to preach the narrative literature in the Old Testament. I have returned to these texts often in more than three decades of pastoral ministry and preaching.

You deserve to know a little bit about my journey in studying and preaching Old Testament stories. This will help you decide if you want me to serve as a mentor. My journey began in the spring of 1986 when I served as a teaching assistant in Hebrew grammar and exegesis to Dr. Ronald B. Allen at Western Seminary in Portland, Oregon. My esteemed professor asked me to fill in for him in his introductory Hebrew exegesis class and teach the lecture on "Exegesis in Hebrew Narrative Literature." This opportunity forced me to start thinking through a methodology for interpreting Old Testament narrative literature. I devoured Robert Alter's book *The Art of Biblical Narrative*, and the journey gained momentum. In fact, the title of my book that you're reading is a tip of the cap to his influence on my thinking. That same spring I completed a master's thesis on an Old Testament narrative text—Genesis 38.

Two years later, my first stab at preaching through an Old Testament narrative took place as I described it above. My struggles in preaching 1 Samuel propelled me further in my quest to learn how to preach Old Testament narratives effectively. I listened to homileticians like Haddon Robinson, Donald Sunukjian, and Paul Borden. I ordered their cassette tapes (remember those?!) and traveled to listen to them in person. I even had the nerve to write, email, and phone them for input. I cringe when I remember the sermon manuscripts from my 1 Samuel series that I sent to Paul Borden to solicit his input.

Eventually, I enrolled in a doctoral program in preaching at Gordon-Conwell Theological Seminary. My mentor was Haddon Robinson, and under his direction, I wrote my dissertation on preaching Old Testament narrative literature. That led to the first edition of this book.

Now, almost two decades later, I have the privilege of writing a second edition. I am grateful to Jim Kinney, executive vice president of Baker Publishing, for inviting me to do so. In the last two decades, I have not changed my basic approach to preaching Old Testament narrative texts, but I have had the opportunity to refine it. I have paid attention to my reviewers. In fact, one theological journal reviewed the first edition seventeen years after it was published! I have also had the opportunity to teach and learn from students at all levels of theological education—undergraduate level, master's level, and doctoral level—at Montana Bible College, Moody Bible Institute, Moody Theological Seminary, Denver Seminary, Trinity Evangelical Divinity School, Heritage Theological Seminary, and Western Seminary. I also enrolled in a PhD program in Biblical Hebrew at the University of Stellenbosch. It is a privilege to work directly with Christo van der Merwe—one of my early mentors from a distance two decades ago when I began applying linguistics to the study of Old Testament narrative texts. The Lord willing, I will finish my dissertation and graduate within a year of the publication of this second edition—and shortly after I turn sixty. Not every pastor needs to pursue a PhD, yet all of us need to be lifelong learners. I still have much to learn. In fact, I am confident I will be learning how to preach Old Testament stories until the day I die.

Most important, I've tried to practice what I preach. Or to be more precise, I've tried to preach what I practice. Over the past three decades of pastoral ministry, I have preached regularly in every narrative book or section of the Old Testament. As I said in the preface to the first edition, I am attempting to write the book I needed when I first started preaching. I have often wished that someone else would have written the book I needed, for though I work hard in the Hebrew Bible, I do not feel worthy to carry the armor of first-class Hebrew scholars. Likewise, I do not envision myself in the starting lineup with the Michael Jordans of modern preaching—both preachers and teachers of preachers. But in the sovereignty of God, he has given me abilities and interests in two fields: Old Testament exegesis and homiletics. I write, then, with a foot in both disciplines.

This volume consists of three parts. Part 1 will prepare you to preach, looking at some of the challenges we face, including how to think about preaching Christ from these texts. Part 2 will take you from text to concept—what we call the *hermeneutical* side of the task. It will teach you a method for studying Old Testament narrative texts. You can apply this method whether or not you can read biblical Hebrew. Then, part 3 will take you from concept to sermon—what we call the *homiletical* side of the task. This part of the book will help you take the raw exegetical material and craft a sermon that achieves accuracy, clarity, interest, and relevance. There are three appendices that provide (A) a sample sermon manuscript from an Old Testament narrative text, (B) instructions for using Hebrew in narrative exegesis, and (C) commentary suggestions for narrative exegesis.

If you're wondering about the differences between this second edition and the first edition, let me reiterate that my basic approach to interpreting and preaching Old Testament narrative texts has not changed. I have added a chapter titled "The Christ-Centered Preaching Debate." I did not deal with this sufficiently (in fact, hardly at all) in the first edition. Also, those who used the first edition will notice that the five sample sermon manuscripts are gone. Sample sermons—both manuscripts as well as audio and video—are more readily available than they were two decades ago. In order to streamline and tighten up this volume, I simply included a single sample manuscript in appendix A.

Finally, here's a personal word to my readers. I write as an evangelical pastor to other evangelical pastors and teachers who have the amazing privilege and awesome responsibility of proclaiming the Word of God to churches week after week. You are my heroes. We're in the trenches together, and I pray that I can help you. This means that I also write to pastors-in-training who are learning to preach. What a privilege to help shape a new generation of preachers. I hope I can help you get your hermeneutical and homiletical acts together in Old Testament stories a lot more quickly than I did. I also write with appreciation for those who communicate the Word of God in a variety of other settings, including Sunday School classes, small group Bible studies, and weekend retreats. The church needs all of you to exercise your preaching and teaching gifts well. I hope this volume helps you communicate Old Testament stories effectively.

Above all, I write for the glory of God, and his Son, Jesus Christ, the central character in the grand story of redemption. I am amazed at what God has provided for me through Jesus Christ. To God be the glory forever and ever.

Acknowledgments

A section of acknowledgments resembles the credits that roll at the end of a movie and don't seem terribly important to the viewer. As the reader, you can afford to skip these acknowledgments. As the writer, I cannot. I deeply appreciate the people who helped me turn my vision for this book into a reality.

It's easy to know where to start. I thank my dear wife, Priscilla, for her encouragement, support, and sacrifice. She never once complained to me about my preoccupation with this project and other writing projects. Her love for Jesus Christ, as well as her love for me, has had a profound impact on my life. Priscilla is the love of my life and the joy of my heart. I also thank my children and their spouses—Erin and Manny, Anna and Grant, Benjamin and Nicole, and Luke and Janzyn for their love, patience, support, and encouragement over the years. I pray that my love for and preaching of the stories of the Old Testament have contributed to their growth in the faith. I pray, too, that it will contribute to the faith of my grandchildren (seven so far).

I am grateful to Haddon Robinson for his interest in this project, as well as his input. Doing doctoral work in preaching under Haddon will rank as one of the greatest privileges of my life. I am a better man for God because of the time spent with such a brilliant, godly mentor.

I thank Paul Borden, Don Sunukjian, Alice Mathews, and Haddon Robinson for graciously sharing their sermon manuscripts with me for the first edition.

I am grateful for my Hebrew and Semitic language professors over the years: Ron Parkhurst, Jerry Vreeland, Ronald Allen, Ralph Alexander, Richard Averbeck (Ugaritic), and Christo van der Merwe (supervisor for my PhD studies).

Along the way, two congregations have given me time to research and write. More importantly, they have shared my vision for how my writing might help to enrich and equip other pastors. I am grateful for Dry Creek Bible Church (Belgrade, MT) and CrossLife Evangelical Free Church (Libertyville, IL).

I also want to thank Carmen Joy Imes for reading the draft of this second edition and providing invaluable feedback. This volume is much stronger because of her suggestions. I am grateful to Jennifer Hale of Baker Publishing for the fantastic work she did as project editor. I have already mentioned Jim Kinney's role in the publication of his volume, yet I want to express my appreciation for his patience and persistence as he encouraged me to complete this second edition.

At this point, I feel like the writer of Hebrews who did not have time to tell about other heroes of the faith at the end of a magnificent discussion (see Heb. 11:32). Like the writer of Hebrews, I, too, have run out of time—or space—in my acknowledgments. So I will simply list the names of others who have helped me, even though I wish I could tell the story behind their contributions. Here, then, are those who have helped me in some way, whether tracking down sources, offering feedback, or simply believing in this book: Jan Halvorson, Claudia Glover, Meredith Kline, Robert Stanbery, John Sailhamer, Warren Wiersbe, Dave Wyrtzen, Brian Larson, Tim Walton, Eric and Lisa Pierson, John Ramer, Eric Price, Thomas Middlebrook, Lance Higginbotham, and Jim Coakley. My three younger brothers each contributed input: David Mathewson, Mark Mathewson, and Kevin Mathewson.

Last, but hardly least, I thank my parents, Maynard and Ruth Mathewson, for modeling faithful and effective service of Christ through the thick and thin of pastoral ministry. The preacher who has had the greatest impact on my life is my father. I'm thankful he got to read the first edition a few months before cancer took his life. The final words I heard him say were, "No matter what happens, remember that God is good." This book has its roots in his commitment to preach the Word of God "in season and out of season" (2 Tim. 4:2).

Part 1

Preparing to Preach

1

The Challenge of Preaching Old Testament Narratives

People crave stories. Just watch folks sitting in an airline terminal waiting to catch a flight. Several are reading novels by the likes of Toni Morrisson, Cormac McCarthy, C. J. Box, or Marilynne Robinson—whether on a Kindle reader or in a hardback edition. Some of the passengers with earbuds are listening to biographies of Michelle Obama or Melania Trump. Another passenger fastens his eyes to his tablet, watching one of the three movies based on J. R. R. Tolkien's fantasy-adventure novel, *The Lord of the Rings*.

Other people tell stories or listen to someone tell them. A thirty-something mom tells her sister about a run-in with her son's fifth-grade teacher. A cluster of business professionals listen to a CEO describe how her company survived the economic downturn during the COVID-19 pandemic. A college student is on his phone, providing a friend with an animated account of a scene in the latest *Star Wars* movie.

When preachers open up the text of Scripture each Sunday morning, they speak to listeners whose "hearts traffic in stories." Indeed, our "very orientation to the world is fundamentally shaped by stories."[1] This is because "stories plant ideas and emotions into a listener's brain."[2] Yes,

---

1. Smith, *Imagining the Kingdom*, 108.
2. Gallo, *Talk Like TED*, 49.

listeners unknowingly get their theology from the stories they consume during the week. How does a preacher address boomers shaped by the "sermons" conveyed via news stories on Fox News or CNN? How does a Bible expositor communicate to millennials who come to church with scenes from a Netflix original dancing in their heads? How does a minister of the Gospel relate God's truth to the fourteen-year-olds who have fed on the sermons preached to them by the "stories" contained in their social media accounts?

The sheer number of stories in the Old Testament seems to give preachers an edge. According to the most conservative estimates, stories account for 30 to 40 percent of the Old Testament. Preachers can cash in on the stories of David, Ruth, Samson, and Jezebel when they stand before their video-saturated, story-driven congregations.[3] Theologian R. C. Sproul once said, "I'm big on preaching from narratives because people will listen ten times as hard to a story as they will to an abstract lesson."[4]

Unfortunately, it is not as simple as it seems. Preachers often neglect Old Testament narratives or, like beginners playing the saxophone, preach them poorly. Neither problem says much about our reverence for God's Word, let alone about our love for the people to whom God has called us to preach. As journalist Terry Mattingly observes, "Most people hear academic lectures at church, then turn to mass media to find inspiring tales of heroes and villains, triumph and tragedy, sin and redemption, heaven and hell."[5]

Preachers who take Scripture seriously must do better. Venerable preaching professor Haddon Robinson argues, "Anyone who loves the Bible must value the story, for whatever else the Bible is, it is a book of stories. Old Testament theology comes packaged in narratives of men and women who go running off to set up their handmade gods, and of others who take God seriously enough to bet their lives on Him."[6] Evangelicals have taken Old Testament stories seriously enough to defend their historicity. Now

---

3. As long ago as 1995, David L. Larsen argued, "This is the milieu and matrix for the explosive rebirth and renewal of interest in the story, a rekindling that has reached and powerfully shaken the world of Christian communication as well. Good storytellers are gurus in our society" (*Telling the Old*, 14–15). One wonders if preachers have made progress since then in capitalizing on the power of stories and storytellers.
4. Duduit, "Theology and Preaching in the 90s," 23.
5. Mattingly, "Star Wars."
6. Robinson, *Biblical Preaching*, 90.

it's time to learn to preach them effectively. While this volume focuses on Old Testament stories, readers can apply much of it to the stories in the Gospels and Acts.[7]

A Commitment to Expository Preaching

I am writing primarily for preachers who are committed to expository preaching. I want to help them do exposition in Old Testament narrative literature. By "expository preaching," I refer to preaching that exposes the meaning of a text of Scripture and applies that meaning to the lives of the hearers. Two well-known preaching professors supply helpful definitions.

> An expository sermon may be defined as a message whose structure and thought are developed from a biblical text, covering its scope, in order to explain how the features and context of the text disclose enduring principles for faithful thinking, living, and worship intended by the Spirit, who inspired the text. (Bryan Chapell)[8]

> Expository preaching is the communication of a biblical concept, derived from and transmitted through a historical, grammatical, and literary study of a passage in its context, which the Holy Spirit first applies to the personality and experience of the preacher, then through him to his hearers. (Haddon Robinson)[9]

When people finish listening to an expository sermon, they should understand the author's meaning and should even be able to track the development of the author's thought in the text. They should also have some idea of what the truth will look like fleshed out in their lives. Listeners who hear expository preaching week after week will get to think through books and major blocks of text. They will learn how to read the Scriptures for themselves, following the argument of a particular text. While a series of expository sermons may cover assorted passages on a particular theme, expositors generally work through individual books of the Bible or major sections in those books. The payoffs are tremendous.

---

7. However, there are issues unique to the Gospels. Preachers will do well to consult a source like Pennington, *Reading the Gospels Wisely*, and J. Brown, *Gospels as Stories*.
8. Chapell, *Christ-Centered Preaching*, 8–9.
9. Robinson, *Biblical Preaching*, 5.

As Tim Keller notes, expository preaching "expresses and unleashes our belief in the whole Bible as God's authoritative, living, and active Word."[10]

At its core, expository preaching is more of a philosophy than a method. That is, it amounts to a set of commitments or convictions rather than a particular method. Let me share a couple of convictions that expositors must bring to the task. Without these convictions, they are likely to pursue methods that sell short their efforts. While these convictions apply to preaching from any literary genre in the Bible, they are especially critical to preaching from Old Testament narratives.

1. Exposition is more than an exegetical lecture. A few expositors to whom I have listened seem to equate exposition with backing up the exegetical dump truck and unloading its contents on their congregations. They may even offer a running commentary on the text without any sense of unity. Hearers who exalt this style frequently describe it as "verse-by-verse teaching." Often, such hearers come from preaching-deficient backgrounds. They are so starved for God's Word that they are willing to receive raw data. They love baskets of exegetical nuggets, and they want preaching that squeezes every ounce of insight out of a Greek or Hebrew term. With this style of preaching, preachers can go until time runs out. It doesn't matter if they quit at verse 4, verse 7, or verse 16. There is no development of a flow of thought—simply a litany of exegetical insights.

Richard Mayhue clarifies that expository preaching "is not a commentary running from word to word and verse to verse without unity, outline, and pervasive drive." Furthermore, "it is not pure exegesis, no matter how scholarly, if it lacks a theme, thesis, outline, and development."[11]

While this approach hampers effective preaching of any literary genre in Scripture, it especially damns the preaching of Old Testament narratives. Stories unfold. Their ideas take time to develop and gel. Furthermore, their ideas may not be as highly concentrated as in other types of literature. In Old Testament narrative, it may take an entire chapter before the theological message of the text emerges. Colossians 3:1–11 is a great choice for a sermon text. Genesis 38:1–11 is not. The former text tells believers how to live as those who have been raised with Christ. However, the first eleven verses of Genesis 38 only provide the background necessary for understanding the story.

---

10. Keller, *Preaching*, 35.
11. Mayhue, "Rediscovering Expository Preaching," 10.

Another unfortunate side effect of reducing exposition to an exegetical lecture is a failure to engage the heart. According to Tim Keller, the neglect of persuasion or illustration or other ways to affect the heart may come "from an inaccurate reading of Paul's warnings in 1 Corinthians 1 and 2 against using 'human wisdom' in preaching." This neglect makes for preaching that is boring and unfaithful to the very purpose of preaching.[12]

2. *There is no form inherent in expository preaching.* Richard Mayhue is on target when he writes, "Exposition is not so much defined by the form of the message as it is by the source and process through which the message was formed."[13] To put it another way, there is no such thing as an expository sermon form. Ideally, the form should come from the text. As Sidney Greidanus argues, an expository sermon should let the biblical text provide clues for shaping the sermon.[14]

Thus, expositors who work in Old Testament narratives need to adjust their style and even discard the captioned survey approach (e.g., I. Abraham's Test, II. Abraham's Obedience, III. Abraham's Reward). We often pan this as the "three points and a poem" method. This style ends up working against rather than for the preacher who employs it when preaching a Bible story. We will return to this problem later in the chapter.

Why We Struggle with Old Testament Stories

Faithful preachers who may shine in Ephesians often preach poorly in 1 Samuel. Why do we struggle to preach Old Testament stories? Answering this question will help us get back on track. It will reveal areas that need adjustment. Several factors contribute to our poor performance in the pulpit when we open Scripture to an Old Testament narrative.

1. We view stories as fluff. Many churches teach Bible stories to children downstairs in the basement while the adults study Paul's epistles upstairs in the auditorium.[15] Wesley Kort explains why we often sell narrative short:

> Generally we hold narrative to be optional, to be a matter of taste rather than of necessity. We may even disdain narrative as a form of discourse

---

12. Keller, *Preaching*, 42.
13. Mayhue, "Rediscovering Expository Preaching," 11.
14. Greidanus, *Modern Preacher*, 18–20.
15. For a discussion of this problem, see Thomas, "Old Testament 'Folk Canon,'" 45–62.

more suited for children than for adults or more for ancient and otherwise underdeveloped people than for the educated and sophisticated. As modern and enlightened adults we have the strength to view our world as it is without the illusions and comforts of narrative wholes. We have little patience for narrative and are tempted to press for an enumeration of facts or a set of clearly and sharply formulated ideas.[16]

However, as N. T. Wright argues, "stories are one of the most basic modes of human life." They do not exist simply to illustrate a point. Wright says, "Stories are often wrongly regarded as a poor person's substitute for the 'real thing,' which is to be found either in some abstract truth or in statements about 'bare facts.'"[17] In fact, J. De Waal Dryden observes that a growing number of Old Testament scholars recognize "the strong wisdom agendas incorporated in these [Old Testament] narratives."[18]

As a result, Eugene Peterson challenges pastors who look down on stories: "Why is the story so often dismissed as not quite adult? Why, among earnest pastors, is the story looked down upon as not quite serious? It is ignorance, mostly. The story is the most adult form of language, the most serious form into which language can be put. Among pastors, who have particular responsibilities for keeping the words of Scripture active in the mind and memory of the faith communities, an appreciation for the story in which Scripture comes to us is imperative."[19]

2. *We get frustrated by the subtlety of narrative.* Old Testament narratives make their point in a subtle way. They typically "show" us rather than "tell" us. This indirect approach frustrates those who want a text to state its point in a direct way. Haddon Robinson asks, "Why didn't God just come right out and say what he meant and not beat around the bush with stories?"[20] This subtlety tends to lead to subjectivity. As Charles Dickson notes, "Interpreters perceive structures in narratives, episodes, and narrative units that are not supported by the text; they see structures in the text that are not there."[21]

16. Kort, *Story, Text, and Scripture*, 12–13.
17. N. T. Wright, *New Testament and the People of God*, 38.
18. Dryden, *Hermeneutic of Wisdom*, 101.
19. Peterson, *Working the Angles*, 119.
20. Robinson, "Heresy of Application," 310.
21. Dickson, *From Story Interpretation*, 239.

3. We minimize the role of Old Testament stories in the canon. In the past, some Bible expositors turned to the Old Testament and its narratives only for illustrations of new covenant truth.[22] However, David C. Deuel offers a needed corrective:

> Using Old Testament narrative *only* to illustrate New Testament teaching, however, results in ignoring much Old Testament instruction that may serve as background for New Testament theology, or else as teaching not repeated in the New Testament. Creation, law, and covenant are in Old Testament narrative which, if ignored or used for illustrations only, will create many problems of biblical imbalance. An adequate theological framework must include the whole Old Testament (cf. 2 Timothy 3:16, "All Scripture . . .").[23]

Iain Provan concurs when he says, "All historiography is also in some sense ideological literature. That is, any story about the past involves selection and interpretation by authors intent on persuading their readership in some way."[24]

More recently, influential pastor Andy Stanley has asked followers of Jesus to consider "unhitching your teaching of what it means to follow Jesus from all things old covenant," including its narratives, for the sake of the next generation's faith.[25] He claims that when we "anchor our story to an old covenant narrative and worldview, we lose our case in the marketplace. . . . In the real world. The world where science is gospel and folks are growing more and more skeptical of all things religious." Not only that, we end up with "the prosperity gospel, the crusades, anti-Semitism, legalism, exclusivism, judgmentalism," and all sorts of "isms."[26] However, it is completely unacceptable for believers to unhitch their Christian faith from the Bible Jesus read. There is a better way to address Stanley's

---

22. For example, see MacArthur, "Frequently Asked Questions," 341–42. Two decades later, in a sermon on Christ in the Old Testament, MacArthur suggested that preaching on Christian living from an Old Testament narrative text misses the point and spiritualizes the text given that "there are no Christians living in the Old Testament" ("Introduction to Christ").

23. Deuel, "Expository Preaching," 283.

24. Provan, *1 and 2 Kings*, 8.

25. Stanley, *Irresistible*, 315. Earlier, he refers to "our incessant habit of reaching back into old covenant concepts, teachings, sayings, and narratives to support our own teachings, sayings, and narratives" (90). These "teachings" that stem from the teaching of the old covenant include all sorts of bizarre behaviors or judgmental attitudes (90–91).

26. Stanley, *Irresistible*, 158.

concerns. Brent Strawn, in *The Old Testament Is Dying: A Diagnosis and Recommended Treatment*, says that the way forward is to "learn the *entire* language of Scripture, Old and New Testaments *together*."[27] Only then can we challenge our own misreadings of the Old Testament, as well as the "massive reductions" of its message by the New Atheists, the Marcionites (old and new), and the "happiologists" (like Joel Osteen and other representatives of the prosperity gospel).[28]

4. *We get intimidated by the language and literature of the Old Testament.* A fourth reason evangelicals struggle with preaching Old Testament stories is more practical: the language and literature of the New Testament seem more manageable. Choosing New Testament studies over Old Testament studies resembles a citizen of the United States specializing in United States history instead of the history of Western civilization. With United States history, there's a smaller body of material to learn, and it's more familiar. A college Greek professor explained to me that he pursued graduate studies in New Testament language and exegesis because there was too much to master in Old Testament studies. The sheer size of the Old Testament, the length of Old Testament history, and his difficulty in learning Hebrew steered him toward the New Testament. Evangelical seminaries reinforce this problem when they require fewer hours in Hebrew grammar and exegesis courses than in Greek grammar and exegesis courses. Fortunately, the easiest reading in the Hebrew Bible resides in its narrative sections. That's why first-year Hebrew students often begin reading the book of Ruth within a few weeks. Appendix B will help preachers ease back into the world of Biblical Hebrew and use it with profit.

5. *We get enslaved to a particular style of exposition.* A final reason why preachers struggle with Old Testament stories is enslavement to a particular homiletical method. Don Wardlaw argues, "When preachers feel they have not preached a passage of Scripture unless they have dissected and rearranged that Word into a lawyer's brief, they in reality make the Word of God subservient to one particular, technical kind of reason."[29] Similarly, Fred Craddock encourages preachers who want to stand at the

---

27. Strawn, *Old Testament Is Dying*, 225 (emphasis original).
28. See Strawn, *Old Testament Is Dying*, 131, as well as chaps. 4–6 in Strawn's volume for a more detailed discussion of each of these "massive reductions."
29. Wardlaw, "Introduction," 16.

threshold of new pulpit power to ask "why the Gospel should always be impaled upon the frame of Aristotelian logic."[30]

As previously noted, some evangelicals preach through an Old Testament narrative text by using the captioned survey form. Basically, this sermon develops through the points of an analytical outline. Usually, the preacher will state these points prominently so listeners leave the sermon with an outline in their minds or at least on paper. For example, the sermon I preached several years ago on 1 Samuel 7 chewed its way through the following outline:

I. The Repentance of God's People (7:2–6)
   A. The determination to seek the Lord (v. 2)
   B. The decree to put away idols (vv. 3–4)
   C. The decision to offer confession (vv. 5–6)
II. The Victory of God's People (7:7–11)
   A. The Philistine advance toward Israel was frightening (v. 7)
   B. The Israelite cry to the Lord was compelling (vv. 8–9)
   C. The divine thunder against the Philistines was overwhelming (vv. 10–11)
III. The Resulting Prosperity of God's People (7:12–17)
   A. God was worshiped (v. 12)
   B. The enemy was subdued (v. 13a)
   C. The land was at peace (vv. 13b–17)

The recipe for such a sermon is simple: (1) slice the text into an analytical outline; (2) season the outline points with parallelism; (3) sprinkle the points with alliteration; and (4) serve for thirty to forty-five minutes on a fill-in-the-blank outline projected on the big screens. Is this an overblown caricature? No. This approach was popular when I began pastoral ministry. More than three decades later, it has not subsided. A while ago, I checked out the website of a prominent midwestern evangelical church. Their senior pastor, a leader in his particular denomination, made his sermons available in sermon notes and in an audio format. He had been preaching through 1 Samuel, so I clicked on some of his outlines. He had

---

30. Craddock, *As One without Authority*, 45.

certainly mastered the analytical outline approach. One of his sermons broke down the text according to three Vs: "the *vilification* of the Lord's glory," "the *vindication* of the Lord's glory," and "the *vengeance* by the Lord's glory." When I listened to the sermon on audio, the preacher made each of his points prominent with statements like, "In verses 1–2, we find the vilification of the Lord's glory," or "Verses 3–5 describe the vindication of the Lord's glory."

The problem is, good storytellers do not convey their stories through analytical outlines. Veteran expositor Warren Wiersbe reminds preachers that a sermon must present biblical truth "in a manner that is reasonable, imaginative, and intrinsic to the text."[31] He adds, "To preach biblically means much more than to preach the truth of the Bible accurately. It also means to present that truth the way the biblical writers and speakers presented it."[32] When Stephen preached a Bible story in Acts 7, he did not organize his material in an analytical outline. This does not mean that an analytical outline sermon is categorically unbiblical. But it does suggest that an expositor is not bound to this type of sermon form even though it remains popular today in evangelical circles. The analytical outline approach presses the story into a mold that often works against it, especially when the outline points are alliterated or parallel.

A Learning Strategy

We're ready to start the process of building or remodeling a method for preaching Old Testament narratives. This volume will build on the methodology presented in Haddon Robinson's classic textbook *Biblical Preaching*. Robinson breaks the task of sermon preparation into ten stages (see table 1.1). The present volume will follow the same strategy. Please do not let this deter you if you slice the pie differently. You may follow a different homiletical approach. That's fine. You should be able to tailor the contents of this volume to fit your own process of sermon development.

Let me add another clarification. The process of developing an expository message from an Old Testament narrative text should be fluid and artistic. You must develop a feel for it. However, to learn the process you

---

31. Wiersbe, *Preaching and Teaching*, 304–5.
32. Wiersbe, *Preaching and Teaching*, 36.

Table 1.1
Robinson's Stages of Sermon Preparation
1. Selecting the Passage
2. Studying the Passage
3. Discovering the Exegetical Idea
4. Analyzing the Exegetical Idea
5. Formulating the Homiletical Idea
6. Determining the Sermon's Purpose
7. Deciding How to Accomplish This Purpose
8. Outlining the Sermon
9. Filling in the Sermon Outline
10. Preparing the Introduction and Conclusion

must break it down into its component parts. Years ago when I learned how to drive, my driver's education manual broke down a left-hand turn into twelve steps. At the time, I thought it was ridiculous. But breaking the process down helped me learn the fundamentals correctly. Learning to preach an Old Testament narrative works the same way. We have to break the process down into mechanical steps so that we can reassemble them into a fluid, artistic motion.

Finally, here's a word about studying narrative texts in Hebrew. Knowing Biblical Hebrew, or learning it, will give you an edge. Thankfully, as already noted, the easiest type of literature to read in the Hebrew Bible is narrative. So you might want to revive your Hebrew or take the plunge and learn it.[33] However, if you don't know Hebrew, don't panic. You can still do quality exegesis and understand what a narrative is saying and what it is doing with what it is saying.

---

33. I highly recommend Howell, Merkle, and Plummer, *Hebrew for Life*.

2

The Christ-Centered Preaching Debate

Early in Michael Jordan's NBA career, the Chicago Bulls coaching staff disagreed over how to run the offense. Doug Collins, the head coach, employed a keep-the-ball-in-Jordan's-hands strategy. One of his assistants, Tex Winter, argued for a "triangle offense" that kept the ball moving from player to player. The disagreement escalated. Collins banished Winter from the bench. Finally, management fired Collins and replaced him with Phil Jackson, another assistant mentored by Winter. The rest is history. Jackson led the Bulls and their star player, Michael Jordan, to six NBA championships.

There is a debate in the field of preaching that stokes the same kind of heated disagreement. It is the debate over whether (or how) to preach Christ in the Old Testament. Your conclusions will shape the way that you study and preach an Old Testament narrative text. So it is worth thinking carefully about it before proceeding.

A Fascinating Controversy

A good entry point into the debate is a controversy that raged in the Reformed churches in Holland just prior to World War II over how to preach "historical texts"—that is, Old Testament narratives. Sidney Greidanus explored this controversy in his 1970 doctoral dissertation, *Sola Scriptura: Problems and Principles in Preaching Historical Texts*. Some preachers within these Dutch Reformed churches advocated an "exemplary approach," which looked to the characters in the stories as models to imitate or avoid. Others in these same churches argued for a "redemptive-historical approach" (or "Christocentric" approach), which proclaimed how the story points forward to the person and work of Christ. Interestingly, this was an in-house disagreement.

The debate raged during the 1930s and early 1940s, but it faded soon after the German armies invaded Holland in May 1940 and occupied it until 1945. As Greidanus observes, "The disruptive influence of this occupation on the normal pattern of life was hardly conducive to carrying on the controversy."[1] A fatal schism in the church toward the end of World War II kept the debate from resurfacing. Greidanus, though, revisited the controversy twenty-five years later and offered his own critique and a model for preaching the "historical texts" of the Old Testament.

The Basic Arguments

Here is a brief overview of each approach. The "exemplary approach" looked at the characters in a narrative as models to imitate or warning examples to shun.[2] It took its cue from three New Testament passages.[3] In 1 Corinthians 10, the apostle Paul cites God's judgment on his rebellious people during their wilderness wanderings as warning "examples" (vv. 6, 11). Furthermore, as one proponent observed, "Hebrews 11 interprets the redemptive history of the O.T. in an 'exemplary sense.'"[4] Finally, "exemplary" preachers pointed to the usage of Elijah's experience in 1 Kings 17–18 by James (5:17–18) as support for their approach. In 1941, N. Streefkerk wrote, "I am told that when I speak about prayer, I may think of Elijah. But am I not allowed to refer to the power of his prayer when I narrate or preach the *history* of Elijah? That seems extremely odd to me."[5]

The "redemptive-historical approach" argued that the Old Testament historical texts have a specific purpose: the revelation of God's coming to

---

1. Greidanus, *Sola Scriptura*, 50.
2. Greidanus, *Sola Scriptura*, 58.
3. Greidanus, *Sola Scriptura*, 113–19.
4. Greidanus, *Sola Scriptura*, 117. Here, Greidanus quotes Ph. J. Hyser.
5. Greidanus, *Sola Scriptura*, 118.

the world in Christ.⁶ Thus, preachers who want to preach on issues like covetousness or prayer should "take a text which presents God's direct revelation on these matters" rather than trying to illustrate them from a narrative text.⁷ Redemptive-historical preachers opposed the exemplary approach as a "fragmentary interpretation which reads the Bible as a collection of biographies." One preacher, T. Hoekstra, warned: "When glittering subsidiary characters appear in redemptive history, the danger is undoubtedly present that the leading character will recede to the background, that Christ will remain in the darkness."⁸ According to the redemptive-historical proponents, this did not mean drawing a magical line or making an acrobatic leap from Christ to the cross or incarnation. Rather, it meant pointing to the person of Christ or signifying his work as Messiah or Mediator. He is the eternal Logos who is actively at work in Moses, Joshua, the judges, and David.⁹

Preachers on the redemptive-historical side of the debate challenged the conclusions of the exemplary approach regarding the New Testament's usage of examples from Old Testament events and characters. They argued that the words translated as "examples" in 1 Corinthians 10—*typoi* (τυποι, v. 6) and *typikōs* (τυπικως, v. 11)—refer to types or prefigurations of events in the messianic age rather than to pedagogical examples.¹⁰ Also, given that Hebrews 11:35–38 includes extrabiblical persons as well as biblical ones, we should take the exemplars of faith as "concrete illustrations" rather than as "pieces of normative interpretation."¹¹ Similarly, the fact that James 5:17–18 uses Elijah as an illustration does not imply that prayer is the specific intent of 1 Kings 17–18. There are many other elements in that narrative, and we must not let them sidetrack us from preaching the intent of the text—the revelation of God's coming to the world in Christ.¹²

Greidanus's Critique and a Later Twist

After pondering the arguments of both sides, Greidanus offered a brilliant critique. Essentially, he argued for a mediating position. He agreed

6. Greidanus, *Sola Scriptura*, 132–33.
7. Greidanus, *Sola Scriptura*, 132.
8. Greidanus, *Sola Scriptura*, 141.
9. Greidanus, *Sola Scriptura*, 144–45.
10. Greidanus, *Sola Scriptura*, 114.
11. Greidanus, *Sola Scriptura*, 117.
12. Greidanus, *Sola Scriptura*, 119.

with the redemptive-historical side that the historical narratives in the Old Testament "do not intend to give biographies of men but to proclaim the redemptive acts of God for man."[13] These narratives bear witness to Christ, the one who has been active from the beginning as the Logos.[14] Greidanus also agreed with the exemplary side that these narratives have normative as well as historical authority. He concluded, "One does not have to turn to another category of texts or fall back on examples to find warning, comfort, and admonition. All of this is already contained in the historical text"—that is, in an Old Testament narrative text.[15] Therefore, the proclamation of these texts must be *relevant*, communicating the "ethical thrust" of a passage within the light of the author's theocentric framework.[16] After all, the historical accounts in the Old Testament proclaim God's acts to God's people in their particular needs.[17]

Thus, Greidanus faulted the redemptive-historical approach for confining Old Testament historical texts in a framework that prevented them from saying what they intend to say. He criticized the exemplary approach for reading them in a biographical, moralistic way.[18]

Eighteen years after his dissertation, Greidanus worked his conclusions into a volume for pastors and aspiring preachers titled *The Modern Preacher and the Ancient Text*. This volume took into account the blossoming field of literary studies and dealt with four types of biblical literature, including Hebrew narratives. Then Greidanus changed his mind. In an interesting twist, Greidanus argued for a much stricter Christ-centered approach in his 1999 volume, *Preaching Christ from the Old Testament: A Contemporary Hermeneutical Method*. He now counsels preachers to move from the Old Testament text to the incarnate Christ.[19]

The Way Forward

I am convinced that the original mediating view of Greidanus is the way forward for faithful preaching of Old Testament narrative texts. What I

---

13. Greidanus, *Sola Scriptura*, 215.
14. Greidanus, *Sola Scriptura*, 223.
15. Greidanus, *Sola Scriptura*, 212.
16. Greidanus, *Sola Scriptura*, 226.
17. Greidanus, *Sola Scriptura*, 212.
18. Greidanus, *Sola Scriptura*, 173.
19. Greidanus, *Preaching Christ*, 36–37, 233.

am suggesting, then, is a mediating view that takes the strengths of both major views about preaching the Old Testament. These views, described below, are the *theocentric* view and the *Christocentric* view. Notice that the alternatives are not the same as they were in the Reformed churches in Holland just prior to World War II. Exemplary preaching from Old Testament narrative literature is still popular. However, the leading practitioners and professors of preaching are not treating it as a viable approach—at least not as an exclusive approach. Those who make room for it do so as a subcategory under either theocentric or Christocentric preaching. I will have more to say about this in a moment.

No one who takes the Scriptures seriously denies that the Old Testament speaks of Jesus Christ. Jesus claimed this in conversations with his followers the day he was raised from death (see Luke 24:25–27, 44–47). The issue, though, is *how* to preach the Old Testament, including its narratives, in light of the way that the Old Testament points to Jesus.

The Theocentric View

Preachers who adopt a theocentric approach stand in the tradition of John Calvin who emphasized preaching a particular text with a view to exposing the intention of the author.[20] For Calvin, unlike Luther, theocentric preaching was implicitly Christ-centered;[21] and Calvin was critical of Luther's Christological exegesis.[22] Perhaps the best current representatives of the theocentric view are Kenneth Langley and Abraham Kuruvilla.

Langley argues that "Old Testament narratives related how God has acted in, through, and despite the actions of the human characters. The agenda is theological. To concentrate on human deeds, then, is often to miss the point." However, "recognizing that God is central in these stories does not mean they have no exemplar value for moral instruction."[23] Langley sees this as the problem with the Christocentric view. In its quest not to treat the Bible as a to-do list or self-improvement manual, "this approach so privileges the indicative that the imperative of Scripture is sometimes oppressed."[24] Yet God's "grace does not preclude exhortation, as indicated

20. Greidanus, *Preaching Christ*, 127–51.
21. Greidanus, *Preaching Christ*, 147. See pp. 111–26 for Luther's approach.
22. Greidanus, *Preaching Christ*, 139.
23. Langley, "Theocentric View," 83.
24. Langley, "Theocentric View," 101. The "indicative" refers to what God has done, while the "imperative" refers to what God calls people to do.

by hundreds of scriptural commands, by our Lord's proclamation, 'Repent and believe the good news' (Mark 1:15), and the indicative-imperative structure of some of Paul's epistles."[25] In Langley's view, then, a sermon works from the textual details to discern the theological message and issues a call for God's people to respond appropriately.

Kuruvilla takes a similar view. He wants preachers to expound the particulars of the specific text they preach so they can reveal its theology (what it affirms about God) and the life change for which it calls.[26] Kuruvilla shrewdly labels his approach "Christiconic" since it "sees each pericope of Scripture portraying a facet of the canonical image of Christ."[27] To put it another way, he argues that preaching is trinitarian. "The text inspired by the Holy Spirit (2 Pet. 1:21) depicts Jesus Christ, the Son, to whose image humans are to conform (Rom. 8:29). As they are so conformed, the will of God the Father is being done and his kingdom is coming to pass (Matt. 6:10)."[28] Kuruvilla's concern with the Christocentric approach is that it risks neglecting the "specific thrusts of individual OT texts."[29] While he sees a place for biblical theology (the tracing of biblical themes) in the teaching program of the church, he believes that "the sermon is not a place for such a display." Instead, "preaching is the event where the specific message of a particular text—its divine demand—is exposited and brought to bear upon the life of the children of God to transform them for the glory of God."[30]

The Christocentric View

In the Christocentric, or redemptive-historical, approach to preaching, the focus is on Jesus Christ, the one to whom all portions of Scripture point. However, there is a rather broad spectrum of "Christ-centered" approaches to preaching.

Sidney Greidanus, as we have already noted, represents a more restrictive Christocentric approach. He places his approach "somewhere between Calvin's theocentric method and Luther's Christological method."[31]

25. Langley, "Theocentric View," 101–2.
26. Kuruvilla, "Christiconic View," 57–58.
27. Kuruvilla, *Privilege the Text!*, 29.
28. Kuruvilla, "Christiconic View," 63.
29. Kuruvilla, *Privilege the Text!*, 239.
30. Kuruvilla, *Privilege the Text!*, 240.
31. Greidanus, *Preaching Christ*, 227.

Greidanus builds his approach on the context in which the Old Testament finds its final interpretation. "For Christians, that context cannot be anything but the New Testament."[32] Thus, the issue that confronts preachers is "how to preach the incarnate Christ from a book that predates his incarnation by many centuries."[33] This means moving from the Old Testament text one is preaching to the New Testament to preach Christ. This move cannot be arbitrary, though. "One must look for a clue, a feature, in the Old Testament text that warrants linking it with a particular New Testament event or one or more New Testament passages."[34] Greidanus identifies seven ways a preacher can make this move: redemptive-historical progression, promise fulfillment, typology, analogy, longitudinal themes, contrast, and New Testament references.[35]

Greidanus insists that the move to Christ from an Old Testament text must align with the author's intended message, and the way to discover this message is through rigorous literary, grammatical, and historical analysis.[36] It is wrong to force a text to say what it does not say.[37] Thus, he identifies shortcomings in the approach of Charles Haddon Spurgeon, who is, perhaps, the prince of Christ-centered preachers. Greidanus faulted Spurgeon for using Old Testament texts as "springboards" for preaching Christ and for traveling "through the swamp of typologizing and allegorizing" to get to Christ rather than through a careful interpretive process.[38]

The narrowness of Greidanus's approach surfaces in the application of Old Testament texts to new covenant believers. For example, he cautions preachers not to present David in 1 Samuel 17 as a model of courage. Instead, the essence of the David-Goliath narrative is that "the Lord himself defeats the enemy of his people. This theme locates the passage on the highway of God's kingdom history which leads straight to Jesus' victory over Satan."[39] The application for today is for God's people to get involved in the battle against the evil one (if prosperity has blinded them to it) and to rely on God who fights for them (if they have been relying

---

32. Greidanus, *Preaching Christ*, 40.
33. Greidanus, *Preaching Christ*, 54.
34. Greidanus, *Preaching Christ*, 54.
35. Greidanus, *Preaching Christ*, 233. See 203–25 for a discussion of the first six ways. Greidanus notes that these ways "are not scientifically precise and overlap considerably" (203).
36. Greidanus, *Preaching Christ*, 284–85.
37. Greidanus, *Preaching Christ*, 37.
38. Greidanus, *Preaching Christ*, 160–61.
39. Greidanus, *Preaching Christ*, 239.

on their own strength). Similarly, Greidanus takes issue with preachers who apply the unique testing of Abraham in Genesis 22 to the testing of God's people in general. The textual theme, or main idea, proposed by some of the better commentators is something like this: "Whenever the sovereign God tests the faith of his people, he demands unquestioning, trusting obedience."[40] However, Greidanus offers this alternative: "The Lord provides a lamb for a burnt offering so that Isaac (Israel) may live."[41] This results in the following sermon theme: "The Lord provides a sacrificial lamb so that his people may live."[42] The goal of the sermon is to "encourage God's people fully to trust their faithful Lord for their salvation."[43]

On the other hand, Bryan Chapell represents a less restrictive Christocentric approach. He is not leery of preaching the instructions of Scripture—its imperatives as well as its indicatives. Rather, his concern is that preaching "matters of faith or practice without rooting their foundation or fruit in what God would do, has done, or will do through the ministry of Christ creates a human-centered (anthropocentric) faith without Christian distinctions."[44] The key is to relate a particular preaching text to the big story of Scripture—its redemptive message that moves through the stages of creation, fall, redemption, and final consummation.[45] This is the task of biblical theology. In recent decades, evangelical preachers have infused biblical theology into their preaching, understanding that the redemptive flow of biblical history is an essential part of a text's context.[46]

Chapell counsels preachers to read with "gospel glasses." These are "not X-ray goggles that make an image or reference to Jesus mysteriously emerge from behind some bush in every biblical account."[47] Rather, they reflect aspects of God's nature that provide redemption as well as aspects of human nature that require redemption.

40. Greidanus, *Preaching Christ*, 303.
41. Greidanus, *Preaching Christ*, 304.
42. Greidanus, *Preaching Christ*, 315.
43. Greidanus, *Preaching Christ*, 315.
44. Chapell, "Redemptive-Historic View," 15.
45. Chapell, "Redemptive-Historic View," 4–7.
46. Chapell, "Redemptive-Historic View," 3. Chapell's list of preachers who used biblical theology in their sermons includes Don Carson, Sinclair Ferguson, John Piper, Steve Brown, James Montgomery Boice, Tony Merida, Jerry Bridges, Ray Ortlund, Danny Akin, and Timothy Keller.
47. Chapell, "Redemptive-Historic View," 17.

Timothy Keller's approach seems to fall between Greidanus and Chapell. I have listened to dozens of Keller's sermons and have appreciated his willingness to preach the Scriptures' appeals to holy living. Yet, in addition to grounding what Scripture tells us to do (imperative) in what God through Christ has done for us (indicative), Keller is eager to point out how Jesus is the fulfillment of the major themes, figures, and images in the Bible.[48] Jesus is the better David, the better Esther, the true king, and the just judge. The key to preaching Christ "is to find out how your particular text fits into the full canonical context and participates as a chapter in the great narrative arc of the Bible, which is how God saves us and renews the world through the salvation by free grace in his Son, Jesus Christ."[49]

The Theocentric-Christocentric View

As noted above, I am advocating for the mediating view Sidney Greidanus argued for in his 1970 doctoral dissertation. Yes, I recognize the danger in taking a mediating view. I lived in Montana for almost half of my life, and I spent the better part of a year working on a cattle ranch. So I have an affinity for the sayings of the Old West. They are often blunt and do not mince words. One of them is, "He who straddles a fence gets a sore crotch." This speaks to the danger of a mediating view. The idea is, make up your mind. You can't have it both ways. However, I believe preachers *need* to have it both ways when it comes to the debate over Christ-centered preaching. I believe we must read the Old Testament in its literary, grammatical, and historical-cultural environment so as to determine its theological message and its "ethical thrust." At the same time, I believe we must locate the theology of this text in the larger storyline of the Bible—the concern of biblical theology.

Although labels are fraught with difficulty, some call this the "Christotelic" view, acknowledging that Christ is the *telos*, or goal, of the Old Testament. John Walton says it well: "In the christotelic approach, we recognize that all of God's revelation reaches a new plateau in Christ, so all of it can be seen as heading in that direction.... Christology, then, cannot be left out of the equation, but it does not replace what the Old Testament authors were doing."[50] Christopher Wright makes a similar point when

---

48. Keller, *Preaching*, 73–82.
49. Keller, *Preaching*, 70.
50. J. Walton, *Old Testament Theology*, 5–6.

he says, "Preaching from the Old Testament is not just preaching *about* Jesus, though it should certainly lead people ultimately to Jesus. . . . It all *points* to Christ. It is not all '*about* Christ.'"[51]

I will present a process for connecting to the Bible's storyline and its hero, Jesus Christ, in chapter 9. For now, here is my plea to those who identify exclusively as theocentric or Christocentric.

To those preachers who identify as "theocentric," I remind you that the divine demand of an Old Testament narrative text must always be grounded in what God has done for you in Christ. The historical accounts concerning Deborah, Abraham, Ruth, or David cannot be understood and applied apart from their connection to the metanarrative of the Bible and the hero of that narrative, Jesus the Messiah. This is where I differ from Kuruvilla. He sees the sermon not as a place for a display of biblical theology but as "the event where the specific message of a particular text—its divine demand—is exposited and brought to bear on the life of the children of God to transform them for the glory of God."[52] Yet how can an Old Testament text be brought to bear on the lives of new covenant believers without noting how its theological message is shaped by the way it finds its fulfillment in Christ? I appreciate Kuruvilla's concern about how a Christ-centered focus can obscure "the specific thrust of individual OT texts."[53] However, if this specific thrust gets "swallowed up" by "biblical-theology transactions,"[54] the fault lies with the preacher—not the methodology itself.

To those preachers who fall on the side of a more Christocentric approach, I remind you of Timothy Keller's warning. He says that "it is possible to 'get to Christ' so quickly in preaching a text that we fail to be sensitive to the particularities of the text's message. We leapfrog over historical realities to Jesus as though the Old Testament Scriptures had little significance to their original readers."[55] This amounts to flattening the text so that every sermon sounds the same and overlooks critical topics—whether the dignity of work, the value of human life, or the way God's people handle suffering.[56] Another danger is to "find" Christ in details

---

51. C. Wright, *How to Preach and Teach*, 52–53 (emphasis original).
52. Kuruvilla, *Privilege the Text!*, 240.
53. Kuruvilla, *Privilege the Text!*, 239.
54. This is Kuruvilla's concern and language in *Privilege the Text!*, 240.
55. Keller, *Preaching*, 60.
56. Langley, "Theocentric View," 103–4; C. Wright, *How to Preach and Teach*, 56–59.

where he is not. Kevin Vanhoozer offers this perspective on how Jesus explained to the disciples on the road to Emmaus "what was said in all the Scriptures concerning himself" (Luke 24:27): "I believe this was not a heavy-handed allegorical reading that made use of fanciful connections between incidental details and the life of Christ, but rather an interpretation that discerned the through-line, the central dramatic thrust, of divine redemptive history—namely the way in which the prophets, priests, and kings anticipated aspects of Christ's own work, and the way in which God's repeated delivery of the people of Israel from their enemies (and ultimately from themselves) anticipated the delivery of the church from sin, death, and destruction."[57] Lucas O'Neill refers to these twin dangers as *missing* the text (that is, "failing to honor the details of the passage we are preaching") and *misusing* the text (that is, mishandling "the details of the text in order to get to Christ").[58]

Christocentric preachers will also do well to remember that Christ-centered preaching does not preclude calling the people of God to behave, as well as believe, in a certain way. I disagree with the kind of strict Christ-centered approach that says: "We do not confront men with Christ by preaching theological ideas nor by ethical exhortations, but by rehearsing the saving events witnessed in Scripture."[59] Such an approach is unnecessarily reductionistic. "When the apostles spoke of the gospel and rehearsed its saving events, they issued a call for nonbelievers to believe (see Acts 2:38–41 and 1 Cor. 15:1–3) and a call for believers to align their behavior with the gospel (see Gal. 2:14)."[60] As Gordon Wenham says, "Old Testament narrative books do have a didactic purpose, that is, they are trying to instill both theological truths and ethical ideals into their readers."[61]

My conviction, then, is that preachers need not pit a theocentric approach against a Christocentric approach.[62] Rather the former should lead to the latter, and the latter should build upon the former. As D. A. Carson observed in an interview with R. C. Sproul, the New Testament

---

57. Vanhoozer, *Hearers and Doers*, 224–25.
58. O'Neill, *Preaching to Be Heard*, 127.
59. Donald G. Miller as quoted by Greidanus, *Preaching Christ*, 235–36.
60. Mathewson, "Prophetic Preaching from Old Testament Narrative Texts," 41.
61. Wenham, *Story as Torah*, 3.
62. For a helpful, in-depth comparison and evaluation of the leading Christocentric proponent (Sidney Greidanus) and the leading theocentric proponent (Abraham Kuruvilla), see Price, "Comparing Sidney Greidanus," 69–93.

writers worked with biblical-theological categories and drew moral lessons as they read the Old Testament.[63] Similarly, Michael Kruger says, "OT stories/figures can function both as a type of Christ and as moral examples of what true faith can produce in the life of God's people."[64] In the next chapter, I will encourage preachers to focus on the theology of the narrative—its prophetic message or "ethical thrust." Sometimes, the characters provide negative or positive models of this message; at other times, their behavior is not the main issue. Furthermore, in chapter 9, I will discuss how to utilize biblical theology in a sermon on an Old Testament narrative while still highlighting the particulars of the text and its theological message. For now, though, my plea is simply not to drive a wedge between biblical theology and the ethical ideals of a particular narrative. Theocentric and Christocentric preaching need not be mutually exclusive.

---

63. See Ligonier Ministries, "RC Sproul Interviews DA Carson." The pertinent section runs from about 21:22 to 23:08. Carson's answer is in response to a question on canonical interpretation. Here is a lightly edited transcript of Carson's answer:

> Many Christian preachers have preached series from the life of Abraham or the life of David, and it has been not uncommon [for them] to preach almost moralizing sermons. David was good here, let's be good. David was bad there, let's not be bad. And that's about all you see from it whether from Abraham or Daniel or David. Everything becomes a moralizing lesson and that's all. Then they become aware of biblical-theological categories and see how David is the beginning of the Davidic dynasty and how . . . through the promises given to Abraham all the families of the earth will be blessed. So they begin to preach in these broader categories and forget the moral categories. But then you . . . remember how Paul in 1 Corinthians 10:1–13 can read Israel's history and draw moralizing lessons. In other words, one of the ways that the Old Testament is read on occasion is precisely to draw moralizing lessons. Elijah was a man as we are, yet he persevered. We should be prayer warriors as he was. There's no deep typology. It is an argument by analogy. He's somebody to imitate. It's application.

64. Kruger, "Are We Allowed to Use OT Figures as Moral Examples?"

From Text to Concept

3

The Journey Begins

The summit of Long's Peak in Colorado's Rocky Mountain National Park towers 14,259 feet above sea level. Reaching it requires an eight-mile hike from the trailhead to the top, with an elevation gain of almost 6,000 feet. Then you have to get back down. Both parts of the journey have their own joys and hazards. I know this from experience, having attempted it three times and reaching the summit twice.

Preaching a sermon is similar. There are two main parts to the journey: ascending from text to concept, and then descending from concept to sermon. The first half of the journey is an exegetical process designed to reach the exegetical summit—an understanding of what a text is saying and what the biblical author is doing with it. The second half of the journey is a homiletical process. The preacher has to descend the exegetical summit and deliver the goods to the listeners. This involves shaping a sermon that unpacks the meaning of the text and applies it to the lives of the listeners.

Here in part two, chapters 3–8 will prepare you to reach the exegetical summit. This chapter will get you started on the journey by helping you with text selection, by introducing an exegetical strategy, and by urging you to saturate your exegetical study in prayer.

Text Selection

Choosing an Old Testament narrative text to preach can be difficult because there are so many options. You can choose from any of the books in your English Bible from Genesis through Esther. Some of them consist primarily of narrative. This is the case with Genesis, the first half of Exodus, and the "historical books" beginning with Joshua. Even books that contain a significant amount of law code or discourse materials—the latter half of Exodus, Leviticus, Numbers, and Deuteronomy—have narratives embedded within them. Plus, their overall structure is narrative. You will also find narrative sections in prophetic books like Isaiah, Daniel, and Jonah.

If you have never before ventured into Old Testament narrative literature, spend some time reading through the narrative books and note the stories that stir your affections. Start with a single sermon on one of them. Or choose a favorite or a familiar story such as Deborah and Jael (Judg. 4), David and Goliath (1 Sam. 17), or Elijah and the prophets of Baal (1 Kings 18). Listeners are often familiar with these stories, yet unfamiliar with the message they communicate. On the other hand, your listeners may not be as familiar with some stories as you might assume. They have heard constant references to Samson and Delilah in popular love ballads, but they may know little of the details.

Planning a sermon series from a narrative book is the next challenge to tackle. A series on Genesis or Samuel makes sense since these books are so foundational to the storyline of the Bible. However, their sheer size may make it wise to begin with smaller narrative units such as the Abraham cycle (Gen. 12–25) or David's wilderness years (1 Sam. 16–31). The book of Ruth is a terrific entry point into biblical narrative. However, while it is natural to base text selection on a personality such as Abraham or David, remember that the writer intended to do more than provide a life of Abraham or David. Besides, some of the most potent stories in 1 Samuel come in chapters 4–7, before David is even introduced in the story.

The key to text selection is to choose a text that constitutes a unit of biblical thought. Preachers who are used to working with one paragraph in the New Testament epistles may be surprised when they have to select several paragraphs, a whole chapter, or possibly two chapters in order to assemble a preaching unit. For example, Haddon Robinson observes, "When exploring an episode such as David's adultery with Bathsheba, we would violate the story were we to preach it a paragraph at a time. Instead we would probably base the sermon on the entire eleventh chapter of 2 Samuel and at least part of the twelfth, because this entire section of 2 Samuel records David's sin and its devastating consequences."[1]

What constitutes a unit of thought in narrative text? A whole story. The limits of a story (where it begins and ends) are determined primarily by analyzing the plot. Stories typically contain an exposition, a crisis, a resolution, and sometimes a conclusion. Additionally, if the narrator uses a chiastic structure, the beginning and final items in a chiasm will mark off the boundaries of a story. Chapter 4 will help you do plot analysis and work with chiastic structure.

Paying attention to changes in *place*, *time*, and *persons* will also help you see breaks in a narrative.[2] Sometimes these changes work in concert. For example, Genesis 18:33 signals closure of a narrative by reporting a change of place: "When the Lord had finished speaking with Abraham, he left, and Abraham returned home." In the next statement, Genesis 19:1, a change of persons indicates the beginning of a new unit. The shift is from the Lord and Abraham to the two angels and Lot. A change of place in Genesis 19:30 begins a new narrative as Lot and his two daughters leave Zoar and settle in the mountains. Then, in Genesis 20:1, a change of both place and persons introduces a new unit as Abraham takes the stage again and moves into the region of the Negev. Changes of time also signal breaks in a narrative. For example, the narrator introduces a new story in Genesis 22:1 by saying, "Some time later . . ." Similarly, a new story begins in Genesis 15:1 with the words, "After these things . . ." (NASB). In Genesis 16–17, the narrator uses Abram's age to indicate a break between two stories. The first story concludes by noting that "Abram was eighty-six years old when Hagar bore him Ishmael" (Gen. 16:16). A new story opens in Genesis 17:1 with the words, "When Abram was ninety-nine years old, the Lord appeared to him."

Sometimes a shift from prose to poetry brings a narrative to a close. Stephen Weitzman argues that early Jews expected their biblical heroes to break into song whenever they were delivered by miracles.[3] He argues that the narrative role of the songs in Exodus 15 and Judges 5 parallels a technique of closure often used in ancient Egyptian battle accounts.[4]

1. Robinson, *Biblical Preaching*, 30.
2. Sailhamer, "Database Approach," 327–33.
3. Weitzman, *Song and Story*, 125, 131.
4. Weitzman, *Song and Story*, 125.

The bottom line is, make sure you select an entire story. You may even choose to group stories together if they develop a similar theme, such as the three stories in 1 Samuel 24–26 that revolve around revenge or the three stories in Exodus 15:22–17:7 that center on complaining.

Nailing down a story to preach is a significant step. Once you have done this, you are ready to begin your exegetical study. Now the real work starts.

An Exegetical Strategy

Meaning is an unavoidable result of communication. This is true for written texts as well as for spoken words. Theologian Kevin Vanhoozer affirms that "there *is* a meaning in the text, that it can be known, and that readers should strive to do so."[5] He asks, "How can we account for a poem moving us to tears, a promise that evokes a firm hope, or a parable that prompts us to sell all our goods and give the profits to the poor? How can we account for the hundreds of daily transactions, punctuated by simple phrases ('Come in'; 'Please be quiet'; 'That will be $4.99, please'; 'I love you'), that shape our lives? Does deconstruction adequately account for what is, after all, an everyday occurrence, namely, communication?"[6]

Philosopher Nicholas Wolterstorff reaches similar conclusions in his response to Jacques Derrida, the father of deconstruction, who argued authorial discourse interpretation is untenable because authorial discourse is untenable. Wolterstorff observes, "Paradoxical as it may seem, he [Derrida] wants us to apply to his own texts that very mode of interpretation against which he launches a general attack; he wants us to interpret his texts for what he was saying and to get that right."[7]

Meaning in Old Testament Narratives

Some challenge this notion of meaning when it comes to reading narratives in the Old Testament. For example, Hebrew Bible scholars David M. Gunn and Danna Nolan Fewell say, "Meaning is not something out there in the text waiting to be discovered. Meaning is always, in the last analysis, the reader's creation, and readers, like texts, come in an infinite variety."[8]

---

5. Vanhoozer, *Is There a Meaning*, 24 (emphasis original).
6. Vanhoozer, *Is There a Meaning*, 202.
7. Wolterstorff, *Divine Discourse*, 153.
8. Gunn and Fewell, *Narrative in the Hebrew Bible*, xi.

The Journey Begins

Similarly, theologian Richard Jensen contends that the stories of the Bible "invite us to participate in their reality, not to understand that reality."[9] Jensen adds, "I have sought to make it crystal clear that I do not believe that the Bible is primarily a book of ideas."[10]

However, Hebrew Bible scholars from a variety of persuasions recognize that Old Testament narratives convey meaning. Take a few moments to ponder their conclusions.

> The Bible's main form of exposition, the narrative, is most appropriately characterized as primary rhetoric, its primary objective being to persuade its audience. (Dale Patrick and Allen Scult)[11]

> The aim of the intrinsic study of literature is to understand the text from inside, guided by the obvious and quite natural question: "What do you mean? What are you actually saying?" This question is simultaneously the most essential question which we could ask of the text or, more generally, of any work of art or, even more generally, of any partner in conversation. (J. P. Fokkelman)[12]

> The biblical authors are of course constantly, urgently conscious of telling a story in order to reveal the imperative truth of God's works in history and of Israel's hopes and failings. Close attention to the literary strategies through which that truth was expressed may actually help us to understand it better, enable us to see the minute elements of complicating design in the Bible's sacred history. (Robert Alter)[13]

> Rather than seeking to let the literature of ancient Israel address us on its own terms—however remote from ours, and however we may finally judge them—it too easily makes of biblical literature a reflection of our own concerns at the end of the twentieth century, whether secular or theological.

---

9. Jensen, *Thinking in Story*, 62.

10. Jensen, *Thinking in Story*, 109. Yet Jensen makes statement after statement in *Thinking in Story* that presupposes a commitment to meaning. For example, he says, "Oral communities tell their stories in such a way that particular stories are the way to grasp more abstract or universal concepts" (22). Later he speaks of "the theme" of the Nebuchadnezzar story in Daniel 4 (86). To be sure, as he observes, "stories work by indirection" (62). But indirection does not negate meaning.

11. Patrick and Scult, *Rhetoric and Biblical Interpretation*, 29.

12. Fokkelman, *Narrative Art and Poetry*, 1:1.

13. Alter, *Art of Biblical Narrative*, 46.

Narrative rhetoric, like any other rhetoric, is designed to create a certain impression on the hearer or reader, and that impression is lessened or confused by a reader's ignorance of the presuppositions of the texts. (Simon B. Parker)[14]

Custodians of narrative texts should not compromise the fundamental characteristics of the material. Required is the recognition that the religious meaning of the material is generated first of all because of features constitutive to its fundamental nature as narrative and text. The religious meaning and significance of biblical material and its literary and textual form are inseparable. (Wesley Kort)[15]

It is through the [literary] techniques [in Hebrew narrative] that the meaning of the facts of the narrative is determined. (Shimon Bar-Efrat)[16]

Communication presupposes a speaker who resorts to certain linguistic and structural tools in order to produce certain effects on the addressee; the discourse accordingly supplies a network of clues to the speaker's intention. In this respect, the Bible does not vary from any other literary or ordinary message except in the ends and the rules that govern the forms of communication. (Meir Sternberg)[17]

John Sailhamer provides a fitting summary. He says, "A text is . . . an embodiment of an author's intention, that is a strategy designed to carry out that intention."[18] To put it another way, Nicholas Wolterstorff says, "The issue is not whether one's interpretation is valuable in one way or another—exciting, original, imaginative, provocative, beneficial—but whether it is true."[19]

Meaning as a Prophetic Message

What kind of truth or meaning should we expect to find in an Old Testament narrative text? When I was growing up, I learned in Sunday School that books like Joshua, Judges, Samuel, and Kings were "historical books."

14. Parker, *Stories in Scripture and Inscriptions*, 4.
15. Kort, *Story, Text, and Scripture*, x–xi. He argues that narrative is "articulated belief structure" (20).
16. Bar-Efrat, *Narrative Art in the Bible*, 10.
17. Sternberg, *Poetics of Biblical Narrative*, 9.
18. Sailhamer, *Introduction to Old Testament Theology*, 46–47.
19. Wolterstorff, *Divine Discourse*, 181.

That is how our English Bibles classify them. Years later, I learned that the Hebrew Bible places Joshua, Judges, Samuel, and Kings in a category called "Former Prophets." Designating these books as "Former Prophets," the Hebrew Bible recognizes that they convey a prophetic message just like the "Latter Prophets" such as Isaiah, Jeremiah, or Amos. Mary Evans describes the Former Prophets as "preached history."[20] Daniel Block argues that "by classifying Judges as a prophetic work, we acknowledge" that it "carries a paraenetic/homiletical agenda" and represents "an extended sermon, or series of sermons." This sermon "draws its 'texts' from the real historical experiences of the Israelites in the premonarchic period. But like a modern preacher, the biblical author selects, organizes, arranges, shapes, and crafts his material for maximum effect."[21]

The situation is the same in the narrative sections of the Torah or Pentateuch, the first five books of the Hebrew Bible. While the term *Torah* is usually translated as "law," it actually is a broad term that means "teaching" or "instruction."[22] So the classification of the first five books of the Hebrew Bible deems them to be books of teaching or instruction.

The placement of so many narrative books and texts in the Torah and Former Prophets reveals their purpose. Although they use narrative as their communication vehicle, these texts communicate a prophetic message or at least offer instruction or teaching. Gordon J. Wenham concludes that there is "a normative claim in historical narrative that fiction for all its interest rarely makes."[23] Yairah Amit concurs, saying, "The biblical authors present their stories as a meaningful history from which the readers must draw a moral."[24]

One important implication is that we cannot pit proposition against narrative. In fact, narrative texts contain propositions, even though they communicate them in a subtle manner. As Gordon Wenham observes, "Old Testament narratives . . . seldom contain explicit moral judgements, but much more often leave the events to speak for themselves."[25] Mary

---

20. Evans, *Judges and Ruth*, 6.
21. Block, *Judges, Ruth*, 52.
22. *Jewish Bible*, 2.
23. Wenham, *Story as Torah*, 12–13. Likewise, Dale Ralph Davis refers to the "theology of a biblical text, that is, what the text means to say about God, his ways and his works" (*Word Became Fresh*, 31).
24. Amit, *Reading Biblical Narratives*, 93.
25. Wenham, *Story as Torah*, 14.

Evans observes that "the way the story is told directs the reader towards a particular perspective."[26] It may be helpful to liken a narrative text to a child's dot-to-dot picture. The picture does not emerge until the child draws lines that connect the dots. Narrative works this way. The exegete must connect the narrative dots in order to see the prophetic message or instruction. As literary critic Erich Auerbach claims in his classic *Mimesis*, "The Scripture stories do not, like Homer's, court our favour, they do not flatter us that they may please us and enchant us—they seek to subject us, and if we refuse to be subjected we are rebels."[27] Likewise, Robert Coles points out that stories offer a challenge to our conscience as well as to our intellect.[28] They "not only keep us company, but admonish us, point us in new directions, or give us the courage to stay a given course."[29]

The Quest for a Big Idea

The notion that an Old Testament narrative issues a prophetic message or provides instruction has an important implication for our exegesis. We are on a quest for the text's big idea—that is, a one-sentence summary of the theological message it communicates.

We live in an age that favors bulleted lists. Not surprisingly, then, preachers often comb Old Testament stories for lists of moral principles they can preach. They may find three strategies for finding God's will or four keys to a healthy marriage or four consequences of idolatry. However, no research suggests that Old Testament authors used narratives as a vehicle for communicating lists. Obviously, biblical writers sometimes compile lists. The writer of Proverbs signals a list by saying, "There are six things the LORD hates, seven that are detestable to him" (Prov. 6:16). In Hebrews 10:19–25, the writer draws three conclusions from the access to the Father provided by Jesus. Each item is introduced by the exhortation "let us."[30] However, the prophetic message of an Old Testament narrative usually comes in the form of a dominant idea rather than a list.

26. Evans, *Judges and Ruth*, 6.
27. Auerbach, *Mimesis*, 12.
28. Coles, *Call of Stories*, 81.
29. Coles, *Call of Stories*, 159.
30. In the Greek text, vv. 22–24 each begin with a hortatory subjunctive. While the NIV includes two more "let us" statements in v. 25, these statements consist of two participial phrases that describe strategies for carrying out the "let us" statement (hortatory subjunctive) in v. 24.

I am not claiming that every Old Testament text contains only one concept or idea. I am saying that the concepts and ideas embedded in a text form a unified whole. Haddon Robinson, the dean of big idea preaching, clarifies it like this: "Sermons seldom fail because they have too many ideas; more often they fail because they deal with unrelated ideas."[31] Multiple ideas work in concert to form a larger, overarching idea. The interpreter sets out on a quest to find the overarching idea that subsumes all the others. This quest, when done properly, is clarifying rather than reductionistic.[32] We will return to this concept in chapter 8.

An Exegetical Process

In the 1996 US Open, my friend Steve Jones stood on the eighteenth tee tied for the lead with his friend Tom Lehman. As a *Sports Illustrated* writer later wrote, Steve stepped up to the ball with his driver and "lasered it down the right side, over some bunkers and into the fairway." Several minutes later, he tapped in the winning putt to clinch his first major tournament win. Developing a lightning-quick swing with such power and grace took years of breaking it down and working on its component parts. Steve had to master the mechanics: grip, stance, shoulder position, arms, backswing, and follow-through. Similarly, interpreting Old Testament narratives requires mastering a set of mechanics. However, the goal is for interpretation to become a fluid process.

Chapters 4–7 will present an exegetical process that will help you understand the prophetic message, or the instruction communicated by an Old Testament narrative. This process is organized by the acronym ACTS. Each letter (*A, C, T, S*) represents a different element of a narrative. These elements are categories that contain the various literary features that writers use to shape their narrative. Initially, this may feel like working through a checklist. Yet the goal is to become a skilled reader who possesses a feel for the text. There is an art to reading; it requires mastering the mechanics by which a narrative text communicates.[33]

31. Robinson, *Biblical Preaching*, 16.
32. For a critique of the big idea approach to preaching, particularly in regard to this concern, see Kuruvilla, "Time to Kill the Big Idea?," 825–46. However, I do not believe the problems Kuruvilla identifies are intrinsic to the big idea approach to preaching when it is properly practiced. See Mathewson, "Let the Big Idea Live!," 33–41.
33. Mark Ellingsen says that if we are to allow Scripture to be its own interpreter, "it is necessary simply to accept it as a piece of literature which functions as a book of the church"

There are a couple of dangers, though, when it comes to the labels and technical terms that biblical scholars use to refer to the features found in a narrative. One danger is that interpreters will reduce the hermeneutical process to slapping labels on elements in the text. The goal of exegetical analysis is not a mere pile of analytical data and labels. Rather, exegetical analysis should produce understanding of a text. Alter argues, "Reading any body of literature involves a specialized mode of perception in which every culture trains its members from childhood. As modern readers of the Bible, we need to relearn something of this mode of perception that was second nature to the original audiences."[34] Simply labeling the plot type as a comedy or classifying a character as a protagonist does not guarantee understanding. Nor does it cause you to experience the story in the way the author intended. As Jean Louis Ska observes, "The object of analysis is the movement of a living being, not the autopsy of a corpse."[35] He further explains, "Analysis should make the text more understandable. If it produces the opposite effect as, for instance, when it atomizes the text into very short segments . . . there is something wrong either in the theory or in its application."[36]

A second danger is contaminating your sermon with these technical terms. Your listeners need to hear you use terms like *protagonist* or *chiastic structure* about as much as you need to hear your dentist tell you that you have a mesio-occlusal distal carious lesion on number 14. All you need to hear is that you have a cavity on your first upper left molar. Shop talk may impress a few listeners, but it will confuse and frustrate most of them. As one of my seminary professors quipped, "We use terms like this so we can justify the high tuition we charge!"

So why even bother with labels and technical terms if we shouldn't use them on others? Fair question. Using the labels and technical terms employed by Old Testament scholars and commentators will help you interact more quickly with important concepts. Ska explains, "All these [literary] categories are indicators of the way to proceed when one enters into a

---

(*Integrity of Biblical Narrative*, 20). To put it another way, Hans Frei says, "Meaning and narrative shape bear significantly on each other" (*Eclipse of Biblical Narrative*, 11). Otherwise, without attention to literary criticism and other aspects of exegesis, we will misunderstand what Scripture says.

34. Alter, *Art of Biblical Narrative*, 62.
35. Ska, "*Our Fathers Have Told Us*," 36.
36. Ska, "*Our Fathers Have Told Us*," 67.

narrative. They are never pigeon-holes to arrange neatly and permanently the texts proposed for analysis which is more often a question of nuance and degree than of mere classification. They are rather a compass and maps that a traveller uses for a journey through the Biblical narratives."[37] Shop talk is necessary. It works for you when you interact with the writings of Old Testament scholars and commentators. It works against your interpretation when you become enamored with the labels and not the story. It works against your preaching when you slip it into your sermon and cause a higher level of confusion.

The Primacy of Prayer

In Bruce Mawhinney's novel, *Preaching with Freshness*, retired seminary professor Dr. William Vickerson coaches a former student who is struggling with his preaching. In one of their conversations, Dr. Vickerson warns his protégé about preaching sermons devoid of the Spirit of God. He says, "Often, we spend so much time gathering information in our studies that we never stop to pray over it. We plunge headlong into our sermon outlines without seeking the Lord's guidance on how to handle the materials before us."[38]

Preachers who hope to preach Old Testament stories with accuracy and power must saturate their study of the text with prayer. As Rick Reed reminds us, "Faithful preaching requires devoted praying."[39] When I sit down to study a narrative text, I begin with a time of prayer. I ask God to help me concentrate and work diligently in the text. At various points in my exegetical study, I rise from my desk and walk down the hall from my office into our worship center. As I wander through the aisles, I pray that God will help me work through a particular gap in my understanding of the story I am studying. Sometimes I even take my notes and pray through them as I kneel near the place where I will stand on Sunday to deliver my sermon. Later in the sermon preparation process, I pray for the Spirit's help in understanding how God wants me, as well as my listeners, to respond to the narrative. Similarly, Matthew Kim urges preachers to pray for the Holy Spirit's presence and power, for transformed lives, and for congregational

37. Ska, *"Our Fathers Have Told Us,"* 94.
38. Mawhinney, *Preaching with Freshness*, 137.
39. Reed, *Heart of the Preacher*, 135.

intentionality.[40] If you do the bulk of your sermon preparation in a coffee shop, take a break and go for a prayer walk. Whatever setting you choose for sermon preparation, make sure you build in times of prayer.

I believe we will all do well to follow the example of William Lane. In the preface to his commentary on the Gospel of Mark, he says, "When a critical or theological decision has been demanded by the text before I was prepared to commit myself, I have adopted the practice of the Puritan commentators in laying the material before the Lord and asking for his guidance."[41]

Alright, let the exegetical study begin! It is time to look at the ACTS of the narrative we have selected to preach. Like hiking to the top of Long's Peak, the challenges of our exegetical climb are formidable. But the result is rewarding.

---

40. Kim, *Little Book for New Preachers*, 117–21.
41. Lane, *Gospel according to Mark*, xii.

4

A is for Action

Like you, I am a busy pastor. My ministry plate is full, so I have limited time to spend on exegesis. The exegetical process I have developed is as lean as possible, yet substantial enough to determine the prophetic message or instruction of the narrative. You can usually do the work in three to eight hours, depending on your exegetical skill level, whether or not you study the text in Hebrew, and the complexity and size of the story you select.

A helpful way to organize this exegetical process is to use the acronym ACTS. Each letter (*A*, *C*, *T*, *S*) represents a different exegetical category for study. It is based on the four key elements found in all stories: plot, characters, setting, and point of view.[1]

To begin, you need your Bible and a word processing program—or a legal pad—for recording some notes. Writing down observations, questions, summaries, and conclusions will force you to think at a higher level.

Initially, do not run to the commentaries. If you study the text in Hebrew, you will need tools such as a lexicon and a grammar. Otherwise, save the reference tools for later. The idea is to think through the passage on your own before diving into commentaries, theological wordbooks, and the like. I will say more about commentaries in appendix C. You will get more out of them if you wait to consult them until you have done your own thinking.

1. Longman, "Biblical Narrative," 71.

The *A* in the acrostic ACTS represents action. The place to start your analysis is the action, or plot, since Old Testament stories focus more on the development of action than on the development of particular characters.[2] It consists of a sequence of events that usually hinges on a conflict or crisis. The events in the story move through this conflict or crisis toward some kind of resolution. Why is tracking the plot so important? Israeli scholar Shimon Bar-Efrat observes, "The plot serves to organize events in such a way as to arouse the reader's interest and emotional involvement, while at the same time imbuing the events with meaning."[3]

Plot Shape

As I read a story the first time, I look closely at the shape of the plot. Plots in Old Testament narrative assume the same basic shape. Generally, they consist of four main stages or elements in the flow of action: exposition, crisis, resolution, and conclusion or denouement (see table 4.1).[4] Sometimes it is hard to tell where the shift from one element to another takes place. Interpreters do not have to agonize over exactly where each change occurs. Often the changes between plot elements reflect the almost imperceptible shift from first to second gear with an automatic transmission. You know the change has occurred, yet it is difficult to pinpoint exactly where it occurred.

To see how these elements work, let's examine three Old Testament stories: the story of Judah and Tamar (Gen. 38), the story of Micah and the Danites (Judg. 17–18), and the story of Esther.

Exposition

The exposition provides the information that sets up the story. It introduces the characters, informing us of their names, traits, physical appear-

---

2. Ska, *"Our Fathers Have Told Us,"* 17. I am using "action" and "plot" interchangeably.
3. Bar-Efrat, *Narrative Art in the Bible*, 93.
4. Some exegetes use slightly different terms to speak of the same phenomena. Yairah Amit analyzes Old Testament narratives with a five-stage plot structure: exposition, complication, change, unraveling, and ending (*Reading Biblical Narratives*, 47). Other scholars speak of exposition, conflict, complication, climax, and denoument. While the four-stage scheme I have presented does not list "complication" or "change" or "unraveling" as a separate step, it recognizes that a crisis and resolution are not neatly packaged events. They may involve rising tension, further complication, and an unraveling that leads to a final resolution.

ance, state in life, and relationships. It may also describe the geographical or historical setting. Ska comments, "In an exposition, the reader finds only short notices about the situation of the main characters. The information is often laconic, generic, and abstract, whereas the first scene is detailed, concrete, and unique."[5] Whatever the story writer includes, it will help the reader understand the action that follows.[6]

Table 4.1
Elements in the Plot
1. Exposition
2. Crisis
3. Resolution
4. Conclusion (Denouement)

In the Judah-Tamar story of Genesis 38, verses 1–6 function as exposition, introducing us to the geographical setting ("went down to . . . Adullam") and the characters who will play a part in the plot (Judah, his three sons, and Tamar). This information, which shows Judah making a break with his brothers and establishing relationships with the Canaanites, tips off the reader that Judah is not walking in fellowship with Yahweh.[7]

The exposition section of the story of Micah and the Danites in Judges 17–18 is quite brief. Likely, the exposition occurs in 17:1, which simply introduces us to Micah and where he lives before plunging into the crisis.

The book of Esther provides another example. Chapters 1 and 2 serve as the exposition. To understand the story of Esther, a reader must grasp King Xerxes's anger and compulsive behavior, Esther's secret nationality, and Mordecai's uncovering of an assassination plot. According to Esther 2:23, Mordecai's heroic deed was recorded in official court records. This information will become crucial in the events of chapter 6.

Crisis

From exposition, the plot moves into the crisis, variously described as the complication, the conflict, or the tension. Once the conflict appears, the tension rises as the story moves toward its resolution. For this reason, some scholars point to an inciting moment or occasioning incident when the problem appears for the first time. Subsequent development is described

---

5. Ska, "*Our Fathers Have Told Us*," 23.
6. Bar-Efrat, *Narrative Art in the Bible*, 114.
7. For an analysis of Gen. 38, see Mathewson, "Exegetical Study of Genesis 38," 373–92. Again, it is hard to determine precisely where the exposition ends. Ska, for example, says the exposition runs through verse 11 ("*Our Fathers Have Told Us*," 23–24).

as complication or rising tension. Scholars describe the highest level of intensity in the conflict as the climax or peak moment.

Returning to the previous three narratives, readers can see examples of the crisis stage in the plot structure. In Genesis 38, verses 7–24 form the crisis (or vv. 12–24, if you believe the exposition occurs in 1–11). There are actually two crises in this story. First, in verses 7–11 Yahweh puts two of Judah's sons, Er and Onan, to death. Tamar, Er's wife, is left as a childless widow when Judah refuses to give her his third son, Shelah, in keeping with the custom of levirate marriage.[8] Rather than moving quickly to a resolution, verses 12–24 build toward another crisis that flares up in verse 24.[9] There, Judah discovers Tamar's pregnancy and sentences her to be burned.

In Judges 17–18, the crisis unfolds as a series of actions that violate the law of Moses. The crisis, or series of crises, runs from Judges 17:2 through 18:10. Technically, the crisis may extend further, but the move toward resolution begins in 18:11 with the Danites setting out for the land of Laish, armed for battle.

In the book of Esther, the crisis occurs in chapters 3–4 where Haman plots to destroy the Jews and Esther decides to bring this matter to the king at the risk of her life.[10]

Resolution

Eventually, the story moves from crisis to resolution. In the resolution, the plot descends rapidly from its climax to a solution of the original conflict.[11] Ska comments, "What matters most in the analysis of a narrative, we think, is to pinpoint the resolution of the plot. This moment, more than any other, is the one the reader is waiting for. It is also easier

---

8. Verses 7–11 could be classified as a "preparatory scene" that "prepares for a decisive meeting and creates the appropriate atmosphere of hope, fear, or curiosity" (Ska, *"Our Fathers Have Told Us,"* 26). Ska discusses this in conjunction with the complication stage or moment of a plot.

9. Bar-Efrat calls this type of plot structure an "illusory conclusion." He writes, "In contrast to . . . examples, where the storyline gradually rises to a climax and then descends rapidly to the serene conclusion, here the narrative does not end after the gradual ascent and the rapid decline, but rises once more to another pinnacle, only then descending to the genuine conclusion" (*Narrative Art in the Bible*, 124).

10. Once again, the fluid changes between plot elements make it difficult to determine if the crisis section ends with chap. 4 or extends into chap. 5 where two more minicrises transpire: Esther delays her request to the king, and Haman builds a gallows on which to hang Mordecai.

11. Longman, *Literary Approaches*, 92.

to uncover the resolution than the other moments. After this resolution, the dramatic tension drops and can even disappear completely."[12]

In Genesis 38, the resolution occurs in verses 25–26 when Tamar produces the objects that indict Judah as the man who impregnated her. This might be described as the climax peak. The tension quickly subsides into resolution as Judah then pronounces her more righteous than himself.

The resolution of Judges 17–18 begins in 18:11, as noted above, and stretches through 18:30. In essence, the two parallel stories, which intertwine, are both resolved. Micah's acts of disobedience in constructing his own shrine, or "house of gods," result in all of it being stolen by the Danites (see 18:18–26). Even his priest abandons him. Then, resolution to the story of the Danites culminates in a brief, yet ominous, notice in 18:30. After the Danites capture Laish, they rebuild the city and name it Dan, living there "until the time of the captivity of the land." Thus, their seemingly happy resolution results in bondage.

In the book of Esther, the resolution takes place in 5:1–9:19 as Mordecai receives the honor Haman intended for himself, Haman receives the hanging he intended for Mordecai, and the Jews triumph over their enemies.

Conclusion (Denouement)

Finally, stories end in a conclusion or denouement. The latter term refers to the tying up of loose ends.[13] The conclusion or denouement generally sums up the outcome of the story or the fate of the main characters in the wake of the resolution. Or the conclusion can offer a special message to the reader. Some narratives do not have a conclusion distinguishable from the resolution. Some narratives "are open-ended or contain elements that prepare for another plot (Joseph story, Jonah, Judges 8:28–35 [Gideon] . . .)."[14] Often the conclusion is marked by someone who returns home or leaves for another destination.[15]

Returning to our examples, in Genesis 38, it is less certain whether verses 27–30 function separately from the resolution. In Judges 17–18, I consider 18:31 to be the conclusion to the narrative since it summarizes the outcome of the Danites' occupation of a new territory: "They continued

---

12. Ska, *"Our Fathers Have Told Us,"* 29.
13. Ryken, *Words of Delight*, 104.
14. Ska, *"Our Fathers Have Told Us,"* 29.
15. Bar-Efrat, *Narrative Art in the Bible*, 130–31. Cf. Alter, *Art of Biblical Narrative*, 65.

to use the idol Micah had made, all the time the house of God was in Shiloh." Esther 9:20–10:3 certainly functions as a conclusion. It informs the reader that Mordecai and Queen Esther established the feast of Purim and that Mordecai rose to greatness in the Persian government and in his people's esteem.

Archetypes

Another way to analyze plot is to identify the archetypes that show up in a story. When applied to the plot, the term *archetype* refers to a repeated pattern. In Old Testament narratives, these repeated patterns occur at the level of overall plot (*plot motifs*) and at the level of episodes or scenes within the plot (*type scenes*). Identifying them will help an interpreter see how a story develops in comparison to other Old Testament narratives or scenes of the same type.

Leland Ryken has produced an extensive list of plot motifs (see table 4.2).[16] Most notable are the comedy and the tragedy. A *comedy* is a "U-shaped story that begins in prosperity, descends into tragedy, and rises again to end happily."[17] The plots in Genesis 38 and the book of Esther take a comic direction. A *tragedy*, on the other hand, is "the story of exceptional calamity. It portrays a movement from prosperity to catastrophe."[18] The plot in Judges 17–18, for example, takes a tragic direction; other examples of tragedies in the Old Testament include the stories of Samson (Judg. 13–16), Saul (1 Sam. 8–31), and Esau (Gen. 25–27).[19]

Simon Parker opens up some additional categories in his comparative study of narratives in Northwest Semitic inscriptions and the Hebrew Bible. He identifies *petitionary narratives* (2 Sam. 12:1–7; 14:1–23; 1 Kings 3:16–27; 20:38–42; 2 Kings 4:1–7; 6:24–30; 8:1–6), *stories of military cam-*

---

16. Adapted from Ryken, *Words of Delight*, 49; and Ryken, *How to Read the Bible*, 53–54, 191–92.

17. Ryken, *How to Read the Bible*, 82. Ryken lists the following elements that have become virtually synonymous with literary comedy: disguise, mistaken identity, character transformation from bad to good, surprise, miracle, providential assistance to good characters, sudden reversal of misfortune, rescue from disaster, poetic justice, the motif of lost and found, reversal of conventional expectations such as the preference of the younger child over the older, and sudden release.

18. Ryken, *How to Read the Bible*, 83.

19. For a specialized study of the Old Testament tragedies of Saul, Jephthah, select members of Saul's house, and David, see Exum, *Tragedy and Biblical Narrative*.

> **Table 4.2**
>
> **Ryken's List of Plot Motifs**
>
> 1. *The quest [heroic narrative, hero story]*, in which a hero struggles to reach a goal, undergoing obstacles and temporary defeat before achieving success. (Examples: Joseph, David, Ruth, Abraham)
> 2. *The death-rebirth motif [pathetic plot]*, in which a hero endures death or danger and returns to life or security. (Examples: Hezekiah, Joseph)
> 3. *The initiation [admiration]*, in which a character is thrust out of an existing, usually ideal, situation and undergoes a series of ordeals as he or she encounters various forms of evil or hardship for the first time. (Examples: Elisha, Daniel, Jacob)
> 4. *The journey*, in which the characters encounter danger and experience growth as they move from one place to another. (Example: Jacob)
> 5. *Tragedy*, or the more specific form of *the fall from innocence*, depicting a decline from bliss to woe. (Examples: Saul, Samson)
> 6. *Comedy*, a U-shaped story that begins in prosperity, descends into tragedy, but rises to a happy ending as obstacles to success are overcome. (Examples: Judah and Tamar, Ruth, Esther)
> 7. *Crime and punishment [punitive plot]*, in which an unsympathetic or villainous character undergoes an adverse change of fortune as a punishment for misdeeds. (Examples: Gehazi, Jezebel, Ahab, Absalom)
> 8. *The temptation*, in which someone becomes the victim of an evil tempter or temptress. (Examples: Eve, Samson and Delilah)
> 9. *The rescue*. (Examples: Esther, Elisha at Dothan)
> 10. *The suffering-servant motif*, in which a character undergoes undeserved suffering for the benefit of others. (Example: Joseph)
> 11. *The Cinderella or rags-to-riches motif*, in which a character overcomes the obstacles of ostracism and poverty. (Example: David, Gideon)
> 12. *The movement from ignorance to epiphany [revelation story]*, in which a character progresses from ignorance to insight and illumination. (Example: Abraham)

paigns (2 Kings 13–14; Josh. 10; 2 Sam. 8), and *stories of miraculous deliverance from a siege* (2 Kings 3:4–27; 6:24–7:20; 18:13–19:37). Parker's analysis of the petitionary narrative in 1 Kings 3:16–27 (Solomon and the two prostitutes who claim to be mother to the same baby) demonstrates the value of his study. He observes, "In all petitionary narratives, the reader's sympathies or interests are engaged on the side of the petitioner rather than the party against whom the petition is lodged."[20] In this story, "the narrator chose to quote fully the petition of the one woman, and the effect of that choice is to dispose the reader in her favor."[21] Thus, this petitionary narrative "engages us morally; we now have an emotional investment in the outcome, and we are not only intellectually satisfied but also emotionally relieved when Solomon exposes the truth."[22]

Within the overall framework of a plot, type scenes recur as well. Type scenes are repeated events or situations that occur in Bible stories. These scenes "are built around understood conventions about what should be included and in what order items should appear."[23] Ryken likens type scenes to a brief interview on the evening news. Such an interview typically starts with a shot of the interviewer in front of an appropriate background. Depending on the news story, the background might be the stands of a sports stadium or the wreckage of a disaster. Then the interviewer begins a question-and-answer dialogue with a point guard or a congressional leader or a biology teacher. Finally, the camera zooms in on the interviewer who looks into the camera and offers a summary or interpretation. Why does virtually every television news interview follow this format? According to Ryken, it is simply the established convention of the genre.[24]

Robert Alter lists some of the most commonly repeated biblical type scenes: the announcement of the birth of a hero to his barren mother, the encounter with one's future spouse at a well, the epiphany in the field, the initiatory trial, danger in the desert and discovery of a well or other source of sustenance, and the testament of a dying hero.[25] Robert Culley also identifies several types of "action sequences" on which plots may be built (see table 4.3). In each action sequence, something arouses an expectation, and then the expectation is fulfilled.[26] Most biblical stories contain more than one action sequence.

What is the payoff for identifying type scenes? Weston W. Fields argues, "In a word, a motif often carries the essential message of a story."[27] Alter

20. Parker, *Stories in Scripture and Inscriptions*, 23.
21. Parker, *Stories in Scripture and Inscriptions*, 24.
22. Parker, *Stories in Scripture and Inscriptions*, 24.
23. Ryken, *Words of Delight*, 50.
24. Ryken, *Words of Delight*, 50.
25. Alter, *Art of Biblical Narrative*, 51.
26. Culley, *Themes and Variations*, 50.
27. Fields, *Sodom and Gomorrah*, 20. "The function of motifs and submotifs, therefore, is *representational*: the intent is to communicate a message or a series of messages beyond the

> **Table 4.3**
>
> ### Culley's List of Action Sequences
>
> **Punishment Sequences**
>
> 1. *Wrong/punished* (Elijah's curse of boys; fate of Lot's wife)
> 2. *Injury/avenged* (Amnon and Absalom; Dinah)
>
> **Rescue Sequences**
>
> 3. *Difficulty/rescued* (Elisha and lost axhead; Elijah and widow's boy)
> 4. *Difficulty/escaped* (Hebrew midwives; Michal's rescue of David)
>
> **Achievement Sequences**
>
> 5. *Desire/achieved* (Ahab and Naboth's vineyard; Gehazi; Isaac's deceit)
> 6. *Task/accomplished* (wife for Isaac; Abraham's test)
>
> **Reward Sequences**
>
> 7. *Good deed/rewarded* (couple who hosts Elisha; Hebrew midwives)
>
> **Announcement Sequences**
>
> 8. *Announcement/happened* (creation story; Abram's call; Micaiah)
>
> **Prohibition Sequences**
>
> 9. *Prohibition/transgressed* (Lot's wife; garden of Eden)

explains what happens when a storyteller came, for example, to the moment of his hero's betrothal: "Both he and his audience were aware that the scene had to unfold in particular circumstances, according to a fixed order. If some of those circumstances were altered or suppressed, or if the scene were actually omitted, that communicated something to the audience."[28]

We find an example in Genesis 38. Throughout Genesis, the motif of the elder serving the younger occurs frequently. Normally, the younger brother would serve the older brother. In Genesis 38, this motif is worked out in the birth of Tamar's twin sons, emphasizing God's sovereign plan of grace in which he accomplishes his purpose by using unexpected and even weaker means. God's blessing is extended to those who have no other claim to it.[29]

---

action, object, character, or situation portrayed, or to offer plastic illustrations which present all the options" (21).

28. Alter, *Art of Biblical Narrative*, 52.
29. See Sailhamer, "Genesis," 225.

Repetition

Another detail to pay attention to when analyzing the action of a narrative is repetition. When I took advanced composition in my junior year of high school, I always dreaded the red-ink symbol "R&R" on my writing assignments. "R&R" meant "redundant and repetitive." Mrs. Blair, my English teacher, frowned upon repeated statements. Her preference was to say it well one time. When it was necessary to refer to something twice, she told us to use a different term the second time. In English literature, repetition is a sin.

In Old Testament narratives, though, repetition is a virtue. It is a technique used by writers to accomplish what we accomplish today through larger font sizes, boldface type, or italics. Thus, plot analysis requires paying attention to repetition.

David M. Gunn and Danna Nolan Fewell comment on the technique of repetition employed in Old Testament narrative literature: "Whereas English prose eschews repetition, so that we are constantly looking for synonyms as we write, ancient Hebrew prose enjoys it. The verbatim repetition of a word, phrase, sentence, or set of sentences, or even the recurrence of words falling into the same semantic range can function to structure the story, to create atmosphere, to construct a theme or character, to emphasize a certain point to the reader, or to build suspense."[30]

Where does repetition occur? Sometimes, a command or prophecy is cited at one point and then is "closely followed by its verbatim fulfillment."[31] For example, Joshua 6:20 describes the Israelite conquest of Jericho by repeating the identical terms that God used in issuing the command in Joshua 6:5:

> Now it will happen when there is a blast of the ram's horn, *when they hear the voice of the shofar,* that *all the people will shout a great war-shout.* Then the city *wall will fall down to the ground, and the people will go up, each one straight ahead.* (Josh. 6:5)

> So the people shouted, and they blew the shofars. Now it happened as the people *heard the voice of the shofar,* that *the people shouted a great*

---

30. Gunn and Fewell, *Narrative in the Hebrew Bible*, 148. Alter also attributes the use of repetition to the oral context in which the Bible was communicated since its audience generally listened to rather than read the text (*Art of Biblical Narrative*, 90).

31. Alter, *Art of Biblical Narrative*, 90–91. See also Bar-Efrat, *Narrative Art in the Bible*, 161.

war-shout. Then the *wall fell down to the ground, and the people went up to the city, each one straight ahead*. (Josh. 6:20)[32]

This kind of repetition highlights the people's precise obedience, indicating "that everything happens exactly as God commanded."[33] On the other hand, Bar-Efrat suggests that "special attention should be paid to the differences which often exist between the first and second versions, such as addition, omission, expansion, summarization, changed order, and substitution."[34] For a classic example, compare the dialogue between the woman and the serpent in Genesis 3:1–3 where God's original command (Gen. 2:16–17) is distorted by the serpent and expanded by the woman.

Repetition may also occur in the recurrence of a key word (*leitwort*).[35] Alter cites David's response to Absalom's death as an example: "The poet-king, who elsewhere responds to the report of deaths with eloquent elegies, here simply sobs, 'Absalom, Absalom, my son, my son,' repeating 'my son' eight times in two verses (2 Sam. 19:1, 5)."[36] The narrative in 2 Samuel 9 provides another example in its repetition of the term *lovingkindness* (vv. 1, 3, and 7, author's translation).

J. P. Fokkelman argues that David's wish to show lovingkindness to Mephibosheth is the driving force of the action: "Not only are there three scenes and three protagonists but the passage II Sam. 9 has three paragraphs of text in which *ḥsd* [the Hebrew term translated "lovingkindness"] appears three times. Also, the manifestation of lovingkindness comes up three times."[37] Similarly, the variations in 1 Samuel 15 on the terms *listen*, *voice*, and *word* stress the theme. This repetition highlights Saul's failure to listen to God's Word and instead to listen to the people's voice.[38]

Linguists have noted that the technique of "renominalizing" (the repetition of a proper name) may mark a climactic point in the text, such as in Genesis 37:28, where the name Joseph occurs three times in the Hebrew (rather than being referenced after the first occurrence by pronouns, as

---

32. Author's translation. The corresponding elements have been italicized.
33. Bar-Efrat, *Narrative Art in the Bible*, 162.
34. Bar-Efrat, *Narrative Art in the Bible*, 162.
35. Alter, *Art of Biblical Narrative*, 92.
36. Alter, *Art of Biblical Narrative*, 92. In English Bibles, the references would be 2 Sam. 18:33 and 19:4. For comments on the slight inversion in the wording between the two laments, see Berlin, *Poetics and Interpretation*, 75.
37. Fokkelman, *Narrative Art and Poetry*, 1:26.
38. Alter, *Art of Biblical Narrative*, 93.

most English translations do).³⁹ Repetition of a proper name to refer to a participant when a pronoun is sufficient may also "indicate that what he says is important, surprising, or unexpected (e.g., Gen. 18:13; 42:14; 46:30; Judg. 6:13; 8:23)."⁴⁰

Time and Pace

While tracking the plot, an interpreter must observe the pace at which a narrative unfolds. Literary scholars differentiate between *narrated time* (or *actual time*) and *narration time* (see table 4.4). Narrated time consists of the time within a narrative. Thus, Yairah Amit refers to it as "internal" time.⁴¹ It describes the length of the actions in the story and is thus measured in "real" units, such as days or years.⁴² Narrated time is subject to gaps, delays, acceleration, and even movement in different directions.⁴³ Bar-Efrat comments on some of the functions of narrated time:

> Apart from its role within the narrative itself, such as providing emphases or implying connections between separate incidents, narrated time can fulfil direct functions for the reader, such as creating suspense or determining attitudes. . . . Since the decision as to what to include and what to omit, what to convey rapidly and on what to dwell at length, is closely bound up with the importance of the various subjects, the character of time as it is shaped within the narrative will be of great value in any attempt to analyze and interpret the narrative.⁴⁴

Narration time refers to the time required for telling or reading the narrative.⁴⁵ To put it another way, narration time equals the length of material—that is, how many words or sentences or paragraphs it takes to tell or read the story.⁴⁶ It is "external time"—that is, something "more or less known and shared by all readers"—whether this involves minutes or hours.⁴⁷

---

39. Van der Merwe, "Discourse Linguistics," 35.
40. Van der Merwe, "Discourse Linguistics," 35.
41. Amit, *Reading Biblical Narratives*, 104.
42. Ska, *"Our Fathers Have Told Us,"* 7.
43. Bar-Efrat, *Narrative Art in the Bible*, 142.
44. Bar-Efrat, *Narrative Art in the Bible*, 142–43.
45. Bar-Efrat, *Narrative Art in the Bible*, 143.
46. Ska, *"Our Fathers Have Told Us,"* 8.
47. Amit, *Reading Biblical Narratives*, 104.

Table 4.4		
Narrated (Actual) Time	vs.	**Narration Time**
Time of actual events		Time needed to tell events
Measured by days/weeks		Measured by story's length

To be honest, I often get the labels mixed up. So why bother with the distinction? As it turns out, there is value in comparing narrative time (length of actual events) with narration time (length of material needed to relate actual events). According to Ska, "The ratio between the two makes it possible for the reader to detect the necessary choices of the narrator and the effects he wanted to produce."[48] Bar-Efrat elaborates on this idea: "By studying the relation between narration time and narrated time the relative weight of the various sections of the narrative will be clarified, as well as their proportions with regard to one another and the narrative as a whole, thereby disclosing the focal points of the narrative. By elucidating the relationship between the two systems we will be able to see in how much detail matters are presented within the narrative, enabling us to draw conclusions about the meaning of the narrative, its central theme, etc."[49]

Jerome Walsh points out that narrators can move a story along more quickly and summarize when "events take longer to happen than to read about." By contrast, a narrator can slow down a story and create delay when "events take less time to transpire than to recount."[50]

For example, the narration in Genesis 38:1–11 moves at a rapid pace to lay the groundwork for the subsequent events in the story.[51] Alter explains,

> Genesis 38 begins with Judah fathering three sons, one after another, recorded in breathless pace. Here, as at other points in the episode, nothing is allowed to detract our focused attention from the primary, problematic subject of the proper channel for the seed. In a triad of verbs that admits nothing adventitious, Judah sees, takes, lies with a woman; and she, responding appropriately, conceives, bears and gives the son a name. Then,

48. Ska, *"Our Fathers Have Told Us,"* 8.
49. Bar-Efrat, *Narrative Art in the Bible*, 143.
50. Walsh, *Old Testament Narrative*, 54–57.
51. Mathewson, "Exegetical Study of Genesis 38," 376–81. Gerhard von Rad writes, "The real action in the Judah-Tamar story begins at vs. 12ff. But for the reader to understand this extremely odd occurrence the narrator must first acquaint him with a few conditions" (*Genesis*, 352).

with no narrative indication of any events at all in the intervening time, we move ahead an entire generation to the inexplicable death of Er, Judah's firstborn, after his marriage to Tamar.[52]

After Genesis 38:12 signals a sizable time gap ("Now after the days became many"[53]), the action slows down as it enters the heart of the story. Verses 12–23 linger on Judah's sexual liaison with the disguised Tamar and his unsuccessful attempt to make payment. The action accelerates again in verse 24. While the quick pace in verses 1–11 served to cover background information, the return to a quick pace in verse 24 enables the narrative to proceed "quickly to its dramatic climax."[54]

To summarize, while the narrated time in Genesis 38:1–11 amounts to approximately eighteen to twenty years,[55] the narration time amounts to about 32 percent of the narrative.[56] In Genesis 38:12–30, the narrated time amounts to approximately nine months, while the narration time amounts to about 68 percent of the narrative.

Genesis 22 provides another good example. In verses 9–10, a string of seven verbs rapidly advances the main storyline, forcing the reader to agonize with Abraham as he reaches the place, builds the altar, arranges the wood, ties up his son Isaac, lays him on the altar, reaches out his hand, and takes the knife.[57] Alter argues that "sudden dense concentrations or unbroken chains of verbs, usually attached to a single subject, . . . indicate some particular intensity, rapidity, or a single-minded purposefulness of activity."[58] By contrast, earlier in the story (v. 2) the narrator suspends the action as he relates God's instructions to Abraham. Four phrases slow down the narrated time, creating suspense. With each phrase, the tension builds as the specificity increases. God said, "Take your son . . . the only son you have . . . the one you love . . . Isaac."[59]

---

52. Alter, *Art of Biblical Narrative*, 6.
53. Author's translation.
54. Rad, *Genesis*, 355.
55. For the chronology of the events in Gen. 38:1–11, see Mathewson, "Exegetical Study of Genesis 38," 382–83.
56. This percentage is based on the number of lines in the Hebrew text (*Biblia Hebraica Stuttgartensia*) of Gen. 38. It is also confirmed by a word count.
57. These are all *wayyiqtol* forms (also called "preterite" or "imperfect with *waw-*consecutive"). Their function in narrative is to advance the main line of the story. Appendix B discusses this feature in detail.
58. Alter, *Art of Biblical Narrative*, 80.
59. Author's translation of the Hebrew text of Gen. 22:2a.

Point of View

How readers experience Old Testament stories depends in part on the perspective of the storyteller. Adele Berlin reminds readers that "a character is not perceived by the reader directly, but rather mediated or filtered through the telling of the (implied) author, the narrator, or another character."[60] We refer to the storyteller's perspective as the point of view. Longman explains, "The narrator is the one who controls the story. His is the voice through whom we hear about the action and the people of the narrative. The narrator's point of view is the perspective through which we observe and evaluate everything connected with the story. In short, the narrator is a device used by authors to shape and guide how the reader responds to the characters and events of the story."[61] So in addition to examining a story's plot, characters, and setting, interpreters must also zero in on a story's point of view or perspective.

Generally, the Old Testament narrators adopt a third-person point of view. The most notable exceptions are certain stories in Nehemiah that are cast in first-person narrative. The following description of the Gospel of Mark's "narrator" applies equally well to the narrators of Old Testament stories: "The narrator does not figure in the events of the story; speaks in the third person; is not bound by time or space in the telling of the story; is an implied invisible presence in every scene, capable of being anywhere to 'recount' the action; displays full omniscience by narrating the thoughts, feelings, or sensory experiences of many characters; often turns from the story to give direct 'asides' to the reader, explaining a custom or translating a word or commenting on the story; and narrates the story from one overarching ideological point of view."[62]

Focalization

A key aspect of the storyteller's point of view is called *focalization*. More specifically, this aspect observes what material in the narrative arises from the *reader's* point of view ("external focalization" or "vision from

---

60. Adele Berlin, *Poetics and Interpretation*, 43. Like Jean Louis Ska, I find the distinctions between "implied author" and "narrator" and between "implied reader" and "narrator" to be "practically irrelevant in most of the Biblical narratives" (Ska, "Our Fathers Have Told Us," 42).
61. Longman, "Biblical Narrative," 75.
62. Rhoads and Michie, *Mark as Story*, 36.

without"), what material issues from the *character's* point of view ("internal focalization" or "vision from within"), and what material comes from the *narrator's* point of view ("zero focalization" or "vision from behind").[63] The first focalization is considered an *external* point of view. The next two focalizations—character and narrator—are considered *internal* points of view (see table 4.5).

In Genesis 38, for example, the story begins with an external point of view. That is, "the reader first has the impression that the narrative is told by an external observer listing facts."[64] But in verse 7, the narrator adopts an internal perspective. More specifically, he shares information from the narrator's point of view, not the character's. The text gives us no reason to assume that the character, Er, was privy to this information. In other words, the narrator is saying more than the character knows. However, in verse 9 the narrator discloses what Onan knows. This internal perspective is assumed by the character as well as the narrator.

Table 4.5

Points of View

External
↓
- Reader—what an observer knows

Internal
↓
- Character—what a character knows (more than a reader knows)
- Narrator—what a narrator knows (more than a character knows)

Interpreters can look for three indicators of a shift in focalization (see table 4.6).[65] First, focalization is often indicated by verbs of perception (to see, to hear, to know, etc.). A second indicator is the expression "to say to one's heart" as in Genesis 8:21 and 27:41.[66] A third indicator is the Hebrew particle וְהִנֵּה, *wehinneh* (often translated as "behold"). This particle sometimes signals a shift from the narrator's omniscient perspective

---

63. Ska, "*Our Fathers Have Told Us*," 66–67.
64. Ska, "*Our Fathers Have Told Us*," 69.
65. Ska, "*Our Fathers Have Told Us*," 67–68.
66. English translations typically translate the expression in these instances as "said to himself" or "said in his heart."

to the character's perspective.⁶⁷ That is, the narrator shows the reader a certain detail through the eyes of the character. For examples, see Genesis 24:63; 28:12–13; 29:25; Judges 3:24–25; 2 Samuel 15:24; 18:24; and 1 Kings 18:7. Sometimes, a more word-for-word translation is necessary, like the English Standard Version (ESV) or the New American Standard Bible (NASB), since some translations, like the New International Version (NIV), leave *wehinneh* untranslated for stylistic reasons. In Genesis 28:12–13a, the particle *wehinneh* ("behold") occurs three times within a short space, each time signifying what Jacob saw in his dream: "And he dreamed, and behold, there was a ladder set up on the earth, and the top of it reached to heaven. And behold, the angels of God were ascending and descending on it! And behold, the LORD stood above it and said . . ." (ESV).

Table 4.6

Indicators of Shifts in Focalization

1. Verbs of perception (to see, to hear, to know)
2. The expression "to say to one's heart"
3. The particle *wehinneh* (*hinneh*, "behold")

Irony

Another feature of the narrator's perspective is irony. Irony refers to an incongruity or discrepancy.⁶⁸ There are three basic types of irony in Old Testament narrative literature (see table 4.7). Ska distinguishes between the first two types: verbal and dramatic.⁶⁹ Verbal irony refers to statements in which a character says one thing and intends the opposite. An example is Michal's speech to David after he returned from the parade that brought the ark of the covenant into Jerusalem. Her words are recorded in 2 Samuel 6:20: "And David returned to bless his household. But Michal the daughter of Saul came out to meet David and said, 'How the king of Israel honored himself today, uncovering himself today before the eyes of his servants' female servants, as one of the vulgar fellows shamelessly uncovers himself!'" (ESV) She meant that David had *not* honored himself.

---

67. Fokkelman, *Narrative Art in Genesis*, 50–55; Bar-Efrat, *Narrative Art in the Bible*, 35–36; Berlin, *Poetics and Interpretation*, 62–63.
68. Ryken, *Words of Delight*, 361.
69. Ska, "*Our Fathers Have Told Us*," 57–61.

Table 4.7
Three Types of Irony 1. *Verbal*—The character says one thing and means something else. 2. *Dramatic*—The character says something but does not understand its full implications. 3. *Situational*—The situation is the opposite of what is expected or appropriate.

On the other hand, dramatic irony occurs when a character says one thing but does not perceive what the reader knows to be true. Bar-Efrat explains that dramatic irony "derives from the fact that the character knows less than the reader, or unknowingly does things which are not in his or her own best interests, or from the course of events leading to results which are the reverse of the character's aspirations."[70] Sisera's speech to Jael in Judges 4:20 offers a prime example. When he seeks refuge in her tent, he instructs her, "Stand in the doorway of the tent. . . . If someone comes by and asks you, 'Is anyone in there?' say 'No.'"

Sisera did not realize the truth behind the answer he instructed Jael to give. There would not be anyone present because he would be dead with a tent peg driven through his temple! Uriah's response to King David provides an additional example of dramatic irony. In 2 Samuel 11:10, David asks Uriah why he had not returned home to his wife to spend the night. Uriah's reply is recorded in 2 Samuel 11:11: "Uriah said to David, 'The ark and Israel and Judah are staying in tents, and my commander Joab and my lord's men are camped in the open country. How could I go to my house to eat and drink and make love to my wife? As surely as you live, I will not do such a thing!'" Bar-Efrat comments on the "ironic sting in his words," assuming that Uriah did not know what David had done with Bathsheba, Uriah's wife, in Uriah's absence:

> To all intents and purposes Uriah simply compares his conditions with those of his comrades in the field, declaring that he will not enjoy any privilege which they cannot share. The sting, however, lies in the fact that an implicit comparison is made between his behaviour and David's. Uriah asserts that he will not go to lie with his wife, and that is precisely what

---

70. Bar-Efrat, *Narrative Art in the Bible*, 125.

David has been doing! ... The subtle irony reaches its zenith when Uriah swears by David's life, namely, by the life of the man who did just what he will not do.[71]

Ryken mentions a third type of irony. Irony of situation occurs when a situation is the opposite of what is expected or appropriate.[72] An example would be Gehazi, Elisha's servant, contracting the leprosy from which Naaman had just been healed (2 Kings 5:27). An additional case including irony of situation would be the story of Saul setting out in search of lost donkeys and coming back with a kingdom (1 Sam. 9).

Chiasmus

Another potential tool for analyzing the action (plot) of a narrative is searching for chiasmus or chiastic structure. To be honest, I am a bit hesitant about recommending this tool for pastors. Identifying a chiastic structure is usually a challenging, time-consuming task. It is also a speculative venture.[73] Therefore, it might be wise to leave chiasmus to the commentators. If they identify a chiastic structure, you can work with it to see if it provides any useful insights into how the narrative flows and fits together. What follows, then, is a brief introduction to this feature and how it works.

In a chiastic structure, "the same language and style elements are repeated in the second part in reverse order—last matching first and first matching last."[74] Thus, a chiastic pattern is diagrammed as follows:

A
  B
    C
    C′
  B′
A′

---

71. Bar-Efrat, *Narrative Art in the Bible*, 126.
72. Ryken, *Words of Delight*, 361. While Ska does not label this category, he seems to include it as an aspect of dramatic irony ("*Our Fathers Have Told Us*," 60).
73. "Discussions on chiasmus in the Bible have offered an abundance of all sorts of writings in which there is chiastic repetition; but there is no one rule for all of them" (Avishur, *Studies in Biblical Narrative*, 15).
74. Avishur, *Studies in Biblical Narrative*, 15.

Sometimes, there is a lone element at the center, on which the pattern turns. In this case, the pattern would be diagrammed as follows:[75]

A
  B
    C
      D
    C′
  B′
A′

Israeli scholar Yitzhak Avishur finds that all examples of chiasmus in the Hebrew Bible should be classified into one of four categories:[76]

1. Chiasmus in a *verse* of prose or poetry.
2. Chiasmus in a *paragraph* of prose and in a *stanza* or *strophe* in poetry.
3. Chiasmus in an *entire work* in prose (a story or a speech) and in poetry (a poem or a speech).
4. Chiasmus in a *literary division* (a cycle of stories, a series of chapters, or a whole biblical book).

What is the value of identifying a chiastic structure? Writers use chiastic structure to limit the boundaries of a section.[77] Also, when a lone item stands at the center of a chiasm, the writer makes it the focal point or turning point.[78] David A. Dorsey cites the body of the book of Judges (chapters 3–16) as an example. In the stories of seven major judges, the rule of Gideon stands at the center and functions as the story's turning point. "Until Gideon's rule, Israel did well under the judges; with Gideon's rule, however, things deteriorated, and from his time to the end of the period, Israel experienced a succession of bad rulers and civil wars" (see table 4.8).[79]

One of the more obvious examples of chiasm appears in Genesis 11:1–9. J. P. Fokkelman has convincingly demonstrated that the chiastic structure

---

75. Jerome Walsh distinguishes between a double-centered structure (ABCC′B′A′) which he refers to as "chiastic" and a single-centered structure (ABCB′A′) which he labels "concentric" (*Style and Structure in Biblical Hebrew Narrative*, 13).
76. Avishur, *Studies in Biblical Narrative*, 15.
77. Pratt, *He Gave Us Stories*, 220.
78. Dorsey, *Literary Structure*, 31.
79. Dorsey, *Literary Structure*, 31.

> **Table 4.8**
>
> **Dorsey's Chiastic Structure of Judges 3–16**
>
> A Othniel and his <u>good wife</u> (3:7–11; cf. 1:11–15)
>   B Ehud and the victory <u>at the Jordan fords</u> (3:12–31)
>   C Deborah: <u>enemy's skull crushed by woman</u> (4:1–5:31)
>   D Gideon: turning point (6:1–8:32)
>   C′ Abimelech: judge's <u>skull crushed by woman</u> (8:33–10:5)
>   B′ Jephthah and the civil war <u>at the Jordan fords</u> (10:6–12:15)
> A′ Samson and his <u>bad wives</u> (13:1–16:31)
>
> Adapted from Dorsey, *Literary Structure*, 31.

consists of an "even six pairs, plus the turning-point flanked by them."[80] Verses 1–4 describe what the human beings do. Verses 5–9 then describe what God does. God's intervention in verse 5 forms the turning point of the story (see table 4.9).[81]

Tim Mackie, cofounder of The Bible Project, says that Bible readers can get the most out of chiastic structure by reading the A elements together, the B elements together, the C elements together, etc.[82] Comparing each section with its matching pair may help readers see the narrator's emphasis more vividly.

If you want to learn more about chiastic structure, I have two suggestions. First, see the brief discussion in *The Modern Preacher and the Ancient Text* by Sidney Greidanus.[83] Second, get a copy of *The Literary Structure of the Old Testament: A Commentary on Genesis–Malachi* by David A. Dorsey. He provides a concise discussion of symmetric (chiastic) patterns in an early chapter.[84] Then, he works through the Old Testament book by book, providing insight into chiastic types of structures in every book.

Creating an Exegetical Outline

Your analysis of a story's plot should culminate in the creation of an exegetical outline. You will not preach from this outline, so you do not have

---

80. Fokkelman, *Narrative Art in Genesis*, 22.
81. Fokkelman, *Narrative Art in Genesis*, 23.
82. Personal conversation with Tim Mackie, May 2019.
83. Greidanus, *Modern Preacher*, 209–11.
84. Dorsey, *Literary Structure*, 30–32.

Table 4.9

Fokkelman's Chiastic Structure of Genesis 11:1–9

```
A   All the earth had one language (1)
 B   there (2)
  C   one to another (3)
   D   Come, let us make bricks (3)
    E   Let us build for ourselves (4)
     F   a city and a tower (4)
      X   And the Lord came down to see (5)
     F′  the city and the tower (5)
    E′  that the humans built (5)
   D′  Come, let us confuse (7)
  C′  everyone the language of his neighbor (7)
 B′  from there (8)
A′  (confused) the language of the whole earth (9)
```

Adapted from Fokkelman, *Narrative Art in Genesis*, 22.

---

to polish it excessively. Try to capture the flow of the narrative. Your main points should reflect the elements of the plot (whether you label them or not)—particularly the narrative's crisis and resolution. Then, you can list key details within these larger sections as subpoints. Also, write out your outline points as sentences. This will force you to think through the ideas you are trying to summarize. Again, this is not a sermon outline; it is an exegetical outline. You will return to it later when you prepare a sermon outline. The following is an example of an exegetical outline of Judges 17–18.

I. Micah builds an idol and appoints a priest for his "house of God" (17:1–13)

II. The Danites decide to seize the distant city of Laish instead of taking over the inheritance assigned to them (18:1–10)

III. The Danites take Micah's idol and priest on their way to capturing Laish, leaving Micah with nothing (18:11–26)

IV. The Danites capture Laish and establish the city of Dan, worshiping Micah's idol until the land ends up in captivity (18:27–31)

Points I and II reflect the two crises in the narrative, while points III and IV reflect the two resolutions. An outline like this is sufficient. However, if you want to go into more detail, you could label the crises and resolutions and then add another level of subpoints.

 I. *Crisis 1:* Micah builds an idol and appoints a priest for his "house of God" (17:1–13)
   A. Micah's mother dedicates the money he stole and returned to Yahweh for him to make an image (1–4)
   B. Micah adds an ephod and some household gods to his "house of God" and installs one of his sons as priest (5)
   C. *Refrain*: In those days, Israel had no king, and everyone did as they saw fit (6)
   D. Micah appoints a young wandering Levite as his priest, believing this act will lead to God's favor (7–13)
 II. *Crisis 2:* The Danites decide to seize the distant city of Laish instead of taking over the inheritance assigned to them (18:1–10)
   A. *Refrain:* In those days, Israel had no king (1a)
   B. The Danites commission an unauthorized spy mission to find a place to live due to their failure to settle in their inheritance (1b–2a)
   C. The Danite spies encounter Micah's priest on their journey and receive his assurance of God's approval (2b–6)
   D. The Danite spies see the peace and prosperity of Laish and encourage the Danites to attack and take the city (7–10)
 III. *Resolution 1:* The Danites take Micah's idol and priest on their way to capturing Laish, leaving Micah with nothing (18:11–26)
   A. The Danite warriors stop at Micah's house on their way to Laish and take his idol, ephod, and household gods (11–17)
   B. Micah's priest initially protests, but eventually he is pleased to accept their offer for him to serve as their priest (18–21)
   C. Micah and his neighbors pursue the Danite warriors, but Micah returns home without his priest and idols (22–26)
 IV. *Resolution 2:* The Danites capture Laish and establish the city of Dan, worshiping Micah's idol until the land ends up in captivity (18:27–31)

A. The Danite warriors overtake the isolated, vulnerable people of Laish who had been living in peace and security (27–28)
B. The Danites rebuild the city and name it Dan (29)
C. The Danites set up the idol, and Micah's priest—a descendent of Moses!—and his sons served until the land went into captivity (30)
D. Meanwhile, the true house of God was in Shiloh (31)

Both outlines—the main-points-only version and the extended version—simply describe how the story unfolds.

Now that you have assessed the narrative's action (or plot), it is time to look more closely at the characters, the people who make the story interesting.

5

C is for Characters

Pixar Animation Studios has created many compelling, unforgettable characters: Dory, Wall-E, Anton Ego, and Woody, for example. Screenwriter Dean Movshovitz argues that these characters are the secret to the success of the movies in which they appear—whether the optimistic and amnesiac Dory, the mute and romantic Wall-E, the snobbish critic Anton Ego, or the loyal cowboy Woody.[1] These characters struggle outside their comfort zones and go through an emotional journey.[2]

The characters in Old Testament narratives are compelling too. As we have already noted, these narratives focus on action (plot development). Yet there is no plot—no conflict, struggle, or journey—without the characters. They infuse these narratives with interest. In the words of a popular rabbinic saying, "God made people because he loves stories." Perhaps the reverse is also true—God made stories because he loves people. Our interest in stories rivets us to the characters. We even identify stories by characters' names: the story of Ruth, the story of David, and the story of Samson and Delilah. Interpreting Old Testament stories requires us to pay attention to the characters and how they develop. Because plot is primary, our analysis should attempt to specify the function of characters in relationship to the plot.[3]

---

1. Movshovitz, *Pixar Storytelling*, 22.
2. Movshovitz, *Pixar Storytelling*, 8.
3. "The predominance of action and the lack of interest in the psychological processes of the characters are two of the main characteristics of Biblical narrative" (Ska, *"Our Fathers Have Told Us,"* 83).

Classifying the Characters

When reading an Old Testament narrative, interpreters should distinguish between major and minor characters (see table 5.1). This distinction arises from the size of a character's role in the story. Furthermore, interpreters should categorize the main characters based on the nature of their roles. Literary scholars identify the following character types: *protagonists* (central characters, those who are most indispensable to the plot), *antagonists* (the main adversaries or forces arrayed against central characters), and *foils* (characters who heighten the central character by providing a contrast or occasionally a parallel).[4]

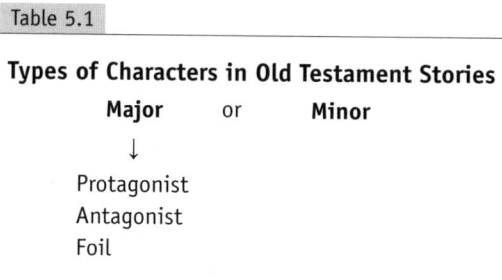

While these categories emerge from Western literary analysis, they seem to transcend Western literature and apply to stories of various cultures, including the Bible. The idea is not to reduce a character to a label but to clarify what role a narrator assigns to a particular character in a particular story.

The David story offers a prime example of how classifying characters aids exegesis. Beginning in 1 Samuel 16, David surfaces as the protagonist while Saul functions as both an antagonist and a foil.[5] Thus, while the conflict in 1 Samuel 17 occurs at one level between David and Goliath, it takes place at another level between David and Saul. Goliath provides the challenge that will reveal the contrast between David and Saul. The future king and the present king respond differently, revealing their fitness to occupy the throne of Israel.[6] David is clearly the hero.

---

4. Ska, *"Our Fathers Have Told Us,"* 86–87; Ryken, *How to Read the Bible*, 43, 54.

5. Brueggemann, *First and Second Samuel*, 124–25. Herbert M. Wolf has suggested that 1 Samuel 15 to 2 Samuel 8 functions as a "dynastic defense," similar in structure and theme to a thirteenth-century Hittite dynastic defense, "Apology of Hattusilis" ("Implications of Form Criticism," 303–6). This section, then, defends the replacement of Saul's house with David's house on the throne.

6. See Brueggemann, *First and Second Samuel*, 134.

In 1 Samuel 25, David remains the protagonist, Nabal functions as the antagonist who opposes David, and Abigail serves as the foil, contrasting David's thirst for retaliation with her discerning plea to let God execute vengeance. Yet Abigail is the true hero in this account. David changes so that by the end of the episode he shares the same conviction as Abigail.[7]

In 2 Samuel 11–12, David continues as the protagonist while Uriah the Hittite serves as the foil. As a foil, Uriah emerges as the hero of the story, demonstrating a level of integrity that David, the leading character, does not. Though Bathsheba is important to the story, her role is minor. Adele Berlin comments, "Throughout the entire story the narrator has purposely subordinated the character of Bathsheba. He has ignored her feelings and given the barest notice of her actions. For lack of a better designation, I will call her an 'agent,' an Aristotelian term which describes the performer of an action necessary to the plot."[8] Later, however, in 1 Kings 1–2, Bathsheba assumes the role of a leading character as she works to secure the throne for her son.[9]

In Genesis 38, Judah is the central character while Tamar serves as a foil. Judah and Tamar are clearly the major characters and everyone else serves in supporting or minor roles (see table 5.2). The terms *major* and *minor* refer to a character's role in a story, not their overall importance in redemptive history. In fact, the same person can play a different role in a different story. In Genesis 37 Judah functions as an antagonist, although a more sympathetic antagonist than his other brothers. In the larger framework of the Joseph story, however, Judah functions as a foil for Joseph.

What do you do once you've labeled the characters? Ryken explains that readers must go through the story as a "traveling companion of

Table 5.2

Character Classification in Genesis 38

Major: Judah—*protagonist*
Tamar—*foil*

Minor: Hirah, daughter of Shua, Er, Onan, Shelah, men at Timnah, midwife, Perez, Zerah

---

7. Some foils, such as Abigail in 1 Samuel 25 and Gehazi in 2 Kings 5, play a major role in the story. Others, such as Orpah in the book of Ruth, play a minor role.
8. Berlin, *Poetics and Interpretation*, 26–27.
9. Berlin, *Poetics and Interpretation*, 27. Berlin notes that there is an "alternation in the narratives [of 1, 2 Samuel and 1 Kings 1–2] between David as the main character and David as subordinate character, and that these correspond roughly to the public and private domains" (33).

the protagonist" and view this protagonist as "someone who undertakes an experiment in living."[10] The key is, "if we can see our own experience in the events and characters of the story, the story has captured something universal about life."[11] Furthermore, Ryken believes that "one of the greatest weaknesses of traditional biblical scholarship is its failure to cultivate an awareness of the genre of hero stories." These stories are "built around a central protagonist who is held up for admiration"—heroes like Daniel or Esther. In fact, he claims that the genre of narrative is "almost synonymous with the subgenre of hero story."[12] The payoff for identifying a narrative as a hero story is the questions it compels us to ask. What represents the right way to live? What constitutes heroic action? What character traits does the story encourage us to emulate or avoid?[13]

Means of Characterization

In John Grisham's novel *The Testament*, lawyer Nate Riley searches for the surprise heir to an eleven-billion-dollar fortune—a missionary named Rachel Lane. Riley finally finds her deep in the jungles of Brazil. At their initial encounter, a group of tribesmen escort Rachel to Riley. Notice how Grisham describes her as he relates the encounter: "Rachel was with them; she was coming. There was a light yellow shirt in the midst of the brown-skinned chests, and a lighter face under a straw hat. . . . She was slightly taller than the Indians, and carried herself with an easy elegance. . . . Nate watched every step. She was very slender, with wide bony shoulders. She began looking in their direction as they grew closer. . . . She removed her hat. Her hair was brown and half-gray, and very short."[14]

Similarly, Louis L'Amour paints a vivid picture of James T. Kettleman, the main character in his novel *Flint*:

> His face was lean and hard, triangular, with high cheekbones, green eyes, and a strong jaw. His sideburns were long in the fashion of the time, his hair dark brown and curly. In the light it showed a tinge of red. His skin was dark, his features, except for his eyes, normally without expression.

10. Ryken, *How to Read the Bible*, 43.
11. Ryken, *How to Read the Bible*, 44. See also 1 Cor. 10:11.
12. Ryken, *How Bible Stories Work*, 101.
13. Ryken, *How Bible Stories Work*, 103–4.
14. Grisham, *Testament*, 254.

James T. Kettleman, financier and speculator, had often been called a handsome man. He had never been called a friendly one.[15]

Our Western literary tradition, particularly the novel, goes to great lengths to paint character portraits. In contrast to a Charlotte Brontë or Charles Dickens, the authors of Old Testament narratives tell their stories in a lean, spare style.[16] Thus, characterization in Old Testament narratives resembles a quick pencil sketch. As Robert Alter notes, "We are given only the barest hints about the physical appearance, the tics and gestures, the dress and implements of the characters, the material milieu in which they enact their destinies."[17] Meir Sternberg observes that elaborate descriptions "perform no other role than realistic fullness."[18] The biblical storytellers do not concern themselves with vivid depictions.[19]

Direct Description

The scarcity of detailed description makes it significant when it does occur. Descriptive details are highly significant because "the ratio of description in general to action and dialogue is relatively low."[20] Therefore, every detail in biblical narrative merits attention. Adele Berlin comments, "The purpose of character description in the Bible is not to enable the reader to visualize the character, but to enable him to situate the character in terms of his place in society, his own particular

---

15. Louis L'Amour, *Flint* (New York: Bantam Books, 1960), 4.
16. T. Long, *Preaching and the Literary Forms*, 78.
17. Alter, *Art of Biblical Narrative*, 114. Alter refers to the "rigorous economy of biblical narrative," which is different from the "Greek tendency to narrative specification that modern literary practice has by and large adopted" (129).
18. Sternberg, *Poetics of Biblical Narrative*, 329.
19. Shimon Bar-Efrat writes,
   The absence of depictions in biblical narrative is connected with the tension which exists in a work of literature between the categories of time and space.... Narration time continues when a more or less detailed description of places or scenes is given, while narrated time comes to a standstill. By stopping narrated time a static element is introduced, and this is incompatible with the dynamic and vigorous nature of biblical narrative. The biblical narrative is wholly devoted to creating a sense of time which flows continually and rapidly, and this is inevitably achieved at the expense of the shaping of space. Because space is fundamentally static and unchanging it is an alien element in biblical narrative. (*Narrative Art in the Bible* [Sheffield, UK: Almond, 1989], 195–96).
20. Berlin, *Poetics and Interpretation*, 34.

situation, and his outstanding traits—in other words, to tell what kind of a person he is."[21]

In most cases, suggests Sternberg, "epithet prefigures drama."[22] The descriptions in Judges 3:15–17 of Ehud as "left-handed" and Eglon as "very fat" prepare the reader for Ehud's successful attempt to sneak an undetected sword (because it was strapped to the side of his body opposite that of most men) into Eglon's quarters and assassinate him. The reference to Joseph's good looks in Genesis 39:6 explains the sexual advance made by Potiphar's wife. Likewise, the description of Esau as a "hairy man" (Gen. 27:11) helps the reader appreciate Jacob's effort when he disguised himself as his brother.

Behavior

Generally, the biblical narrators show us rather than tell us. Thus, interpreters get insight into a character's nature by paying attention to his or her actions. For example, in Judges 17, the narrator does not come right out and state that Micah is corrupt. However, this is an inescapable conclusion as we see Micah break one biblical command after another. He has a shrine—"a house of gods"—in violation of the command in Deuteronomy 12:4–7 for one central place of worship in Israel (v. 5). Then, in violation of Exodus 20:4–6 and Deuteronomy 5:8–10, Micah makes an ephod and household gods to go along with the idol his mother had commissioned (Judg. 17:4–5). He even installs one of his sons as priest (v. 5) in violation of the requirement for priests to be descendants of Aaron (Num. 3:9–10). Finally, he upgrades to a wandering young Levite who shows up at his house (Judg. 17:7–12). This is dubious since priests were supposed to live in Levitical towns (Josh. 21:9–16) and since Micah is looking to this young Levite to be a spiritual father. Besides, Micah has no authority whatsoever to install priests.

Notice as well how the writer describes Peninnah's actions toward Hannah in 1 Samuel 1:6–7: "Because the LORD had closed her [Hannah's]

---

21. Berlin, *Poetics and Interpretation*, 36.
22. Sternberg, *Poetics of Biblical Narrative*, 342. J. P. Fokkelman observes, "The description of people, thoughts, landscapes and buildings can take up many pages in modern narrative. In the Bible it is extremely scarce. If the narrator leaves the action for a moment and tells of a woman that she is 'fair of face,' this is never just because of this quality in its own right. He will only mention something like that if it is going to be a factor in a plot" (*Reading Biblical Narrative*, 71).

womb, her rival [Peninnah] kept provoking her in order to irritate her. This went on year after year. Whenever Hannah went up to the house of the Lord, her rival provoked her till she wept and would not eat." The writer does not need to inform us that Peninnah is a bitter, jealous woman. Her actions clearly demonstrate these traits.

Names

Certain cultures attach a special significance to names. When I lived in Montana, I was fascinated by the starting lineups at high school basketball games whenever teams from Native American[23] communities were playing. I heard names like Tawny Whistling Elk, Jonathan Takes Enemy, Staci Big Hair, and Elvis Old Bull. These names reflect either the circumstances attending the child's birth or a virtue that will hopefully characterize the child's life.

In Old Testament narrative, the characters' names play an important role. As Ska points out, "A very common way to 'characterize' a personage is to give him or her a name."[24] Obvious examples include Abraham (a variant of his old name, Abram, which sounds more like the Hebrew for "father of many nations"), and Nabal in 1 Samuel 25 (whose name means "fool").

John Stek argues for the significance of the names in Judges 4, the account of the defeat of Sisera, the cruel Canaanite commander.[25] Ironically, the Israelite warrior, "lightning" (the meaning of Barak), remains passive, doubtful, and silent. The glory goes to two faithful and fearless women: "bee" (the meaning of Deborah) and "mountain goat" (the meaning of Jael). Stek sees the names forming a pun that captures the gist of the story. Deborah, the bee, dispensed her sweet justice under a honey tree and kept prodding (stinging?) Barak to attack Sisera. Jael, the mountain goat, provided the fleeing Sisera with nourishing milk and then stabbed him when he lay down to rest. As a result, peace is restored to the Promised Land of milk and honey.

The book of Ruth provides another example of how names contribute to characterization. Irony occurs when "My God is King" (Elimelech) flees

---

23. This is the expression in common parlance when I lived in Montana. I am aware that "First Nations" is more appropriate in a Canadian context.
24. Ska, *"Our Fathers Have Told Us,"* 88.
25. Stek, "Bee and the Mountain Goat," 53–86.

his king's territory because of a famine.[26] If the names Mahlon and Chilion mean "sickly" and "failing," they foreshadow the early demise of these men and highlight the severe effects of the famine on Elimelech and his wife, Naomi.[27] Naomi, whose name means "pleasant one," demonstrates the irony of her name when she responds angrily to the women of Bethlehem who call out her name when she returns.[28] Ruth 1:20 may be translated, "But she said to them, 'Do not call me Pleasant One [*naomi*, נָעֳמִי]. Call me Bitter One [*mara*, מָרָא] because Shaddai has made me extremely bitter.'"[29] Even more intriguing is the expression Boaz uses in Ruth 4:1 in reference to a potential kinsman-redeemer. Boaz addresses him with the Hebrew expression *peloni almoni* (פְּלֹנִי אַלְמֹנִי). Hubbard captures the intention of this expression by translating verse 1 like this: "Boaz hailed him: 'Come over here and sit down, Mr. So and So!'"[30] The intrusion of this odd expression "serves a literary, not a historical, purpose. Perhaps the spotlight cast on the man's namelessness implied judgment: the one who refused to raise a name over the inheritance of his deceased kin deserves no name in the story."[31]

Names of characters contribute to the author's intent by highlighting character qualities, but they also form puns and create irony. In Genesis 21:1–7, Sarah's laughter of joy at her son's birth replaces her laughter of disbelief (Gen. 18:12). God, of course, gets the last laugh when Abraham follows his command (Gen. 17:19) and names the boy Isaac, which means "laughter." The delightful pun, though it contains some aesthetic value, serves to highlight God's faithfulness to fulfill promises even when he seems slow in doing it.

Designations

Designations also contribute to characterization. For instance, a designation may betray how one character is perceived by the narrator or

---

26. Hubbard, *Book of Ruth*, 88.
27. Daniel I. Block argues for this interpretation of the names (*Judges, Ruth*, 625). Hubbard, who has doubts about this interpretation of the names, provides a helpful summary of the arguments for and against it (see *Book of Ruth*, 89–90).
28. Hubbard, *Book of Ruth*, 89.
29. Author's translation from the Hebrew text of Ruth 1:20. Unfortunately, the meanings of Ruth and Boaz, names of two prominent characters, have not been settled. Suggestions for the meaning of Ruth range from "refreshment/comfort" to "friendship," while Boaz is most likely related to "strength." See Hubbard, *Book of Ruth*, 94, 134–35.
30. Hubbard, *Book of Ruth*, 232.
31. Hubbard, *Book of Ruth*, 234–35.

by other characters in the story.[32] In Genesis 21:9, the narrator betrays Sarah's resentment when he withholds Ishmael's name and says, "But Sarah saw that the son whom Hagar the Egyptian had borne to Abraham was mocking." David reflects an attitude of contempt toward Goliath by referring to him as "this uncircumcised Philistine" (1 Sam. 17:26). Later the text betrays David's attitude toward Bathsheba by mentioning her as "a/the woman" (2 Sam. 11:1–5) though her name had already been given.[33]

On the other hand, suggests Sternberg, "A character's emergence from anonymity may correlate with a rise in importance. It is no accident that the text [1 Sam. 16:1–13] consistently withholds David's name . . . till the very moment of anointment and elevation."[34]

Alright, you should now have a good handle on how to study the people who make stories interesting. If you take time to classify the characters and to notice how the writer has characterized them, you're well on your way to understanding the theological message of the text. Yet there is more work to do. The next feature of the narrative to consider is what the characters and the narrator say.

---

32. Bar-Efrat, *Narrative Art in the Bible*, 37. Christo H. J. van der Merwe describes the "withholding of full reference to a participant . . . in which a persona is developed first and then finally assigned a name" as a "marked way" of "participant reference" ("Discourse Linguistics and Biblical Hebrew Grammar," 35). See appendix B for an explanation of marking.

33. Bar-Efrat, *Narrative Art in the Bible*, 36. See also Berlin, *Poetics and Interpretation*, 59–60.

34. Sternberg, *Poetics of Biblical Narrative*, 330.

6

T is for Talking

Near the end of Norman Maclean's semiautobiographical novella, *A River Runs through It*, Norman and his father, the Rev. John Maclean, reminisce about the tragic death of Norman's youngest brother, Paul. When the elder Maclean asks his son if he has shared all the details he knows, Norman said, "Everything. His father replied, 'It's not much, is it?'" To this, Norman responded, "No, but you can love completely without complete understanding." Agreeing, his father ended the conversation and said, "That I have known and preached."[1] Norman's response captures the message of the novella. You can love completely without complete understanding.

When studying an Old Testament narrative, interpreters must also focus on the statements or speeches made by the characters—as well as on editorial insights shared by the narrator. The "talking" done by the characters in a story and by its narrator plays a significant role in shaping the story's meaning.

Dialogue: What the Characters Say

The place to begin is with what the characters say. Alter speaks of "the highly subsidiary role of narration in comparison to direct speech by the

---

1. Norman Maclean, *River Runs through It*, 103.

characters."[2] Cynthia Miller notes that "speech permeates the Bible, from the creative word of divine speech in Genesis to the decrees of a Persian king at the end of Chronicles."[3] For example, Joshua 1 consists almost entirely of four speeches: Yahweh to Joshua (1:1–9), Joshua to the officers (1:10–11), Joshua to the Transjordanian tribes (1:12–15), and the people to Joshua (1:16–18). The so-called David-Goliath story in 1 Samuel 17 provides another example. Brueggemann observes, "The action does not take very long. As is characteristic of Israel's narrative art, the speeches are of more interest and importance than the action."[4] Furthermore, Fokkelman makes this observation about the David-Mephibosheth story in 2 Samuel 9: "In this section, [there is a] ratio of 25 lines of narrative to 23 lines of direct speech . . . yet it is the direct speech that carries the action. The other lines have mainly auxiliary function: some of them provide us with information about Ziba and Mephibosheth in their nominal clauses; thirteen lines are only introductory statements ('X said to Y'); six pave the way for a meeting; and the nominal sentences at the end show how David's commands become a lasting reality."[5]

While speech dominates, interpreters should expect it to be compressed. Bar-Efrat explains that "conversations in biblical narrative are never precise and naturalistic imitations of real-life conversations. They are highly concentrated and stylized, are devoid of idle chatter, and all the details they contain are carefully calculated to fulfil a clear function."[6]

What function, then, does the speech of the characters play in a narrative? It has at least four functions.

Insight into Character Traits

One of the functions of speech by the characters is to provide insight into their traits. Esau's blunt request for stew in Genesis 25:30 portrays him as a man controlled by his cravings. On the other hand, Abigail's lengthy speech to David in 1 Samuel 25:24–31, calling him not to take revenge on her foolish husband, reflects her wisdom and insight. Similarly, Uriah's

---

2. Alter, *Art of Biblical Narrative*, 65. Text linguists point out that dialogue is embedded into the main line of a story; however, dialogue often has a significance that transcends its subordinate role in a storyline.
3. Miller, *Representation of Speech*, 1.
4. Brueggemann, *First and Second Samuel*, 133.
5. Fokkelman, *Narrative Art and Poetry*, 1:24.
6. Bar-Efrat, *Narrative Art in the Bible*, 148.

refusal speech to King David's offer of a night at home during a heated battle portrays him as a man of honor and integrity (2 Sam. 11:11). We see the development of Judah in Genesis based on what he says. In response to the news that his daughter-in-law Tamar is "guilty" of prostitution and is pregnant, he says, "Bring her out and have her burned to death!" (Gen. 38:24). This statement is callous and heartbreaking, reflecting an utter lack of compassion for Tamar's plight. Yet after he recognizes that he is the one who impregnated her, he says, "She is more righteous than I, since I wouldn't give her to my son Shelah" (Gen. 38:26). That is, Tamar's actions reflected a more faithful adherence to the cultural standards of levirate marriage than Judah's did. He recognized that she was in the right, while he was in the wrong.

An Indicator of Meaning

Even more significantly, conversation points to meaning. According to Alter, "Dialogue is made to carry a large part of the freight of meaning."[7] For example, when Isaac asks Abraham where the lamb is for the burnt offering, Abraham's response in Genesis 22:8 foreshadows the outcome and supplies the conviction by which he passes God's test: "God himself will provide the lamb for the burnt offering." Joseph summarizes the meaning of the entire Joseph cycle, as well as the immediate story in Genesis 49:29–50:26, when he states, "You intended to harm me, but God intended it for good to accomplish what is now being done, the saving of many lives" (Gen. 50:20). Similarly, statements by David in 1 Samuel 17:34–37 and 45–47 provide the key to the David-Goliath story, and Abigail's impassioned speech in 1 Samuel 25:24–31 (noted above) moves the reader toward the theme of vengeance belonging to God. Thus, interpreters should look to speeches for clues to the author's prophetic message or instruction.

A Summarizing Function

A third role of speech flows out of the previous one. Alter observes that direct speech set in formal verse often has a summarizing or ceremonial function.[8] For example, in Genesis 2:23, Adam's poetic outburst has a ceremonial function, celebrating God's creation of a "suitable helper" for

---

7. Alter, *Art of Biblical Narrative*, 37.
8. Alter, *Art of Biblical Narrative*, 28.

him (2:20).[9] Hannah's speech in 1 Samuel 2:1–10 has more of a summarizing function as it highlights the themes that the remainder of the book of Samuel will develop. Mary Evans is certainly right when she calls Hannah's song "the beginning of the book's main theologizing statement."[10]

Highlighting a Contrast

Finally, Alter points out the technique of "contrastive dialogue" where the contrasting speech of two characters accomplishes "differentiation"—that is, a contrast between ideas or concepts.[11] As examples he cites "Esau's inarticulate outbursts over against Jacob's calculated legalisms in the selling of the birthright (Gen. 25); Joseph's long-winded statement of morally aghast refusal over against the two-word sexual bluntness of Potiphar's wife (Gen. 39); [and] Saul's choked cry after David's impassioned speech outside the cave at Ein Gedi (1 Sam. 24)."[12]

Omniscience: What the Narrator Says

Readers must also pay attention to the "insider information" or "editorial comment" that the narrator shares. Literary scholars refer to this as a narrator's *omniscience*. Sternberg explains, "To say that he [the biblical writer] is omniscient is to invest him with a storytelling privilege that the same writer would hardly lay claim to in his everyday life."[13] Ska elaborates on the notion of omniscience and an omniscient narrator:

> The classical narrator of ancient and traditional narratives is "omniscient." He is almost like God: he knows everything and speaks with an unabashed authority. This privilege is felt especially when he reveals the thoughts of the characters through "inside views." In modern novels the narrator often gives up this privilege and has a knowledge limited to the external world or to the interior world of one character who is used as the "eye of the

---

9. The notion in Gen. 2:20–23 that the woman was created as a "suitable helper" for Adam is in no way demeaning to the woman! After all, God is frequently described as the "help" or "helper" of his people (e.g., Gen. 49:25; Exod. 18:4; Pss. 46:1; 121:1–2). If this concept is demeaning to anyone, it is to Adam. He needs help!
10. Evans, *1 and 2 Samuel*, 20.
11. Alter, *Art of Biblical Narrative*, 72.
12. Alter, *Art of Biblical Narrative*, 72.
13. Sternberg, *Poetics of Biblical Narrative*, 68.

camera" or the "center of consciousness" of the narration. This narrator knows in general only what a normal person can see, hear, and experience.[14]

In Genesis 22:1–19, for example, the narrator informs the audience at the outset that the subsequent events amount to a God-given test. This piece of omniscient information functions as a sort of disclaimer. Sailhamer says, "Without it [v. 1] God's request that Abraham offer up Isaac as a 'burnt offering' would be inexplicable. By stating clearly at the start that 'God tested Abraham' (v. 1), the writer quickly allays any doubt about God's real purpose."[15]

Genesis 38 provides another example of the narrator's omniscience. In Genesis 38:7, he discloses that Er was wicked in Yahweh's sight and Yahweh killed him. His omniscient perspective appears again in verse 9 when he reveals Onan's motives for refusing to impregnate Tamar. Likewise, in verse 10, the omniscient narrator conveys Yahweh's feeling of displeasure about this action as well as the insight that Yahweh took Onan's life. In verse 11, the narrator exposes another piece of privileged information: Judah's reason for not giving his third son, Shelah, to Tamar. Judah believed that Shelah might die like his brothers. Further examples appear in the story: Tamar's motivations for setting up shop as a temple prostitute at a location Judah would pass (v. 14); Judah's lack of perception and failure to recognize Tamar (v. 15); and again, Judah's ignorance that the prostitute was his daughter-in-law (v. 16). Thus, the narrator can disclose a character's opinions, feelings, and intentions—whether the character is God or a human being.[16]

In Judges 17–18, the narrator comments on the moral climate in Israel with two editorial comments. First, Judges 17:6 says, "In those days Israel had no king; everyone did as they saw fit." Then, Judges 18:1 says, "In those days Israel had no king." These refrains—the longer and the shorter—will appear in mirror image in the final narrative in Judges. The shorter refrain begins the narrative in Judges 19:1, and then the longer refrain ends the narrative and the book in 21:25.

A further example occurs in 2 Samuel 11–12. After relating the death of Uriah, his wife's subsequent marriage to David, and the birth of a son,

14. Ska, *"Our Fathers Have Told Us,"* 44.
15. Sailhamer, "Genesis," 209.
16. Bar-Efrat, *Narrative Art in the Bible*, 20.

the narrator offers this perspective in 11:27: "But the thing David had done displeased the Lord."

So far, we have considered the action (plot), the characters, and the talking. Now we need to turn our attention to a final major element in our exegetical process: the setting of the narrative.

7

S is for Setting

Understanding a narrative requires looking at the ACTS. After scrutinizing the action (A), the characters (C), and the talking (T), the interpreter needs to consider the setting (S). There are two issues related to the setting. One issue concerns the specific time, place, and culture in which the story occurs. The other issue concerns the position of the story within the flow of stories that make up a book.

These issues resemble those faced by students who research a Civil War battle. If I intend to understand the Battle of Gettysburg, I have to look at two settings. The first setting consists of the actual location and time period of the battle. The Union and Confederate armies converged unintentionally at the little town of Gettysburg, Pennsylvania, on July 1, 1863. The battle raged for three days, ending on July 3 with Confederate Major General George E. Pickett's fateful charge. Students who study the battle in more detail will observe the role of topographical features like Cemetery Ridge, Round Top, Little Round Top, Devil's Den, and Seminary Ridge.

The second setting consists of the position of the Battle of Gettysburg in the overall flow of the Civil War. The battle occurred roughly in the middle of the Civil War which ran from 1861 to 1865. The Union victory at Gettysburg, coupled with Grant's victory at Vicksburg, reversed the war. Even more significant is what happened in the aftermath of Gettysburg. Union General George Meade missed his chance to finish off Lee's army and end the war. His caution in pursuing Lee gave Lee's troops time to recoup from their exhaustion and escape to Virginia. Understanding the Battle of Gettysburg, then, requires a look at the physical setting in which the battle took place as well as its location in the larger flow of Civil War battles.

When we study an Old Testament narrative, we must pay close attention to both the historical-cultural setting as well as the literary setting.[1] The historical-cultural setting refers to "the space in which the characters perform the actions that constitute the plot."[2] Longman observes, "We must realize that in the historical narrative that dominates the narrative genre of the Bible, the author's choice of setting was usually restricted. Authors simply placed action where it actually occurred. Of course, these authors controlled the selectivity of detail in the description of settings, requiring the reader to pay close attention to these textual signals."[3] On the other hand, the literary setting refers to the location of a story in the larger narrative framework. Both are critical for understanding the meaning of a narrative.

Historical-Cultural Setting

An interpreter discovers the historical-cultural setting by asking and answering several important questions.

- Where did the story happen?
- Is there any significant geographical movement within the story?
- When did this story take place? During what season of the year?
- What was happening in Israel's history at this time?

Robert Chisholm notes that while details of physical setting serve merely to lend realism to the story or create a certain mood, "at other

---

1. In the first edition of this volume, I referred to the historical-cultural setting as the *inner-textual setting* and the literary setting as the *inter-textual setting*. I coined these expressions to remind me to keep my conclusions based on the text. They reflect the distinction between the expressions *inner-textuality* (the composition of a text; links within a text) and *inter-textuality* (the interrelationship of texts; links between texts). For a discussion of the latter two expressions, see Sailhamer, *Introduction to Old Testament Theology*, 155, 212. However, the expressions I coined add more technical language to the mix. So I am going to revert to the standard, simple expressions for the two settings: historical-cultural and literary.
2. Longman, "Biblical Narrative," 74.
3. Longman, "Biblical Narrative," 75.

times physical setting can have symbolic value and contribute to the story's theme."[4] He cites an example: "In 2 Kings 1:9, the king's arrogant officer demands that the prophet Elijah 'come down' from his perch 'on the top of a hill.' Elijah refuses to come down and instead calls fire down on the officer and his men. Elijah's elevated position symbolizes his authority as God's spokesman over the king and his messengers."[5]

In the book of Ruth, the movement of the setting from Israel to Moab and back to Israel is significant. By leaving Israel for Moab, Elimelech abandons the covenant community in search of a solution to his hunger. Furthermore, the temporal information that introduces the narrative, "in the days when the judges ruled" (Ruth 1:1), suggests that the physical problem Elimelech sought to escape was due to a spiritual problem.[6]

In 2 Samuel 11–12, the text identifies the story's beginning as the springtime, when kings typically go out to war. We expect, then, to find King David with the Israelite army at the battlefield. To our surprise, we learn that David remained in Jerusalem. This leads to a crisis that would not have evolved if David had been with his army.

Literary Setting

"To understand fully the significance of a narrative one must examine its placement within the larger whole of which it is a part."[7] This is the story's literary setting. John Beck reminds us that "no story in the Bible was designed to function completely on its own. Every Bible story lies at the heart of a concentric circle of stories that surround it."[8] For example, the story of Solomon and the two prostitutes in 1 Kings 3:16–28 has a verifying function. It authenticates the previous story (1 Kings 3:1–15), which narrates how God gave Solomon a wise and discerning heart.

The story of David, Abigail, and Nabal in 1 Samuel 25 is sandwiched between two stories in which David refrains from taking revenge against King Saul. Thus, the story is part of a larger unit that hinges on the theme

---

4. Chisholm, *From Exegesis to Exposition*, 151.
5. Chisholm, *From Exegesis to Exposition*, 151.
6. The expression "in the days when the judges ruled" is an allusion to the book of Judges. The allusion presupposes an understanding of the cycles that Israel experienced. See Judg. 2:11–19.
7. Chisholm, *From Exegesis to Exposition*, 168.
8. Beck, *God as Storyteller*, 21.

of revenge. In 1 Samuel 24, David refuses to take revenge against the Lord's anointed. In 1 Samuel 25, he learns not to take revenge against an ordinary (nonroyal) fool like Nabal. Even more important, David learns not to take revenge when the death of the prophet Samuel (25:1) weakens his claim to the throne and when everyone seems to be against him. In this story, Abigail arises as a new prophetic voice and reminds David that he does not need to seek vengeance because God will make a lasting dynasty for him and will defeat his enemies (25:28–29). So David's attitude toward revenge comes full circle in 1 Samuel 26 where he seeks Saul out to pursue reconciliation and to emphasize his refusal to inflict harm on the king. In its broader context, 1 Samuel 25 and the immediately surrounding stories are part of a larger unit (1 Sam. 16–2 Sam. 8) that functions as a "dynastic defense," exposing Saul's failure as king and David's qualification to be king.

Another noteworthy example of the literary setting is Genesis 38. While the location of the story within the Joseph narrative has confused many interpreters, its location contributes to the larger story.[9] It interrupts the story just when Joseph has been sold into prison. This heightens the tension, forcing the reader to wait until the story resumes in Genesis 39 before finding out what happens to Joseph. Also, Judah serves as a foil to Joseph. Judah's sexual indiscretion contrasts with Joseph's sexual purity. Furthermore, Genesis 38 is part of the larger story of God developing in Abraham a nation through which he would bless the earth. The continuation of the line of blessing is threatened by Judah's failure to produce an heir. In the end, the righteous Tamar is responsible for continuing the line from which the Messiah would come. Potiphar also serves as a foil to Tamar. Both seduce, yet Tamar's act of seduction was "righteous."[10]

The placement of Judges 17–18 in the book is especially fascinating. The book consists of a double introduction (1:1–3:6), a double conclusion (17–21), and a main section that is commonly referred to as the "cycles" section.[11] The cycles section is actually a downward spiral, with each ad-

---

9. For a summary of the discussion about the problematic location of Gen. 38, see Mathewson, "Exegetical Study of Genesis 38," 373–74. Genesis 38 uses a technique called "resumptive repetition" in which the author of a Biblical Hebrew narrative interrupts a story to insert something and then resumes the original narrative by repeating the last sentence before the break (Talmon, "Presentation of Synchroneity," 9–26).

10. I am grateful to Carmen Joy Imes for this observation (in personal correspondence, September 2020).

11. Younger, *Judges/Ruth*, 30.

ditional cycle showing further moral deterioration in the nation of Israel. The double introduction focuses on the problem of the war of destruction (1:1–2:5) and the problem of idols (2:6–3:6). Then, the double conclusion mirrors the introduction by focusing on the same problems in reverse order. Judges 17–18 deals with the problem of idols, while the narrative in chapters 19–21 concentrates on the problem of the war of destruction. This creates the following *inclusio*:[12]

   A The external problem of the war of destruction (1:1–2:5)
      B The external problem of idols (2:6–3:6)
      B′ The internal problem of idols (17–18)
   A′ The internal problem of the war of destruction (19–21)

In the book's introduction, Israel fails to carry out the war of destruction against the inhabitants of Canaan as God commanded (1:1–2:5). In the book's conclusion, they end up carrying it out against themselves (chaps. 19–21)! The problem with idols worsens as well from the book's introduction to its conclusion. In Judges 2:6–3:6 the struggle is with "foreign" idols—the Baals and the Ashtoreths (2:11, 13). However, in the conclusion (chaps. 17–18), the problem relates to a "domestic" idol—an idol made by an Israelite named Micah (17:1–4; 18:31).[13] Furthermore, in 2:6–3:6, the people of Israel fall into a pattern: idol worship, God's retribution, a cry for help, God's provision of a deliverer, and the restoration of the land to peace—only to fall back into idolatry and begin another cycle. However, in Judges 17–18, there is no repentance whatsoever. The nation—at least the Northern Kingdom as represented by the tribe of Dan—never experiences even a temporary escape from the grip of idol worship.

Our examination of the ACTS of a narrative is finished. Now, we need to draw some conclusions about the message the narrator communicates through the telling of the story.

---

12. See Younger, *Judges/Ruth*, 30. I have put the narrative under consideration, Judg. 17–18, in bold print.
13. Younger, *Judges/Ruth*, 30–31.

8

Drawing Conclusions

By now you will have studied the text from every major angle. Table 8.1 summarizes the major features that you will need to examine when studying an Old Testament story. You might need to keep it handy at first. Eventually, looking for the features of Old Testament narrative texts will become second nature to you, and your reading of the text will be more of a fluid experience rather than a mechanical procedure. As Ska points out, "A text is like a score of music. The music remains dead unless somebody plays or sings what is written in the score. A Biblical text remains dead unless the reader interprets it."[1]

Now you are ready to reflect on your study of the text and draw some conclusions. This is the time to interact with the insights of scholars and teachers. Ideally, you have saved the bulk of your interaction with commentaries until this point in the process. Since you've done your homework, you will be much better prepared to listen to them and debate with them. Not all commentaries are created equal. Some delve so deeply into historical criticism or textual criticism that they avoid the literary dimension of the text. Appendix C lists the more useful commentaries for each narrative book of the Old Testament.

In addition to reading commentaries, plan to consult the standard works on Old Testament narrative literature for discussions of particular texts.

1. Ska, *"Our Fathers Have Told Us,"* 63.

Table 8.1

A Summary of Features to Examine in Old Testament Narratives
Action (Plot)

- *Plot Stages:* Determine the story's exposition, crisis, resolution, and conclusion.
- *Archetypes:* Identify plot patterns or motifs (comedy, tragedy, petitionary narratives, etc.).
- *Repetition:* Notice key words, changes or duplication in command fulfillment, and unnecessary repetition of names and pronouns.
- *Time and Pace:* Compare narrative time (length of events) to narration time (length of telling).
- *Point of View:* Notice whether the perspective is external (the reader's) or internal (the character's or narrator's). Identify any verbal, dramatic, or situational irony.
- *Chiasmus:* Note chiastic patterns (a b c c' b' a') which mark boundaries or turning points.

Characters

- *Classifications:* Identify characters as major (protagonist, antagonist, foil) or minor.
- *Direct Descriptions:* Look for the occasional statement about a character's appearance.
- *Behavior:* Observe the characters' actions for insight into their personalities and nature.
- *Names:* Notice the significance behind names of characters.
- *Designation:* Pay attention to how the narrator or other characters describe a character.

Talking

- *Dialogue:* Listen to what the characters say (direct speech) for insight into their moral character and for clues that point to meaning.
- *Omniscience:* Notice what the narrators say that provides inside views or privileged information.

Setting

- *Historical-Cultural:* Look in the text for the story's temporal, geographical, and cultural setting.
- *Literary:* Look at the context for the story's role in the larger narrative framework.

Drawing Conclusions

If I am preparing a sermon on 1 Samuel 17, I will turn to the indices of works on Old Testament narrative literature to locate any discussions of this particular text (see table 8.2). You may recognize these resources from the footnotes in earlier chapters of this book.

Table 8.2

Works on Old Testament Narrative Literature

1. Robert Alter, *The Art of Biblical Narrative*
2. Shimon Bar-Efrat, *Narrative Art in the Bible*
3. J. P. Fokkelman, *Reading Biblical Narrative: An Introductory Guide*
4. Adele Berlin, *Poetics and Interpretation of Biblical Narrative*
5. Meir Sternberg, *The Poetics of Biblical Narrative*
6. Jerome T. Walsh, *Old Testament Narrative: A Guide to Interpretation*
7. Jean Louis Ska, "Our Fathers Have Told Us"
8. David M. Gunn and Danna Nolan Fewell, *Narrative in the Hebrew Bible*

In my opinion, every preacher who works through an Old Testament narrative book should purchase copies of *The Art of Biblical Narrative* by Robert Alter and *Narrative Art in the Bible* by Shimon Bar-Efrat. Alter, Professor of Hebrew and Comparative Literature at the University of California, Berkeley, published his watershed volume in 1981. It remains a classic in the field of interpreting Old Testament narrative literature, and I recommend it as a first-read for preachers who plan to preach Old Testament narrative texts. Alter writes in the style of a well-crafted *Time* magazine article. Bar-Efrat's work serves as an excellent companion volume. Formerly the head of biblical studies at the Hebrew University secondary school in Jerusalem, Bar-Efrat provides a catalog of literary techniques and devices found in Old Testament narratives. Neither book requires expertise in Hebrew.

If you want more than Alter and Bar-Efrat, the footnotes and bibliography in this book will give you direction. Let me share a few recommendations, though, for further resources. You may want to do more reading in the field, or you may want further works available as references. Start with J. P. Fokkelman's recent work, *Reading Biblical Narrative: An Introductory Guide*. He uses twelve Old Testament stories to help readers pay attention to narrator, character, action, hero, quest, plot, time, and space. Also get a copy of Adele Berlin's slim volume, *Poetics and Interpretation of Biblical Narrative*. Berlin focuses especially on character and characterization and point of view. She then applies these to the book of Ruth. Ambitious preachers may want to tackle Meir Sternberg's massive and at times verbose volume, *The Poetics of Biblical Narrative*. Sternberg, Professor of Poetics and Comparative Literature at Tel Aviv University, covers the entire terrain from theoretical issues to particular literary conventions. Next, try the volume by Jerome T. Walsh, *Old Testament Narrative: A Guide to Interpretation*. This is the most recent full-length monograph on the topic, and it practices its methodology on the Jeroboam story (1 Kings 11:26–14:18), the Elijah story (1 Kings 17:1–19:21), and the Ahab story (1 Kings 20:1–22:40).

If you want to explore even further, try the manual titled *"Our Fathers Have Told Us": Introduction to the Analysis of Hebrew Narratives* by Jean Louis Ska, an Old Testament scholar at the Pontifical Biblical Institute in Rome. Ska aims to help beginners through the forest of new terms used by specialists like Alter, Berlin, Sternberg, and others. He distills the insights of these specialists into concise summaries. Finally, preachers will find helpful insights in *Narrative in the Hebrew Bible* by David M. Gunn and Danna Nolan Fewell, professors at Columbia Theological Seminary in Atlanta and the Perkins School of Theology at Southern Methodist University, respectively. Despite their presupposition that meaning is the reader's creation rather than the author's creation, they offer help on strategies for reading, on characters and narrators, on plot designs, on the lure of language, and on readers and responsibility. Among these topics, they have interspersed chapters on specific Old Testament narratives. None of the books mentioned above require a knowledge of Hebrew.

If you possess Hebrew language skills, you will want to consult appendix B, "Using Hebrew in Narrative Exegesis." This will introduce you to discourse analysis.

The Components of a Big Idea

One of the most challenging stages in the interpretive process is identifying the story's exegetical idea. While you may find several ideas in a story, you need to ask: What is the unifying center? What message is the writer conveying through the story? Identifying this message and writing it in a clear sentence is a significant accomplishment.

Before we discuss finding the exegetical idea of a particular Old Testament narrative, we must make sure we are clear on what an idea is. Thought, whether expressed verbally or in writing, consists of ideas or concepts. An idea or concept consists of two essential elements: a subject and a complement (see table 8.3). A big idea distills the particulars of a text into a summary by isolating what several ideas have in common. When preachers talk about the big idea of a Scripture passage, they often refer to it as an exegetical idea since it emerges from their exegetical study of the text.

Table 8.3

Components of a Big Idea

Subject—What am I talking about?
Complement—What am I saying about what I am talking about?

To find the big idea of a thought unit (paragraph, story, etc.), determine the unit's subject. The term *subject* does not refer to the grammatical subject of a sentence. Rather, it refers to the complete answer to the question, What am I talking about? While a grammatical subject is often a single word, this is not the case with the subject of a big idea. Take a moment to read the following paragraph, and then try to identify its subject. The selection is from Neil Postman's work *Amusing Ourselves to Death*.[2]

> President Ronald Reagan is a former Hollywood movie actor. Former nominee George McGovern has hosted the popular television show, "Saturday Night Live." So has a candidate of more recent vintage, the Reverend Jesse Jackson. Former President Richard Nixon, who once claimed he lost an election because he was sabotaged by make-up men, has offered Senator Edward Kennedy advice on how to make a serious run for the presidency: lose twenty pounds. Although the constitution makes no mention of it, it would appear that fat people are now effectively excluded from running for high political office. Probably bald people as well. Almost certainly those whose looks are not significantly enhanced by the cosmetician's art. Indeed, we may have reached the point where cosmetics has replaced ideology as the field of expertise over which a politician must have competent control.

2. Postman, *Amusing Ourselves to Death*, 4.

Alright, what is the subject of this paragraph? What is this paragraph talking about? Perhaps you note that the paragraph talks about presidents and people who run for political office. This is a good start, but the subject is still too broad. More precisely, the subject is, *What politicians have to pay attention to if they hope to get elected.* Notice the use of the word *what* at the beginning of the subject. Using the questions that journalists ask—what, why, when, where, how, and who—will help you narrow your subject. In fact, I find it helpful to preface each subject I identify with one of these questions. If I wanted to, though, I could state the subject like this: *The area of expertise that politicians must pay attention to if they hope to get elected.* Either way, you have correctly identified the subject.

Once you have nailed down the subject, you look for the complement. As the term suggests, the *complement* completes the subject. It answers the question, What am I saying about what I am talking about? In the above example from Neil Postman, the subject is, *What politicians have to pay attention to if they hope to get elected.* The complement is, *Their personal appearance, not just their platform of issues.* When you put together the subject and complement, a big idea emerges: *In order to get elected, politicians must pay as much attention to their personal appearance as they do to their platform of issues.*

Here is another example from Jamar Tisby's book, *The Color of Compromise*. After reading this paragraph, try to identify its subject and the complement. Tisby writes, "Christianity served as a force to help construct racial categories in the colonial period. A corrupt message that saw no contradiction between the brutalities of bondage and the good news of salvation became the norm. European missionaries tried to calm the slave owners' fear of rebellion by spreading a version of Christianity that emphasized spiritual deliverance, not immediate liberation. Instead of highlighting the dignity of all human beings, European missionaries told Africans that Christianity should make them more obedient and loyal to their earthly masters."[3] The first sentence reveals the topic that Tisby talks about. Which question, though, does Tisby raise? Is he concerned with the what, why, when, where, how, or who of Christianity's role in constructing racial categories in colonial America? I suggest that Tisby's subject (what he is talking about) is, *How did Christianity help construct racial*

---

3. Tisby, *Color of Compromise*, 39.

categories in the colonial period? Perhaps we could substitute "European missionaries" for "Christianity." They are the primary agents of Christianity in this discussion. This is the kind of issue we consider when we wrestle with an author's thought. Tisby's complement (what he is saying about what he is talking about) is, *by emphasizing spiritual deliverance and teaching obedience to earthly masters.* This complement has two parts to it, and so we call it a "multi-complement." The advantage of this is specificity; the disadvantage is complexity. More complexity means more difficulty in mental processing of a summary—and a summary is what a big idea is trying to provide. The big idea that results from combining this subject and complement is: *Christianity helped construct racial categories in the colonial period by emphasizing spiritual deliverance and teaching obedience to earthly masters.*

If we want to simplify the big idea, we could distill the two parts of the complement into a single one. We could state the complement as, *by its teaching.* The big idea then becomes: *Christianity helped construct racial categories in the colonial period by its teaching.* The advantage of this big idea statement is its clarity and brevity. However, it lacks specificity. This is the tension we face when crafting a big idea statement. Another option is to focus the complement on either "emphasizing spiritual deliverance" or "teaching obedience to earthly masters." This assumes that one element is a subset of the other. Yet the paragraph does not suggest this is the case.

If this seems like a lot of work simply to develop a big idea statement, it is! Yet the ability to drill down and summarize the heart of what a text is communicating is critical to preaching clear, compelling sermons.

Developing the Big Idea

In *Biblical Preaching*, Haddon Robinson applies the big idea concept to preaching. He breaks the big idea down into two expressions: the exegetical idea and the homiletical idea. The exegetical idea is stating a biblical concept in such a way that it accurately reflects what the author intends. In a later stage of sermon development, the preacher will take this exegetical idea and state it as a homiletical idea. A homiletical idea is stating a biblical concept in such a way that it accurately reflects the Bible and meaningfully relates to the congregation.

Some of Robinson's followers have added a third expression by subdividing the exegetical idea stage into *exegetical idea* and *theological idea* (see table 8.4).

While I prefer to keep things as simple as possible, I see the value of this extra stage when working in Old Testament narrative literature. In the three-expression approach, the first expression of the big idea is the exegetical idea. This is a one-sentence statement of the author's intended meaning that reflects the time and culture of the original audience. It uses the language of the text, including the names of characters in the story. The next expression is the theological idea. The theological expression states the big idea in timeless language that applies to God's people living in any stage of salvation history. Finally, the preacher will craft the big idea in a homiletical expression. This preaching idea or homiletical idea makes the statement in a more personal, contemporary way. We will develop the preaching or homiletical idea at a later stage of the process. For now, we are concerned with developing an exegetical idea and turning it into a theological idea.

Table 8.4

Expressions of the Big Idea

Exegetical Idea
↓
Theological Idea
↓
Homiletical or Preaching Idea

Clues for Nailing Down the Big Idea

To find the exegetical expression of the big idea in an Old Testament narrative, expositors must sift through the exegetical data they have amassed and attempt to identify a subject. Remember, the subject must be broad enough to account for the entire range of material—plot twists, dialogue, and so on—that makes up the story. For example, Paul Borden states the exegetical idea of 2 Samuel 11–12 like this: *David learns to accept what the grace of God has given him and what the grace of God has not.*[4] The subject of this big idea is, *What David has to learn about responding to the grace of God*. The complement is, *That he must accept what the grace of God has given him and what the grace of God has not.*

But wait. The subjects of most sermons on this text are, *How to avoid adultery*, or *What the consequences of adultery are*. I even listened to a

---

4. Borden and Mathewson, "Big Idea of Narrative Preaching," 279.

sermon on 2 Samuel 11–12 in which the preacher's subject was something like, *Why honesty is the best policy*. However, these are examples of "right idea, wrong text." Sermons built on these subjects use the narrative in 2 Samuel 11–12 as an illustration of ideas found in other Scripture texts. They miss the theology or prophetic message the narrator of 2 Samuel 11–12 was communicating.

Borden's exegetical idea rests on solid footing because he accounts for the data in the text. Borden did his homework, observing that God identified a bigger sin in David's life that stood behind the sins of adultery, deception, and murder. When Nathan came to David with God's message, Nathan began by rehearsing the gifts that God had given to David. These gifts were an expression of God's grace. Then Nathan asks, "Why did you despise the word of the Lord by doing what is evil in his eyes?" (2 Sam. 12:9). The term *despise* means "to regard with contempt." The very next verse reports Nathan's summary, and the same assessment emerges again: "Because you despised me and took the wife of Uriah the Hittite to be your own" (2 Sam. 12:10). Most sermons I've heard from 2 Samuel 11–12 stop there and do not account for the death of David and Bathsheba's first child. In his exegesis, Borden observes that through the death of this child, David learns to accept what God in his grace gives and does not give. Borden also sees a contrast between Uriah and David. Uriah turned out to be the faithful, obedient man that David was not.

Obviously, determining the big idea of Old Testament narrative poses a steeper challenge than other literary genres. Stories work through indirection, conveying their ideas in a more subtle way than other kinds of biblical literature. Thankfully, there are a couple of additional clues that will help the preacher put the details together and determine what the author intended. Haddon Robinson counsels preachers to look for these clues when they study any text of Scripture.[5] I find them particularly helpful in Old Testament narratives.

Vision of God

The first clue is a passage's vision of God. Most passages focus on a particular aspect of God's character, for example, God as Creator or God

---

5. Robinson, *Biblical Preaching*, 64–65.

as Judge. In 2 Samuel 11–12, the narrator's vision of God is the giver of gifts. That's the issue in the text. Again, Nathan's message begins with a litany of the gifts God had given to David. Paul Borden describes this gift giving as God's grace. So the vision of God is the giver of gifts, or the God of grace.

Depravity Factor

A second clue to look for is what Haddon Robinson calls the *depravity factor*.[6] What in humanity rebels against the text's vision of God? What sin keeps God's people from responding properly to a particular aspect of his character? Bryan Chapell calls this the text's FCF or *fallen condition focus*.[7] Returning to our example in 2 Samuel 11–12, the depravity factor is David's (and our) tendency to despise God by being discontented with what his grace has given us.

Determining the big idea resembles splitting wood: sometimes you get stuck in a knot. The way to get out of the knot is to identify the story's vision of God and the depravity factor that works against this vision. These clues will get you back on target.

Examples of Big Ideas in Old Testament Narratives

Let's consider four Old Testament narrative texts and how to move from the exegetical idea to the theological idea for each one. I want to return to 2 Samuel 11–12 and look at a couple possible ways of stating the exegetical idea. Then, we will look at three additional texts: Genesis 13, Judges 17–18, and 1 Samuel 17.

2 Samuel 11–12

I have suggested that Paul Borden's exegetical idea for 2 Samuel 11–12 hits the bull's-eye: *David learns to accept what the grace of God has given him and what the grace of God has not*. But is this the only possible big idea? Yes and no. While an interpreter is bound to the author's theo-

---

6. I am using the language of a previous edition. In his third edition of *Biblical Preaching*, Robinson refers to this as the "human factor" (65).

7. Bryan Chapell defines the *fallen condition focus* (FCF) as "the mutual human condition that contemporary believers share with those to or for whom the text was written that requires the grace of the passage" (*Christ-Centered Preaching*, 42).

logical message, there may be more than one legitimate way to describe it. Any big idea of 2 Samuel 11–12 must account for the exegetical data. Since "preaching is the bringing of truth through personality,"[8] as Phillips Brooks famously said in Yale's 1877 *Lectures on Preaching*, each expositor will focus on the truth from a unique angle.

For example, Scott Wenig states his exegetical idea for 2 Samuel 11–12 like this: *When David abused his kingly power, he was severely disciplined by the* Lord; *but when David properly used his kingly power, God blessed him with honor and glory.*[9] Wenig notes that his exegetical idea "is rooted primarily in the [narrator's] editorial comments, the use of the word 'send,' Nathan's parable to David, and the description of his final victory over the Ammonites."[10] Preachers frequently miss the significance of the end of the narrative—David's victory over the Ammonites in 12:26–31. Yet our understanding of the narrative must take it into account since the narrative does not end until David and his army return to Jerusalem (12:31).

Benjamin Walton proposes an exegetical idea that aligns with Scott Wenig's: *The* Lord *will use repentant kings of Israel to fulfill the Davidic Covenant, but despising the* Lord's *word brings discipline.*[11] Like Wenig, Walton bases his idea on the prophet Nathan's rebuke of David for "despising" God and his word as well as David's repentance and subsequent military victory over the Ammonites.[12]

Like Borden, both Wenig and Walton recognize that the narrative says more than "you shall not commit adultery." Yet how do we account for the different emphases in their exegetical idea statements? The reality is that different exegetes give different weight to the details in a narrative. Borden's idea reflects the contrast between David and Uriah, while Wenig and Walton place more weight on the result of David's repentance—the victory over the Ammonites.

This can seem rather discouraging. We want our exegetical process to lead us to the "exact" exegetical idea. Yet, while our big idea should reflect the details of the text, it cannot possibly include all those details.

---

8. Brooks, *Lectures on Preaching*, 5.
9. This is a condensed version of Wenig's exegetical idea that appears in Wenig, "Different Exegetical and Homiletical Approach," 15.
10. Wenig, "Different Exegetical and Homiletical Approach," 13.
11. B. Walton, *Preaching Old Testament Narratives*, 87. Walton refers to the exegetical idea as the "Original-Theological Message."
12. B. Walton, *Preaching Old Testament Narratives*, 86.

It is worth remembering that a big idea is not a sermon. The sermon will be the place where we unpack all the stunning aspects of the narrative. It is inevitable that our big idea—both in its exegetical and homiletical expressions—will not say everything. However, if we can show that it reflects a careful reading of the narrative—with sensitivity to the action, characters, talking, and setting—then we can proceed with confidence. The exegetical ideas suggested by Borden, Wenig, and Walton are each faithful to the text. We can (and should) debate which reflects the narrator's emphasis the closest. Yet at some point we have to settle on a particular statement. Sunday is coming.

Now notice how these exegetical ideas from 2 Samuel 11–12 can be transformed into theological ideas. Let's start with Paul Borden's exegetical idea.

> Exegetical idea: *David learned to accept what the grace of God had given him and what the grace of God had not.*

> Theological idea: *Believers must learn to accept what the grace of God has given them and what the grace of God has not.*

The theological expression of the big idea assumes that what is true for David in this case is true for believers in any age. When moving from a specific character such as David to a more timeless identity such as believers, preachers must grapple with the range of possibilities (see table 8.5). One possibility is abstracting from "David" to "leaders" since David was Israel's king. This is legitimate, but nothing in the story requires that the teaching applies only to God's people who occupy leadership positions. On the other hand, changing "David" to "people" is too general. God's dealing with David is based on the covenant relationship between them, so the timeless element is "believers." Expositors, then, must search for a timeless element that is neither too specific nor too broad.

Table 8.5

Range of Possibilities for Making an Element Timeless (2 Sam. 11–12)

Person
↑
Believer
↑
Leader
↑
David

Let's see how Scott Wenig moves from his exegetical idea to his theological idea.

> Exegetical idea: *When David abused his kingly power, he was severely disciplined by the LORD; but when David properly used his kingly power, God blessed him with honor and glory.*

> Theological idea: *If you abuse power, it will bring God's judgment but if you use it to serve God and others it brings His blessing.*[13]

Notice from this example, as well as the previous one, how past tense language shifts to present tense. This happens because the theological idea moves away from an event-specific description to a timeless description. Also, the theological idea can often be stated more concisely.

Benjamin Walton moves from his exegetical idea to his theological idea in the following manner.

> Exegetical idea: *The LORD will use repentant kings of Israel to fulfill the Davidic Covenant, but despising the LORD's word brings discipline.*

> Theological idea: *God will use us to fulfill his plan of salvation, but sin brings discipline.*[14]

Walton chooses to abstract from "despising the LORD's word" to "sin," suggesting that the former statement refers to sin in general, not only to heinous sins. He also argues that the move from "repentant kings of Israel" to "us" (present-day believers) is legitimate since the issue in this text is not the job description of a king but the character qualities of a king—the same qualities that should characterize Spirit-led believers today.[15] His decisions illustrate the kind of thought process in which preachers must engage when they move from the exegetical idea to the theological idea.

---

13. Wenig, "Different Exegetical and Homiletical Approach," 15.
14. B. Walton, *Preaching Old Testament Narratives*, 87. He refers to the theological idea as the "Take-Home Truth."
15. B. Walton, *Preaching Old Testament Narratives*, 87.

Genesis 13

The storyline in Genesis 13 is not complicated. Abram moves into Canaan, accompanied by his nephew Lot. Their respective holdings—flocks, herds, and tents—make it difficult for the land to support both of them. As a result, a dispute arises between Abram's herdsmen and Lot's herdsmen. A note in verse 7 about the presence of the Canaanites and Perizzites makes readers aware that neither Abram nor Lot could simply move a few miles away. Other occupants were vying for the same grazing ground. The lone statement Abram makes to Lot in verse 8 is highly significant: "Do not let there be any quarreling between me and you, or between my herdsmen and your herdsmen, because men, brothers, we are" (my translation of the Hebrew text). Abram suggests parting company and offers Lot first choice of where he will go. Abram agrees to take whatever is left. Lot chooses the cities of the Jordan plain, so Abram remains in Canaan. The story closes with God appearing to Abram and reconfirming his gift of the land to Abram and his descendants.

Identifying the vision of God and the depravity factor of this story helps interpreters isolate the exegetical idea. The vision of God is the giver who blesses his people. The depravity factor is the greed or anxiety that leads people to fight with those closest to them over the blessings or rights God has provided. As a result of this analysis, I would identify the subject of Genesis 13 as, *How Abram, a man under God's blessing, handled conflict.* The complement would be, *He took the initiative to resolve it.* When you put subject and complement together, the exegetical idea becomes, *Abram, a man under God's blessing, handled conflict by taking the initiative to resolve it.*

Determining the precise wording can be maddening. Don't let it be. Perhaps it is better to state the subject as, *How Abram preserved God's blessing when he faced conflict.* The complement remains the same, but this changes the exegetical idea to read, *Abram preserved God's blessing when he faced conflict by taking the initiative to resolve it.* When you get this close, don't spend precious time agonizing over which expression will be best. Write one down and go with it. Now, notice the development from exegetical idea to theological idea:

Exegetical Idea: *Abram preserved God's blessing when he faced conflict by taking the initiative to resolve it.*

> Theological Idea: *God's people preserve God's blessing when they face conflict by taking the initiative to resolve it.*

Judges 17–18

As we have already noted, the narrative in Judges 17–18 is about idolatry. In fact, it begins and ends with the idol Micah made. Clearly, idolatry is the depravity factor, and this provides helpful direction for formulating the text's exegetical idea. The vision of God is a bit harder to identify. It is not as prominent as it is in some passages. However, the final statement about "the house of God" (18:31) provides a clue that the vision of God is his desire for his people to relate to his presence at a central place of worship. This is in contrast to Micah's possession of his own "house of gods" (17:5, author's translation).

On the basis of this understanding, we can begin working with the questions journalists ask—what, why, when, where, how, and who—to help us identify the subject. Is the emphasis on *how* Micah and the Danites pursued idolatry, on *why* they engaged in idolatry, or on *what* idolatry is? The resolution of the narrative suggests that the emphasis is on *what* is the outcome or the result of committing idolatry. Micah ended up empty handed. The Danites ultimately ended up in captivity. Behind both consequences, though, is a greater one. Both Micah and the Danites missed out on the presence of God. The final clause of the narrative reminds us that "all the time the house of God was in Shiloh" (18:31). Thus, we can state the subject of Judges 17–18 like this: *What did the idolatry of Micah and the Danites result in?* The complement is, *missing out on the presence of God*. The resulting exegetical idea is, *The idolatry of Micah and the Danites caused them to miss out on the presence of God*. It is not difficult to move to a theological idea since Micah and the Danites belong to Israel—the people of God. Nothing in the narrative suggests that their experience is limited to those living under the law of Moses or to a particular subset of Israel, such as kings or priests. Thus, the move from the exegetical to the theological idea looks like this:

> Exegetical Idea: *The idolatry of Micah and the Danites caused them to miss out on the presence of God.*

> Homiletical Idea: *The idolatry of God's people will cause them to miss out on the presence of God.*

1 Samuel 17

Previously, we observed how the narrative in 1 Samuel 17 appears near the beginning of a section (1 Sam. 15 to 2 Sam. 8) that defends the replacement of Saul's house with David's house as the ruling family. Sandra Richter suggests that 1 Samuel 17 is the final of three call narratives reported for David near the beginning of the section.[16] The first (1 Sam. 16:1–13) identifies David as God's choice, while the second presents David as empowered by God's Spirit (1 Sam. 16:14–23). The third call narrative in 1 Samuel 17 continues to argue for the replacement of Saul's house with David's house.

The narrative presents David as qualified to serve as Israel's king because he faces Goliath with faith instead of fear. When David speaks to the Israelite soldiers standing near him, he refers to Goliath simply as a "disgrace" and questions the authority of this "uncircumcised Philistine" to "defy the armies of the living God" (v. 26). This stands in stark contrast to Saul's dismay and terror in verse 11.

In case we wonder if David's oldest brother, Eliab, is right when he interprets David's bold response as conceited and the product of an evil heart (v. 28), we must recall the instructions in Deuteronomy 20:1–4 for going to war. Israelite soldiers were not to be afraid because of the presence of Yahweh who delivered Israel from Egypt and who fights for his people to give them victory. Thus, David is not acting presumptuously as a brash youth who does not understand the realities of warfare. He is acting out of faith in God and God's promises.

The intensity of David's conviction heightens when he speaks to Saul in verses 34–37. David is the only character in this narrative to factor God's empowering presence into the crisis. David's confidence in God's past acts of rescue—from the lion and the bear—provides confidence in the face of a new challenge, the giant Goliath. Finally, the intensity of David's conviction reaches its zenith when he taunts Goliath and announces that as a result of his impending defeat of Goliath, "the whole world will know that there is a God in Israel" and that "all those gathered here will know that it is not by sword or spear that the LORD saves; for the battle is the LORD's, and he will give all of you into our hands" (vv. 46–47).

---

16. Richter, *Epic of Eden*, 199.

In this narrative, then, David shows that he is qualified to serve as Israel's king because he is a man of faith. He trusts God's promise to lead his people into battle (Deut. 20:1–4) because he has confidence in God's power to save. As a result, I would articulate the exegetical idea and theological idea as follows.

> Exegetical Idea: *Yahweh defeats Goliath through David rather than Saul because David trusted in Yahweh's power to save.*

> Theological Idea: *Yahweh wins victories through leaders who trust in his power to save.*

Several important commentators verify this conclusion. Robert Chisholm describes the big idea of this passage in similar terms: "Faith in the Lord's power to save can be the catalyst for victory."[17] Mary Evans speaks of "David's supreme confidence that God was on their [Israel's] side."[18] Similarly, Robert D. Bergen says that "this account demonstrates the power of a single faith-filled life to inspire an entire army to victory and the vulnerability of all who 'defy the armies of the living God' (vv. 26, 36) when confronted by individuals who possess courageous faith in the Lord."[19]

J. P. Fokkelman takes this a step further in his magisterial work on the books of Samuel, seeing the reason for faith given in verse 47 as the most important line in the story. Whereas verse 46 provides a general revelation to the whole world that there is a God in Israel, verse 47 serves as special revelation to Israel ("all this assembly," ESV): "It is not by sword or spear that the LORD saves; for the battle is the LORD's, and he will give all of you into our hands." Fokkelman views this "universal statement in v. 47" as "the clear successor to and relative of the equally universal statement of faith by Jonathan in 14:6"[20]—"Nothing can hinder the LORD from saving, whether by many or by few." In Fokkelman's view, then, David does not teach *that* Yahweh delivers but rather *how* Yahweh delivers. Thus, on the basis of Fokkelman's analysis, we could state the theological message

---

17. Chisholm, *1 & 2 Samuel*, 116.
18. Evans, *1 and 2 Samuel*, 84.
19. Bergen, *1, 2 Samuel*, 187.
20. Fokkelman, *Narrative Art and Poetry*, 2:182, 184.

of the narrative like this: *Yahweh delivers his people by his power, not through human weaponry.*

Still, this great declaration by David serves a larger purpose. It establishes his qualification to serve as Israel's next king in place of Saul whom God has rejected (see 1 Sam. 15:23). This is what the author is doing with what he is saying. Thus, I conclude that the theological idea of 1 Samuel 17 is: *Yahweh wins victories through leaders who trust in his power to save.*

Nailing down the exegetical idea and theological idea is hard work. It requires wrestling with thought. Don't give up if you get stumped. You may wrestle with the data for an hour at your desk and have only a page of crossed out items on a legal pad to show for it. That's fine. Set it aside and return to it later. In fact, Eugene Lowry counsels preachers to conclude sessions of sermon preparation at points of "felt difficulty."[21] Quit for the day or for a few hours when you have *not* achieved a point of closure rather than when you feel pretty good about what you've accomplished. The reason? Your preconscious mind keeps working on the sermon and wrestling with the problem point. So do something else. Make a hospital call. Play tennis. Take your child to the park. Fix dinner. When you return later, your thoughts may crystallize and lead you to the passage's big idea. You'll say, "It's so simple! Why didn't I see this yesterday?!" For this reason, Jared Alcántara encourages preachers to "walk, jog, or ride a bike as a way to generate new ideas or transform good ideas into better ideas." He asks, "What if the real thief of productivity is *not* the time wasted through activities like walking? What if the real thief is the absence of time to think?"[22] Yes, nailing down the big idea is hard work, but doing it will keep you on track to producing an effective sermon.

---

21. Lowry, *Sermon*, 98–100.
22. Alcántara, *Practices of Christian Preaching*, 181.

Part 3

From Concept to Sermon

9

Starting the Second Half of the Adventure

Jon Krakauer cleared the ice from his oxygen mask, hunched a shoulder against the wind, and straddled the summit of Mount Everest. It was 1:17 p.m. on May 10, 1996. Krakauer, an accomplished climber and journalist, had not slept in fifty-seven hours. He had not eaten much more than a bowl of ramen soup and a handful of peanut M&Ms in three days. Still, he had reached the top of the earth's tallest peak—29,028 feet. In his oxygen-deprived stupor, he had no way of knowing that storm clouds forming below would turn into a vicious blizzard that would claim the lives of five fellow climbers. Yet he knew his adventure was hardly finished. In his book *Into Thin Air*, Krakauer describes what he felt: "Reaching the top of Everest is supposed to trigger a surge of intense elation; against long odds, after all, I had just attained a goal I'd coveted since childhood. But the summit was really only the halfway point. Any impulse I might have felt toward self-congratulation was extinguished by the overwhelming apprehension about the long, dangerous descent that lay ahead."[1] David Breashears, the first American to scale Everest twice, concurs and offers this counsel to climbers: "Getting to the summit is the easy part; it's getting back down that's hard."[2]

1. Krakauer, *Into Thin Air*, 181.
2. Krakauer, *Into Thin Air*, 277.

In this respect, preaching an Old Testament narrative resembles an Everest expedition. Arriving at the exegetical summit—the narrative's theological message—is the easy part. It's getting back down to deliver the goods to the congregation that's hard. The trek down the mountain includes biblical theology, application, sermon structure, and delivery.

This descent from concept to sermon calls for increased fervency in prayer. The summit or halfway point in the process is an important place to pause and worship God for who he is and what he has done. A careful study of the narrative will have yielded new or fresh insights about God's person and work that should move a preacher to praise or repentance. The descent from concept to sermon is no time for a preacher's prayer life to wane.

The chapters in part 3 will explore the stages of sermon development as the expositor descends from concept to sermon. These stages may be the most difficult in the entire process because they involve a high level of thinking. In some ways, I find them harder than studying the narrative text, even if you study it in Hebrew. These stages require synthesis—putting back together what you've taken apart in analysis—and a more abstract type of thinking. Yet as challenging as these stages may appear, they will make the difference between a mediocre sermon and a life-transforming one.

The focus of this chapter is the fourth stage in Robinson's stages of sermon preparation: analyzing the exegetical idea.[3] I suggest analyzing the exegetical idea by asking and answering four questions:

1. How does this theological message connect to the Bible's storyline?
2. What do my listeners need me to explain?
3. Where do my listeners say "I don't agree with that"?
4. How does God want me to respond to this theological message?

Some of the most important sermon preparation occurs when a preacher wrestles with these questions. They require prayerful, rigorous thinking.

Connection (to the Bible's Storyline)

The first question to ask is, *How does this theological message connect to the Bible's storyline?* Every Old Testament narrative we preach belongs to

---

3. In Robinson's methology, this fourth stage uses three developmental (or functional) questions to analyze the big idea.

a larger storyline (metanarrative) that finds its center in Jesus the Messiah. As N. T. Wright has observed, the Old Testament is "a story in search of a conclusion."[4] This conclusion, he argued, must "incorporate the full liberation and redemption of Israel" and should correspond to and grow out of the rest of the Old Testament's story.[5] This is what the New Testament does, and Christian preachers must do it too.

Biblical Theology

The quest to connect a narrative to the storyline of the Bible leads us into the world of biblical theology. According to D. A. Carson, this discipline "focuses on the inductive study of the biblical texts in their final form." The goal is "to uncover and articulate the unity of *all* the biblical texts taken together, resorting primarily to the categories of those texts themselves."[6] The emphasis, then, is on tracing the arc of the Bible's storyline by noting the development of major themes such as covenant, redemption, temple (the presence of God), the image of God, the city of God, the kingdom of God, and many more.

Although it is not advisable to reduce the "center" or organizing principle of the Old Testament to one of these themes,[7] it is possible to summarize the storyline of the Bible in one sentence. Here is my suggestion. *The Bible is the story of God reestablishing the gift of his presence.*[8] The Bible begins and ends in a garden paradise where God dwells with his people. It moves from a potential building site in Genesis 1–2 to a finished city in Revelation 21–22.[9] In between, God dwells with his people in various temples: the tabernacle, the Jerusalem temple, Jesus (Immanuel, "God with us," Matt. 1:23), and the church (Eph. 1:19–22).[10]

---

4. N. T. Wright, *New Testament and the People of God*, 217. Wright says that this is how the "great story of the Hebrew scriptures" was read in the Second Temple period. Yet his observation still applies in our current world.

5. N. T. Wright, *New Testament and the People of God*, 217.

6. Carson, "Systematic Theology and Biblical Theology," 100.

7. This is the conclusion of Gerhard Hasel, *Old Testament Theology*, 139–71.

8. Similarly, John Walton proposes that the primary theme that progresses throughout the entire Bible is "the establishment of God's presence among his people." Furthermore, he does "not consider this to be the 'center' of Old Testament theology, but it is an overarching theme, arguably the most dominant and pervasive of themes, the trajectory along which the program of God moves" (*Old Testament Theology for Christians*, 26).

9. See Alexander, *From Eden to the New Jerusalem*, 14, 19–31.

10. For helpful studies on the theme of God's presence as it relates to the storyline of the Bible, see the following: Beale, *Temple and the Church's Mission*; Beale and Kim, *God Dwells*

None of this denies that the story of the Scriptures is the story of redemption. However, my suggestion presses in more specifically to the purpose of our redemption. God redeemed his people from sin's bondage and exile to restore us to life in his presence. The hero of this story is the one who accomplished redemption for us—Jesus the Messiah, the Lamb of God, who redeemed us by his blood (Gal. 3:13–14; Titus 2:14; 1 Pet. 1:18–19).

Establishing the Connection

Exactly how can preachers make a connection to the storyline of the Bible? First, preachers need to remind listeners that they can only respond properly to a narrative's prophetic message or ethical thrust in the grace provided by Jesus Christ and his gospel. Second, listeners need to understand any lines of continuity or discontinuity between the theological message of an Old Testament narrative and the new covenant. How can we proclaim a narrative from Judges or Chronicles without discussing how its theological message is shaped by its fulfillment in Christ? At a minimum, expositors need to speak to these first two issues.

There are a couple more ways, though, that preachers can establish a connection to the larger story of the Bible. These ways may not show up in every sermon, but they should be a regular part of our preaching. Third, preachers can note any major biblical-theological themes in their narrative and reveal how they culminate in the person of Jesus Christ. I cannot imagine preaching Judges 9 without reflection on the theme of God's justice and judgment for wickedness. Finally, preachers can note any ways that a text prefigures or anticipates Christ.[11] I find this approach to be more natural when preaching narratives where David is a character, given the fact that the New Testament explicitly identifies Jesus as "the Son of David."[12] For example, in 1 Samuel 17, it is appropriate to talk about how David anticipates Jesus, the ultimate warrior-king who defeats the beast and the kings of the earth who try to oppose the living God (Rev. 19:11–21)—even as Goliath did. It can also be appropriate to point out

---

among Us; Lister, *Presence of God*; Alexander, *City of God and the Goal of Creation*; and Duvall and Hays, *God's Relational Presence*.

11. See Greidanus, *Preaching Christ from the Old Testament*, 227–77, for seven ways of moving from the Old Testament to Christ.

12. See, for example, Matt. 1:1; Luke 2:4, 11; Acts 13:32–41; Rom. 1:3; 2 Tim. 2:8; Rev. 22:16.

that Jesus is "the true and better Abigail" when preaching 1 Samuel 25 or "the true and better Josiah" when preaching 1 Kings 22–23. The key is not to force typology or to let it eclipse the theological message of the text.

Explanation

The second question to use in analyzing the exegetical idea is the explanation question. *What do my listeners need me to explain?* Haddon Robinson identifies this question and the next two as the "functional" or "developmental" questions that preachers need to ask about the exegetical idea in relationship to both the text and the audience. These questions probe the dimensions of understanding (explanation), belief (validation), and behavior (application). Robinson counsels preachers to begin by asking, Did the author develop his point by explaining, proving, or applying? Then they should ask, Will my audience respond to this idea by saying, "Explain it, validate it, or apply it"?

When preparing sermons on Old Testament narrative texts, I have found it more helpful to ask these questions in relationship to my listeners rather than to the text. Specifically, I need to know what concepts or details in the text my listeners need explained, proved, or applied. This helps me know what to include or leave out of my sermon. The sequence of these questions is important since we are dealing with how thought forms. You cannot prove or validate what people do not understand. You cannot apply what people do not accept.

The explanation question anticipates places in the narrative where our listeners will say, "I don't understand" or "Please explain that." Contemporary listeners may have questions about customs, geography, theology, and language that an ancient storyteller would assume the audience knew. An expositor who preaches the story of Ruth may have to explain:

- The meaning of names like Elimelech, Naomi, Ruth, Boaz, and Obed
- The theological implications of leaving the land of Israel for Moab
- Who the Moabites were and why Israel despised them
- The plight of a childless widow in Israel
- The kinsman-redeemer concept
- The custom of allowing the poor to glean at the edge of the field

- How much an ephah of grain equals—a small or large amount?
- What the expression "loyal love" (Hebrew, *hesed*, חֶסֶד) means
- The significance of Ruth uncovering Boaz's feet
- Why Boaz sat at the town gate and what the town elders were doing there
- The sandal-removal ceremony (even the writer explains this one!)

Obviously, preachers must not turn the sermon into an exegetical lecture. A sentence or two of explanation will do for most questions. We must not overexplain, nor can we afford to underexplain.

Validation

The third question to use in analyzing the exegetical idea—and the contents of the narrative—is *Where do my listeners say "I don't agree with that"?* The focus here is on validity. A listener may hear a detail or an idea in the narrative and ask, Is it true? In other words, Can I believe it? I have heard Haddon Robinson refer to this as "the C. S. Lewis question" since Lewis was such a genius at anticipating and responding to peoples' objections to the ideas in Scripture. Today, I would call this "the Tim Keller" question since Keller is so astute in his familiarity with the objections of late-modern people.[13]

When we anticipate where our listeners will raise this question, we mimic the biblical writers. For example, as noted previously, the section from 1 Samuel 15 to 2 Samuel 8 resembles a dynastic defense which, in the ancient Near East, defended the replacement of one dynasty with another. The writer anticipates people saying, "I'm not sure I buy the idea of David replacing Saul as king. Prove to me that this was a legitimate move." This section of Samuel, then, validates David's fitness to be king as well as Saul's unworthiness to serve as Israel's king. Similarly, the story in 1 Kings 3:16–28 has a validating function. It tells of two prostitutes who came to King Solomon with a dispute over the maternity of a baby and proves that Solomon did receive wisdom from Yahweh as the previous narrative in 3:1–15 claims.

Even people who take the Bible seriously can struggle with its truth claims. We loudly affirm, "God says it, I believe it, that settles it." Yet we

---

13. See Keller, *Reason for God*, and Keller, *Making Sense of God*.

can still struggle with emotional and intellectual doubts. For example, in a sermon on the book of Esther, you might raise a question that your audience is thinking: How can I really be sure that God is working in my life when I can't see or hear him? Suppose your big idea for Esther is, *Even when you can't see or hear God, he is still in control of your destiny*. When confronted with that idea, a listener might respond, "Is it true? Can I buy this?" Your answer to the listener's question comes right out of the text. From the story of Esther, you can show how God overcomes the poor spiritual climate around you, the impossible people, the unpredictable events of life, the circumstances you can't change. He does all of this in ways you won't recognize if you don't look closely.

Here is another example. When you preach Genesis 13, you might anticipate listeners challenging the notion that believers should initiate conflict resolution. Perhaps some listeners got burned when they tried to resolve a conflict with a longtime friend or with a coworker. When they hear you say, "Believers should take the initiative to resolve conflict," they may respond, "Is it true? I'm not sure I buy it." By anticipating this question, you can use the latter part of the story to validate the idea that God blesses his people when they take the initiative to resolve conflict. You can point out that while the short-term payoffs may be deceiving, the long-term payoffs will reward the risk you take to resolve a conflict.

Application

The final question to use in analyzing the exegetical idea is the application question. *How does God want me to respond to this theological message?* This question takes its cue from 2 Timothy 3:16–17: "All Scripture is God-breathed and is useful for teaching, rebuking, correcting and training in righteousness, so that the servant of God may be thoroughly equipped for every good work." However, as Haddon Robinson quips, "More heresy is preached in application than in Bible exegesis."[14]

Moralizing

One of the pitfalls of applying an Old Testament narrative to listeners' lives is moralizing. This is reducing application to moral lessons from the characters' lives—especially those lessons that are peripheral to the

---

14. Robinson, "Heresy of Application," 306.

theological message or ethical thrust of the narrative. Graeme Goldsworthy warns against this approach:

> We must not view these recorded events [historical narrative] as if they were a mere succession of events from which we draw little moral lessons or examples for life. Much that passes for application of the Old Testament to the Christian life is only moralizing. It consists almost exclusively in *observing* the behaviour of the godly and godless (admittedly against a background of the activity of God) and then *exhorting* people to learn from these observations. That is why the "character" study is a favoured approach to Bible narrative—the life of Moses, the life of David, the life of Elijah and so on. There is nothing wrong with character studies as such—we are to learn by others' examples—but such character studies all too often take the place of more fundamental aspects of biblical teaching.[15]

However, we must not overstate the problem. The problem with these applications is not that they are based on the example of the characters. After all, the apostle Paul recognized the validity of looking at Old Testament narratives for examples of how or how not to live (1 Cor. 10:6, 11). Daniel Doriani observes, "If some rush to draw ethical points from Scripture, others so fear moralism that they resist the idea of using narratives for moral lessons. But Jesus himself justifies the search for ethical principles from biblical narratives."[16]

The problem with calling listeners to follow or not follow the example of the characters usually takes one of two directions. First, such application can rest on a careless or faulty reading of a narrative. For example, some preachers have used Gideon's placement of a fleece on the threshing floor (Judg. 6:36–40) as an example of how to discover God's will by seeking a sign. This misses the point, though, that Gideon already knew God's will! He simply lacked the faith to do it and sought reassurance. As Mary Evans observes, "Gideon's need for God's repeated action shows that signs per se are rarely really convincing."[17]

---

15. Goldsworthy, *Gospel and Kingdom*, 24.
16. Doriani, *Putting the Truth to Work*, 88. The problem is not a "do" or "don't" kind of application, but the *wrong* kind of "do" or "don't" application. See Kromminga, "Remember Lot's Wife," 35.
17. Evans, *Judges and Ruth*, 94. She also notes that "Jesus' somewhat sceptical approach to signs was perhaps influenced by reflection on this passage (see Matt. 12:39; 16:4; Mark 8:11–12; Luke 16:31)" (94n32).

A second problem is basing application on details that are peripheral to the theological message communicated by the author. These details may be critical to the narrative, but they do not reflect the ethical thrust of the narrative. For example, I have heard sermons on 2 Samuel 11–12 that focus much of their application on King David's "failure" to go out to war with his army in the spring. If he had done so, he would not have put himself in a circumstance where he faced sexual temptation. Times of idleness can make us more vulnerable to temptation. However, while David's decision to stay home from battle provided the occasion for temptation, it does not explain why he committed adultery and murder. The narrator shines the spotlight on the sins behind adultery and murder—the sins of despising God's grace and abusing power.

Furthermore, I have heard preachers draw their application primarily from Nathan's parable. They urge listeners to "create a parable when you need to confront someone with their sin." I am not arguing that preachers should remain silent about these elements of the story. Nor am I suggesting that preachers should never draw an application from them. However, they cannot serve as the primary points of application if the preacher's goal is to preach a sermon that communicates the theological message of the text.

A More Excellent Way

How then shall we apply Old Testament narratives to the lives of new covenant believers? I find it helpful to begin by asking, What does this story teach me about God and his relationship with human beings? Haddon Robinson reminds preachers that "the purpose of Bible stories is not to say 'you must, you should.' The purpose is to give insight into how men and women relate to the eternal God and how God relates to them."[18]

This takes us back to two concepts we worked with earlier: a story's vision of God and the depravity factor. We should build application around the contours of these concepts. This is what distinguishes God-centered application from mere moralizing. Like the maxims in the book of Proverbs, our applications may sometimes sound like good business advice, yet they must always be rooted in the fear of God.

18. Robinson, "Heresy of Application," 310.

Identifying the vision of God and the depravity factor helps the interpreter move from the ancient situation to the theological message it conveys. The preacher can then bring the theological message into the modern world and examine what it looks like when a listener lives his or her life in response to it (see fig. 9.1). The exegetical idea you have already developed will usually express the ancient situation. The theological message is essentially the theological expression of the sermon's big idea.

Figure 9.1

The Process of Application

Theological Message
↗ ↘
Ancient Situation   Modern Situation

There are four questions that preachers will do well to ask as they attempt to move from the ancient situation to the modern situation via the theological message.

1. Should I base the application on what the characters do and say? This is tricky because sometimes the positive or negative actions of a character line up with the theological message of the narrative. However, this is not always the case. Judges 3:12–30 is a prime example. When I preach this narrative, my theological idea is: *God delivers his people from hopeless situations in unexpected ways.*[19] Some preachers have called their listeners to use their "unique characteristics" or "weaknesses" to serve God just like Ehud used his left-handedness.[20] Yet in the climax of the narrative, Ehud makes a statement that gives us the clue to the author's intended message: "'Follow me,' he ordered, 'for the LORD has given Moab, your enemy, into your hands'" (Judg. 3:28). This is a story about *how* God delivers his people from situations that appear hopeless. Ehud's left-handedness is only one of the unexpected ways that God used to bring about deliverance. "There is surprise at every point in the story: A left-handed warrior from a tribe with a right-handed name. A secret message. An escape made possible by the delay caused by the smell of a king presumably going to

---

19. Mathewson, "Story of the Left-Handed Assassin," 48.
20. Ehud's left-handedness is unique, but it is doubtful that it is a weakness. The Hebrew expression for "left-handed" in Judg. 3:15 means "bound in his right hand." As Evans observes, "There is not much support for this view, probably because the same idiom when used in [Judges] 20:16 cannot have that implication" (*Judges and Ruth*, 67). Block helpfully suggests that the adjective "bound"—or "shut, restricted"—"suggests Ehud and his fellow Benjamites in 20:16 were not naturally left-handed. On the contrary, they were a specially trained group for whom dexterity with the left hand was inculcated by binding up the right hand" (*Judges, Ruth*, 161).

the bathroom."[21] Thus, it is better to challenge listeners not to give up in hopeless situations rather than to use their unique characteristics to serve God.

On the other hand, the theological message of the narrative in Judges 4 lines up with the characters' actions. In Judges 4, the prophet Deborah relates a message to Barak from God, calling Barak to lead troops to Mount Tabor where God would give him victory over a Canaanite army. Judges 4:8 records the response: "Barak said to her, 'If you go with me, I will go; but if you don't go with me, I won't go.'" Perhaps this sounds noble and godly. Barak will not go into battle without a prophet of God. However, Deborah's response suggests otherwise. She agrees to go with him. "But," she says, "the honor will not be yours, for the LORD will deliver Sisera into the hands of a woman" (v. 9).[22] We expect this woman to be Deborah, a prophet and leader. Instead, the woman who takes down the enemy general, Sisera, turns out to be an unlikely hero—Jael. She is a woman who rises to the occasion and does what is right even though she has severe limitations. First, she lacks a clear word from the LORD like Barak. Second, she does not have military weapons, so she has to resort to household implements—a tent peg and a hammer. Finally, she was supposed to be an ally of Sisera, given that her husband had made an alliance with Sisera's "boss"—Jabin, the king of Hazor. Thus, I summarize the theological message of the narrative like this: *God accomplishes his will through people who have the courage to obey his call to serve.*[23] So then, it is legitimate to call listeners not to be like Barak, but to be like Jael since their behavior does line up with the meaning of the story.

The point is, we can only point to the actions of characters as normative examples to follow or avoid when we ground their actions in the theological message of the narrative.

---

21. Mathewson, "Story of the Left-Handed Assassin," 47. Note that the Hebrew name "Benjamin" means "son of the right hand."

22. According to Mary Evans, Barak's response seems "to indicate that his trust is in her and maybe her connection to God, rather than in God himself" (*Judges and Ruth*, 76). Barry G. Webb describes Deborah as "clearly taken aback, as her rejoinder in verse 9 shows. . . . She will go with him if he insists, but he will have a price to pay" (*Book of Judges*, 184). Similarly, David J. H. Beldman calls Barak an "unwilling leader" and says that he "seems to prefer the presence of Deborah rather than the presence of Yahweh" (*Judges*, 85).

23. This idea finds support in the Song of Deborah in Judg. 5. The song celebrates the willing volunteers in Israel (5:2, 9), yet it offers strong words of condemnation for those who "did not come to help the LORD" (5:23). It also devotes a movement to blessing Jael for her exploits (5:24–27).

2. *What is the ethical thrust of the narrative?* To put it another way, what admonition or exhortation does this story offer? This is an important question because the big idea of a narrative is not an exhortation. The big idea states the theological message of the narrative, and this message implies an exhortation or ethical thrust. Yet it does not state it. Here, we have to ask ourselves what a narrator is doing with what they are saying. This is based on a helpful distinction in linguistics between "semantics" and "pragmatics." Semantics refers to what a saying *means*. Pragmatics refers to how a saying *functions* in its context. For example, take the statement, "A car is coming."[24] In terms of semantics, it means that a four-wheeled vehicle is approaching. However, in terms of pragmatics, the statement can function as either a warning or an encouragement. If my grandkids are playing football in our front yard (and sometimes needing to enter the street to retrieve the football after a missed pass), I will utter the statement as a warning not to go into the street lest they get hit by the car. Yet, if they are waiting impatiently for a pizza delivery, the same statement can be an encouragement. In the same way, preachers must determine how the theological message of a narrative functions—as a warning, an encouragement, or a call to action.

As previously noted, the theological idea of Judges 3:12–30 is: *God delivers his people from hopeless situations in unexpected ways.* That idea describes what the narrative means in terms of semantics. In terms of pragmatics, though, the statement functions as a challenge to trust God and not give up when you face a hopeless situation.

3. *How does the message of the narrative relate to a new covenant believer?* As Klein, Blomberg, and Hubbard suggest, "We can assume neither that all of the OT carries over into the NT without any change in application nor that none of it carries over unchanged. Rather, we must examine each text to discover how it has been fulfilled in Christ (Mt 5:17)."[25] This loops us back into our discussion of biblical theology. The storyline and context of the entire Bible will help us determine what continues and what discontinues as we move from the old covenant—which Old Testament narratives reflect—to the new covenant. For example, the problem of idolatry in Judges 17–18 is not unique to the Old Testament. The apostle John ends his first epistle by warning its recipients to keep

---

24. I have adapted this example from Matthews, *Concise Oxford Dictionary*, 313.
25. Klein, Blomberg, and Hubbard, *Introduction to Biblical Interpretation*, 488–89.

themselves from idols (1 John 5:21), while the apostle Paul equates greed with idolatry in Colossians 3:5.

4. What implications does the theological message have for the concrete situations my listeners face? I am convinced that vague application leads to vague Christian living. Or, as Jared Alcántara says, "Concrete preaching helps our sermons matter more on Monday mornings."[26] So moving from a more abstract theological message to concrete situations in my listeners' lives is imperative. Even when we get specific, it is easy to get tunnel vision. We tend to think about applying the theological message to people like ourselves. The challenge is to think outside our immediate circumstances. What difference will this text make in the lives of believers who are different than a preacher in terms of their life stage, social-economic background, ethnic identity, gender, marital status, occupation, and education? Matthew Kim's volume, *Preaching with Cultural Intelligence*, is worth reading. He reminds us that loving the people to whom we preach requires us to know them beyond their names and professions. "Who are they? What cultures and subcultures do they most identify with? What dreams do they have, and what are their fears? What beliefs do they hold closely? What causes them pain?"[27]

Suppose you are preaching Genesis 13. We have already expressed its theological idea as *God's people preserve God's blessing when they face conflict by taking the initiative to resolve it.* How might your listeners apply it in their particular circumstances? Imagine a single mom with two children who is embroiled in a dispute with the child's father over the details of weekend custody. How might she honor God by taking the initiative to resolve the conflict? Of course, these situations are very difficult because there is always more than one biblical principle or teaching in play. Still, what might it look like in this mom's circumstances to take the initiative to resolve a conflict? What will it look like for a teacher to resolve a conflict with a student's parents over the student's struggle with an attention deficit disorder? How can the teacher honor God by initiating an attempt to resolve their conflict?

Yes, there may be more heresy preached in the application of Scripture than in its exegesis. This is especially true when preaching Old Testament narrative texts. Yet we serve our congregations well when we talk specifics about what it looks like for them to respond to the narratives we proclaim.

---

26. Alcántara, *Practices of Christian Preaching*, 133.
27. Kim, *Preaching with Cultural Intelligence*, 6.

10

Adding the Finishing Touches

Before moving further into the journey from concept to sermon, it is time to add some finishing touches to the work that has already been done. For the sake of clarity, interest, and focus, preachers must think about how they will package their big idea and what purpose they hope to accomplish.

Packaging the Big Idea

People act on ideas. But ideas stick only when a communicator packages them properly. A few years ago, the United Parcel Service (UPS) made this claim: "We run the tightest ship in the shipping business." This claim worked because it was concise, clear, concrete, and creative. It consists of only nine words. Its language is vivid, and it plays off of the word "shipping." As a result, the idea is memorable and compelling. It sticks.

Effective preachers must figure out how to make their ideas stick. "People are more likely to think God's thoughts after Him, and to live and love and choose on the basis of these thoughts when they are couched in memorable sentences."[1] Your sermon big idea needs to be concise, clear, concrete, and creative. The Heath brothers, Chip and Dan, counsel idea creators to be "masters of exclusion. We must relentlessly prioritize."[2] The more words we stuff into an idea, the more mental processing we require of our listeners.

---

1. Robinson, *Biblical Preaching*, 104.
2. Heath and Heath, *Made to Stick*, 16.

Often, less is more. The fewer words we use, the more clarity and memorability we achieve. Our big idea also needs to be concrete and creative—just like proverbs. The following idea is true: *One value of a relationship is the way the two parties bring about personal growth in each other.* This idea is as forgettable as it is true. It is fairly clear, but it is not compelling. However, stating it like this makes it stick: *As iron sharpens iron, so one person sharpens another.* This statement, of course, is Proverbs 27:17.

As preachers, we work with words. So it is worth some time and effort to state our theological idea in a more memorable, compelling way. We refer to this final expression of the big idea as the "homiletical idea" or the "preaching idea." We want our homiletical idea to be concise (9–15 words is ideal), clear, concrete (vivid, specific words), and creative (a striking image or an analogy).

Let me offer four caveats, though. First, a big idea is not a sermon. We are preaching a text, not just a big idea. Exposition is unpacking the nuances and intricacies and surprises of the narrative we are preaching. We want our listeners to enter the story and feel its twists and turns. The big idea is simply the peg on which everything on our sermon hangs. As Laurence Turner observes, "Any sermon must focus on matters of central importance if it is to communicate with a congregation in a relatively brief time."[3] Of course, as important as a big idea is, it is not everything. While we must devote some time to it, we cannot afford to obsess over the perfect big idea statement. There are other aspects to our sermon that require our time and attention.

Second, clear is better than clever. Creativity is good; cleverness is not. It can make grand theological ideas sound cheap, trite, or silly. We are not creating a jingle to sell toothpaste. We are communicating the life-changing truth of God's Word. To be honest, over the years I have often used my theological idea as my homiletical idea. I may make another attempt at whittling away a few words so that it is concise. But I don't spend hours—or even an hour—trying to fashion a statement that will blow away my listeners. If a catchy statement comes to mind, I go with it—as long as it is not too clever and as long as it does not dilute the content of the big idea. If it fails these tests, I scrap it. By the way, even if I come up with a creative idea that passes the "cleverness test" and the

---

3. Turner, "Preaching Narrative," 22.

"content test," I will still use the theological expression of my big idea in the sermon. That is, I use the language of both my homiletical idea *and* my theological idea in the sermon.

Third, introducing an additional expression of the big idea can be confusing. When I have trained preachers in the big idea approach to preaching, I have found that most understand the move from the exegetical to the theological idea. However, there is something about adding an additional expression—the homiletical or preaching idea—that causes confusion. Remember that the content of each expression is supposed to be the same. The exegetical idea summarizes the meaning of a text in "then" language. The theological idea summarizes it in "now" language—that is, in a timeless way that can apply to present-day listeners. The homiletical idea simply states it in a more creative way. To repeat an earlier point, if I can't state my theological idea in a more creative way, I'm fine with that. I simply use my theological idea as my homiletical idea. Perhaps I can state it more concisely, but maybe not.

Here is a fourth caveat about the big idea. Ironically, the pursuit of a creative homiletical idea can result in one that is too generic. The creative language can squeeze out the specific details that make it distinct. The idea then becomes a sound bite that does not really capture the unique teaching of the text. For example, I might be tempted to word my big idea for Judges 17–18 like this: *When you do what is right in your own eyes, nothing in life can be right.* The effectiveness of the first part of the idea is debatable. It picks up on a key detail in the text—people doing what was right in their eyes (17:6). However, the specific way this is expressed in Judges 17–18 is through idolatry. It's the last part of the statement that fails. While there is a nice play on the word "right," the notion that "nothing in life can be right" is too abstract to capture the specific consequences for idolatry that this text reveals.

Let's look at some examples to see how a big idea develops from an exegetical idea to a theological and finally to a homiletical idea. When we run the exegetical idea of Genesis 13 (see table 10.1) through the lens of Jesus's teaching and the entire New Testament, it is apparent that what was true for Abraham is true for the people of God today as well. The theological idea in table 10.1 reflects this, and it is a clear, precise statement. Chances are, though, that it will not stick like Velcro to a listener's mind. However, stating it in a condensed, memorable way can make it linger in

Table 10.1
Big Idea Development in Genesis 13
Exegetical Idea: *Abram preserved God's blessing when he faced conflict by taking the initiative to resolve it.*
Theological Idea: *God's people preserve God's blessing when they face conflict by taking the initiative to resolve it.*
Preaching Idea: *God's people guard God's blessing by operating on a "no conflict" basis.*

a listener's memory: *God's people guard God's blessing by operating on a "no conflict" basis.* This works for a preaching idea because it does not take away from the precision or specificity of the text.

Earlier, I suggested the following theological idea for 1 Samuel 17: *Yahweh wins victories through leaders who trust in his power to save.* This may be sufficient for a preaching idea. Another possibility is: *When God has big business, faith always gets the contract.* This is certainly catchy. The question is, does it dilute the theological message of the text? It highlights the importance of faith over fear—a key idea in 1 Samuel 17. However, it obscures the focus of faith, which is God's power to save. This is a case where I might use both statements in a sermon on 1 Samuel 17.

When I preach Judges 17–18, I might simply use my theological idea as my homiletical idea: *The idolatry of God's people will cause them to miss out on the presence of God.* However, this doesn't sound as personal or as conversational as I might like. The idea strikes with a bit more force when I word it like this: *When we pursue idolatry, we miss out on God's presence.* This statement is clear and concise. However, I might make one more tweak to the first few words so it comes out like this: *When we turn from God to idols, we miss out on God's presence.* The change in language is a play on the phrase "turned to God from idols" in 1 Thessalonians 1:9. Of course, listeners who are unfamiliar with the Bible will not pick up on this. But the wording might catch the attention of listeners who know the Scriptures.

Developing your big idea in this way requires high-level thinking. But the result is an idea that will stick in your listeners' minds. Once you give your big idea sticking power, you are ready to move on and think about your sermon's purpose.

Determining the Sermon's Purpose

Wise preachers take the time to wrestle with a sermon's purpose. Forming a purpose statement forces preachers to think through what they expect to happen within their hearers as a result of hearing the sermon.[4] If the sermon's big idea resembles an arrow, the sermon's purpose resembles the target. The big idea states the truth. The purpose describes what the truth should accomplish.

In order to discipline their thinking, preachers should write out the purpose statement in a sentence that describes the intended outcome. Ask what should happen in the listeners as a result of hearing the sermon. Then write this in a sentence. Effective purpose statements exhibit at least two characteristics.

First, effective purpose statements reflect the purpose of the author. A preacher should start with the author's purpose by asking, What did the writer expect to accomplish by putting this story here and telling it in this manner? With the answer in hand, the second step is to ask, What do I expect to happen in the lives of my audience after listening to this story? The preacher's purpose should be in line with the biblical author's purpose.

In 1 Samuel 17, the writer's purpose is to show the audience that David was more qualified to serve as Israel's king than Saul was because David trusted in God's power to save when he faced Goliath. When I think in terms of the listeners to whom I will preach, my purpose might be to show them what kind of leader God uses.

The purpose of your sermon can be different than the author's purpose as long as it is in line with the author's purpose. However, it must not go in a completely different direction than the biblical author went. We must always ask, Would the narrator be comfortable with the way I am using their story to address this particular situation? Would the biblical author have done that? Effective purpose statements reflect the purpose of the author.

Second, effective purpose statements describe measurable results. Here, it is helpful to state the sermon's purpose as an instructional objective. Think about the purpose of a sermon from Genesis 13. We have already stated the preaching idea like this: *God's people guard God's blessing by operating on a "no conflict" basis.* Perhaps your purpose will be for your

---

4. For a fuller discussion, see Robinson, *Biblical Preaching*, 107–12.

listeners to take a meaningful step to resolve a conflict they have with another believer. This, of course, is not measurable. So you will need to think through what kind of meaningful steps the people in your church family need to take if they are to resolve conflict. These steps might include inviting someone to dinner, sending a note of appreciation, or granting a request. It helps to think about specific conflicts which you have witnessed or in which you have been caught.

If the intended outcome of your sermon on 2 Samuel 11–12 is for listeners to appreciate what God's grace has given them and what it has withheld, then you might state your purpose like this: *Listeners will write out a list of God's specific gifts to them and then offer daily, five-minute prayers of thanksgiving to God for these gifts.* Here is another possible example: *Hearers will use their mealtime prayers to recite God's specific blessings in their lives and to ask him to help them be content.*

Whether or not your listeners will actually write out a list of items or use their mealtime prayers to recite God's blessings, you should preach as if they will. You can even present these as examples of how they might respond to the message of 2 Samuel 11–12. The Spirit of God may even use your sermon to accomplish a different purpose than you intended. But identifying the purpose for your sermon will help you aim your big idea more accurately.

11

Shaping the Sermon

For years, aspiring preachers have received this sage advice: "Tell them what you plan to tell them; tell them; then tell them what you've just told them." This turns out to be lousy advice when preaching a story. To preach an Old Testament narrative effectively, preachers must wrestle with the most effective means of shaping their sermon. This brings us to the next stage in the sermon development process.

At this point the preacher must ask, What kind of form will I use to accomplish the purpose I determined based on the big idea? What shape will my sermon take?

Many pastors opt for shaping their sermons around a list of principles they have combed during their study. A few years ago, I perused a year's worth of issues from a popular publication on preaching. Most of the published manuscripts on Old Testament narrative texts followed this tactic. One pastor shaped a sermon from Exodus 3:1–12 around three keys to impossible living gleaned from Moses's life. Another pastor preached Genesis 45:1–13 by listing the techniques Joseph used to put his painful past behind him. Still another preacher handled the story of Abraham's test in Genesis 22 by sharing four principles about the testing of our faith. Yet another preached the Genesis 39 account of Joseph overcoming temptation by highlighting four reasons why we should say no to sexual temptation. As previously noted, this approach usually does not reflect the strategy or style of the authors who composed Old Testament narratives.

Often, it does not do justice to the prophetic message of the narrative. Instead, it simply uses the narrative to illustrate principles a preacher supposedly finds in a text.

What shape should a sermon from an Old Testament narrative take? The story form is the obvious choice. As David C. Deuel argues, "If the preacher's goal is to be expositional, what is more expositional than preaching the text in its storyline form?"[1] This is not as easy as it sounds, however. Sidney Greidanus explains, "The narrative form has to strike a delicate balance between simply narrating the story and providing explicit statements for right understanding."[2] The key is to plot your sermon by taking your cue from the way the story unfolds. While you need to do more than retell the story, you cannot do less than that. Ideally, you will follow the same set of tracks as the biblical storyteller. What implications does this have for the development of your sermon's big idea?

Inductive Preaching

For one thing, following the contours of the storyline means preaching inductively rather than deductively. The terms *inductive* and *deductive* describe the way people reason and present ideas (see figure 11.1). In deduction, you start with the conclusion or the whole and then work to the specific pieces. The answer is front-loaded, and then you break it down. Arranging a sermon deductively can make it clear. It can also make it boring. Unless your idea creates tension, your listeners will check out. Don Sunukjian preaches an effective deductive sermon on 2 Corinthians 12:7–10 in which he develops the big idea, *The thing you pray most that God would change is the thing you most want to keep.* When listeners hear that idea, their response is not, "Good, I've got the answer. Let's go home." Their response is most likely, "No way! That's crazy." They are ready to debate, to argue, and, yes, to listen to your defense of the idea.

The opposite approach is induction. Induction starts with the specific pieces and then works its way through them to the conclusion or the

---

1. Deuel, "Expository Preaching," 275. By "storyline," Deuel refers to the plot or general plan of a story. Likewise, Sidney Greidanus observes, "The most appropriate form for a sermon on a narrative text is, not surprisingly, the narrative form" (*Modern Preacher*, 226).
2. Greidanus, *Modern Preacher*, 225. Haddon Robinson comments, "Narratives are most effective when the audience hears the story and arrives at the speaker's ideas without the idea being stated directly" (*Biblical Preaching*, 130).

whole. The answer is unknown at the beginning. The idea does not emerge until the end. When done poorly, induction can be unclear. Your listeners may struggle to stay on track since they're not sure where you're going. When done well, though, induction gives the preacher an edge. Arranging a sermon inductively creates suspense and produces a sense of discovery.

> **Figure 11.1**
>
> **Types of Reasoning**
>
> Deductive
> Whole → Parts
> ● → •••••
>
> Inductive
> Parts → Whole
> ••••• → ●

Years ago, my teenage daughter, Erin, and I watched an episode of Dick Van Dyke's hit television series *Diagnosis Murder*. In the first five minutes, a priest intentionally drove his car onto a sidewalk to hit a man who was standing on a street corner. The man lived, but the priest murdered the victim by sneaking into the victim's hospital room and tampering with his IV. My daughter complained, "Oh, I don't like it when they show us at the beginning who committed the murder." She explained to me that *Diagnosis Murder* usually did not reveal the identity of the murderer until the final segment. She preferred it that way because it creates more suspense. In other words, she preferred an inductive arrangement. In this episode, the producers used a deductive arrangement to tell the story. They relied on other means of creating suspense. The story raised questions designed to hold the viewer's interest. Why did a priest commit a murder? How could Dr. Mark Sloan, the leading character played by Dick Van Dyke, prove that the good guy—a man of the cloth—was actually the bad guy? Still, my daughter expressed her preference for an inductive shape.

Since stories operate inductively, most sermons that preach Bible stories should operate inductively as well. A preacher should maintain the story's sense of "strategic delay." In other words, the big idea is not front-loaded but saved for the end. Early in my preaching of Old Testament narratives, I always told the congregation up front what I planned to tell them. I was so concerned they might miss my big idea that I distrusted the story form and gave away my big idea at the beginning of the sermon. I would say something like, "This morning, we're going to see in 1 Samuel 5–7 that *God is not just a power source you can exploit, but a powerful person you must worship.*" In essence, I was saying, "Before I tell you the story this morning, let me skip to the last chapter and read you the ending." However, beginning with the ending leads to a less satisfying, less exciting journey.

Paul Harvey was a master of strategic delay. For years, he charmed his radio audience with his "rest of the story" anecdotes. Author Paul Aurandt compiled these stories in three paperback volumes.[3] These stories model how a storyteller maintains tension and saves key details for the end.

For example, read the following account written by Paul Aurandt, describing how he came to work for Paul Harvey:

> I've always been a fan of Paul Harvey. The quality of his voice and the timing of his words never failed to mesmerize me, even as a young boy who understood little of the News. I listened to him every day, at the encouragement of my parents. And I suppose you might say that the Paul Harvey timing even influenced my music later. The dramatic pauses, the careful, warm pacing.
>
> Anyway, I had known for quite some while that Paul Harvey, my childhood hero, was looking for a writer. On an impulse day . . . when I was practicing for an upcoming concert . . . I sat down and wrote a REST OF THE STORY just as I imagined Paul Harvey would have written it. The topic was a musical one . . . something I'd researched once.
>
> When I was finished, I showed the story to my mother . . . another Paul Harvey devotee. And she was impressed! "It sounds just like him!" she told me.
>
> To make a long story short, I applied for and got the job. I've had to set aside a lot of concerts, but I'm really having fun. So far, at least.
>
> Oh, there's something you might be interested in learning about Mr. Harvey. When you work for someone, you learn things about him no one else knows.
>
> Paul Harvey is not his complete name.
>
> Now, don't tell anybody you heard it from me, but Harvey is his middle name. He dropped his last name because it was difficult to spell and to pronounce.
>
> I kept it.
>
> I'm his son.
>
> And now you know the rest . . . of THE REST OF THE STORY.[4]

Imagine the lack of impact the same information would have if Paul Aurandt had simply written a preface saying, "It's a privilege to serve as editor and writer for my father, Paul Harvey. Just so you know, Paul

---

3. Aurandt, *Paul Harvey's The Rest of the Story*; Aurandt, *More of Paul Harvey's The Rest of the Story*; Aurandt, *Destiny*.

4. Aurandt, *Paul Harvey's The Rest of the Story*, 179–80.

Harvey is not his complete name. It is his first name and middle name. His last name, like mine, is Aurandt. He simply dropped it because it doesn't work as well on the radio." The information is interesting, but the telling is bland. It lacks build-up and intrigue.

Strategic delay is not difficult to build into your sermon because the narrators often practice it. For example, in Judges 17–18, the narrator informs us early on, in 17:5, that Micah had "a house of God."[5] However, the narrator withholds a key clarifying detail until the end of the story: "all the time *the house of God* was in Shiloh" (18:31).[6] Wise preachers will simply reserve comment on this detail until they reach the end of the narrative.

Sometimes, it may be effective to wait until the end of a narrative to emphasize key details that appeared earlier in the story. It's not that you skip these details. You simply refrain from highlighting them until you reach the story's end. For example, in a sermon on 2 Samuel 11–12, you might delay your comments on Uriah's noble words in 11:11 until later in the narrative when you can contrast them with David's actions. By doing so, you show your listeners that Uriah is the hero of the story, while David is its villain. Ironically, Uriah ends up losing his life because he had the integrity to do what David did not—refrain from making love to Bathsheba.

Although following the contours of the storyline means placing the big idea at the end, it also means riding the tension created by the crisis or complication of the story. As a storyteller, tension is your best friend. Lucas O'Neill reminds us that tension is "the suspense that is generated when someone discovers there is something of interest that will soon be revealed." It is a sense of "expectation and anticipation." This does not mean that listeners feel tense. "Tension is simply the desire for resolution."[7] Keeping your listeners in suspense keeps them listening.[8] So plan to play

---

5. The Hebrew expression, בֵּית אֱלֹהִים, is translated as "shrine" by the major English translations. However, the more precise translation is either "house of God" or "house of gods." The ambiguity is tantalizing and prepares us for the end of the narrative.

6. The italics are mine. Note the contrast between "a house of God" in 17:5 and "the house of God" (בֵּית־הָאֱלֹהִים) in 18:31.

7. O'Neill, *Preaching to Be Heard*, 18.

8. Eugene L. Lowry has proposed five sequential stages for a sermon that develops like a story unfolds: (1) upsetting the equilibrium, (2) analyzing the discrepancy, (3) disclosing the clue to resolution, (4) experiencing the gospel, and (5) anticipating the consequences (*Homiletical Plot*, 25). In his most recent work, Lowry slightly modifies his earlier sermon plot, opting for four stages rather than five: (1) conflict, (2) complication, (3) sudden shift, and (4) unfolding. He notes that the gospel component of his previous plot diagram can fit after the sudden shift,

up the tension rather than downplay it. For example, in Genesis 22:2 the tension builds when God commands Abraham to offer Isaac as a sacrifice. A wise expositor will point out how Abraham's apprehension must have increased with each level of specificity: your son . . . your only son . . . the one you love . . . Isaac. Perhaps the preacher will take the time to draw an analogy of how God today puts us in situations that leave us apprehensive, afraid, or even angry. Instead of rushing to the resolution, the preacher will allow the hearers to experience the tension in the text.

Paul Borden perfectly describes how an inductive sermon from an Old Testament story should flow to create tension and then to release it. The starting point is developing the crisis or spiritual disease of the story: "Your job as a preacher is to develop for your congregation how people relate, interact, and struggle with the same spiritual disease. You pick those aspects of the story that enable you to illustrate this disease. Rather than thinking of which verses do this, demonstrate how the plot, character development, scenes, actions, design, tone, and so on develop the disease. You use these elements to state, elaborate, and build the first half to two-thirds of your sermon."[9] According to Borden, the final one-third to one-half of the sermon will develop the remedy:

> You demonstrate how God's people successfully or unsuccessfully embraced the divine remedy for their spiritual sickness. This idea is applied to your congregation. In this way, your preaching idea becomes the reversal (the remedy) to the disequilibrium you have created (the spiritual sickness).
>
> Last, you use the closing minutes to demonstrate the implications of accepting or rejecting this remedy. You show how acceptance brings spiritual health, while rejection brings further illness. You appeal to people to choose health (life) over disease (death).[10]

Borden then explains the payoff for using this kind of an inductive flow to preach an Old Testament narrative:

> Preaching this way enables you and your people to feel the story as drama. The sermon, which has its own plot, uses the pieces of the story that reflect

---

or sometimes it is the sudden shift. Sometimes the good news even takes place before the sudden shift (*Sermon*, 81–89).

9. Paul Borden, "Is There Really One Big Idea," 78.
10. Borden, "Is There Really One Big Idea," 79.

the disequilibrium, reversal, and resolution they felt when they first read or heard the story. However, you have used the story as story, and the idea of the story has caused the congregation to wrestle with the disequilibrium of humanness, to understand and feel the reversal of divine truth, and choose the resolutions that provide life. Both the sermon and the text (a narrative) have been treated as story.[11]

The Flashback Approach

A variation of the inductive approach would be to use a flashback. In other words, start at the conclusion and show how the character arrived there. This technique works particularly well with tragic stories. For example, you might begin a sermon on 2 Samuel 18:1–19:8 with King David's lament over the death of his son Absalom in 18:33. Similarly, you might begin the story of Samson in Judges 13–16 with the final scene—the implosion of the Philistine temple that took blind Samson's life.

The flashback technique can also work in a narrative with a comic structure. The expositor could begin the story of Esther with Esther on the throne and ask, How did a Jewish girl whose nation was in jeopardy of a holocaust end up on the Persian throne? Or the expositor might start the story of Ruth with the ending: How did a Moabite widow end up being part of the line from which King David would come?

The Inductive-Deductive Approach

Occasionally, if the big idea requires an extra dose of explanation or validation, a preacher may choose an inductive-deductive arrangement. Suppose a preacher decides to preach the following big idea from the book of Esther: *Even when you can't see or hear God, he is still in control of your destiny.* Ordinarily, the preacher will work through the story inductively, and this big idea will emerge at the end. However, a preacher may determine that the hearers will not readily buy into this idea. Maybe several teens from their church died in a bus accident. Or perhaps listeners live in a community where God has never done anything dramatic. No revival has taken place there. No Christian leaders or missionaries have arisen

---

11. Borden, "Is There Really One Big Idea," 79.

from the congregation. The preacher may sense the need to tell the story, let the idea emerge about halfway through the sermon, and then go back to point out more specifically from the story that circumstances don't stop God from staying involved. God is still in control despite the insensitivity of people around you. He's still attentive even though you face impossible people in prominent places. What's more, he still guides your destiny when unpredictable events take place. And finally, God remains in control in spite of circumstances that no human being can change.

This arrangement is inductive-deductive because the first part of the sermon tells us the story inductively, while the second part spends time developing the idea. In this case, the development takes the form of validation.

The Semi-inductive Approach

Sometimes sermons from Old Testament narratives can take a semi-inductive form. This happens when the big idea has a multiple complement. The sermon is semi-inductive because the big idea emerges in sections. The expositor raises the subject in the introduction. Then the complement emerges as a series of ideas. For example, I have heard Paul Borden preach a sermon on 1 Samuel 17 in which his big idea is, *David succeeded under pressure because his perspective was different, because he learned the habit of trusting God, and because he let God do the fighting.* The subject of this sermon—*Why David succeeded under pressure*—is introduced at the beginning of the sermon. The three parts of the complement emerge throughout the sermon at the appropriate places in the storyline.

As noted earlier, though, preachers must be careful not to find lists in Old Testament narratives where they really do not exist.

First-Person Narratives

Another decision the preacher must make relates to point of view. Usually, preachers will adopt the third-person point of view and tell the story from the perspective of the biblical narrator. This approach gets its name from the third-person pronouns that dominate the narration: *she* wept, *he* went up, *she* ran, *he* said.

Another option is to tell the story as a major or minor character in the story, similar to Dr. Watson relating a Sherlock Holmes story. This is called a first-person narrative because telling the story as a participant requires using the first-person pronoun: *I came to the throne, I saw, I kept quiet.* Some refer to this kind of sermon as a "dramatic monologue."

In most cases, the sermon will develop along the lines of the story as in a traditional third-person narrative. The form allows the preacher to relive the story in greater depth, seeing what the character sees and hearing what the character hears.

It is fair to ask, though, if this is a wise approach. Does a first-person narrative communicate a Bible-shaped word in a Bible-shaped way? Or is it simply a gimmick? To answer this question, consider the prophet Jeremiah. In Jeremiah 13:1–11, God told Jeremiah to buy a linen belt, put it around his waist, then bury it in some rocks, and eventually dig it up and observe its worthlessness. The ruined belt served as a picture of Judah—bound to God like a belt around one's waist but useless. Furthermore, why did God command Jeremiah to use a communication gimmick to communicate to the priests and people of Judah? In Jeremiah 27–28, God commanded Jeremiah to make a yoke out of straps and crossbars and to put it on his neck. He wore this yoke when he gave a message to King Zedekiah and when he spoke to the people and the priests. Eventually, the prophet Hananiah broke this yoke as he and Jeremiah explained that God would break the yoke of the king of Babylon. Warren Wiersbe comments, "The episodes involving the linen belt (chap. 13), the potter (chaps. 18–19), the yokes (chaps. 27–28), and the burial of the stones in Egypt (chap. 43) were in a sense 'action sermons' for the communicating of abstract truth."[12]

Likewise, Ezekiel used drama to communicate God's Word. Wiersbe observes, "As a sign, he [Ezekiel] was bound with ropes (3:24–27); he 'played war' (4:1–17); he played barber (5:1–17); he clapped his hands and stamped his feet (6:11; see 21:14); he acted like he was going on a trip (12:1–16); he trembled as he ate (12:17–20) and groaned like a man in grief (21:6, 12); he played road-builder (21:18–23); he was not allowed to mourn his dead wife (24:15–27); and he made two sticks into one (37:15–17)."[13]

To be sure, drama can be done poorly, or it can be overdone. Yet the way in which the prophets communicated God's truth seems to give biblical and theological credence to a creative form such as a first-person narrative. The Bible does not stifle the limits of a preacher's creativity as long as the

12. Wiersbe, *Preaching and Teaching with Imagination*, 145.
13. Wiersbe, *Preaching and Teaching with Imagination*, 147.

form complements the content. While this form should not be overdone, mixing in a first-person narrative once or twice a year can add some zing to a preacher's homiletical stew.[14] In fact, I encourage preachers who plan to preach a third-person message to practice it as a first-person narrative sermon. This helps them enter the story and prepares them to tell it more creatively—even when they revert to a third-person approach.

Finding a Place for Application

Another issue preachers face when shaping a sermon relates to application. Where should they include application? Basically, preachers have two choices. Save application for the end when the big idea fully emerges, or weave application throughout the sermon. The decision depends on when ideas come into focus.

The point at which the crisis emerges or picks up steam is a logical place for an application image. If preachers want listeners to understand how their situation resembles Jael's (Judg. 4) or Ruth's predicament, they might stop to sketch what this predicament or disease looks like in the life of a twenty-first-century listener. At this point in the sermon, the application does not consist of a principle to practice. Rather, it's a picture of what the problem looks like in the life of the present-day listener. It's an attempt to get hearers to see themselves in the story. Later, when the resolution surfaces, it's time to picture how the reader will put the remedy into effect for the disease developed in the story.

Obviously, this stage in the process forces you to wrestle with thought. But thinking yourself clear at this stage will equip you to do well at the next stage. Once you have in mind the way you will develop your purpose, you are ready to plot out in detail your plan for preaching the story. You are ready to prepare an outline.

---

14. Arthurs, "Performing the Story," 30.

12

Outlining the Sermon

Twenty students and two professors stared at the handwriting on the wall. One by one, students in a seminary preaching class were projecting their first attempts at a sermon outline from an assigned passage. I nervously sat waiting for my turn. My friend Rod was up first. Rod looked at the transparency he placed on the overhead and read aloud his main points for a potential sermon on 1 Samuel 17, the David and Goliath story:

    I. Goliath Challenges God's People
   II. Saul Cowers with God's People
  III. David Conquers for God's People

After a silent pause, Haddon Robinson, the lead professor, growled, "That sounds like it came out of a book called *Simple Sermons for Sunday Evening*." The class erupted with laughter. Nervous laughter. Sympathetic laughter. "Nobody talks like this anymore, except in the pulpit," he continued. Duane Litfin, guest professor, chimed in, "What Haddon is saying is that he's afraid you might go out and actually preach that sermon!" More laughter.

    The outline stage in sermon preparation is, for some, the most intimidating step in the process. Bryan Chapell relates, "In the classroom and in seminars around the country, I find that preachers have more questions about structure than they do about any other aspect of preaching."[1] Most preachers can relate to feature writer Jon Franklin's frustration about putting stories in the standard outline form. Franklin, a two-time Pulitzer Prize winner, laments, "As near as I can figure it, such outline systems were specifically designed to convince budding writers that outlining is impossible, and that the only way they can create worthwhile copy is to hack their way through the words like a hunter slashing a path through a seven-canopy jungle. The Roman numeral type of outline will . . . be recognized for what it is, the English Teacher's Revenge, or ETR for short."[2]

Tips for Effective Outlines

Let me share some tips that will help you relax and relate to an outline as a friend rather than a foe (see table 12.1). First, don't try to create outlines that people will remember. It took me years of preaching to figure this out.

Table 12.1

Tips for Effective Outlines

1. Don't try to create outlines that people will remember.
2. View main points as endings, not beginnings.
3. State your outline points in full sentences.
4. Think in terms of moves rather than points.
5. Aim for 2–4 main points.
6. Include your big idea in the outline.

The first tip may not be hard for a younger generation of preachers. However, a lot of contemporary preaching still thrives on creating memorable outlines. Early in my preaching, I believed listeners needed to take my outline points home with them—either in their heads or, better yet, on paper. Without a captioned survey of either the passage or its ideas, how would people get the text into their lives? For years, I heard preachers like Warren Wiersbe say, "An outline is not a sermon." But I didn't get it. Eventually, I learned that an outline resembles a map. It gives preachers

1. Chapell, *Christ-Centered Preaching*, 157.
2. Franklin, *Writing for Story*, 110.

directions. It offers a plan. The preacher has to have it in mind but the congregation does not. Donald McDougall reflects on one of the greatest compliments he received after a sermon. The listener said, "I came to realize that you didn't have an outline; it just flowed." McDougall recalls, "Actually I did have an outline I was following, but it was inconspicuous; that is how it should be."[3]

When people relate to me on a personal level, is my skeleton important? Absolutely. Without it, I could not sit, stand, walk, or embrace. But do the people to whom I relate need to see my skeleton? Absolutely not. In fact, it's better when they don't see my bones protruding through the skin. An outline works the same way. It must be there for the sermon to have structure, but the outline does not need to be "Exhibit A." I want people to leave with ideas formed in their minds. Ideas gel in people's minds through images and pictures, not outlines. I want people to go home with God's truth in mind, and particularly with a picture of what that truth looks like when lived out in their lives. While I need my outline to help me communicate the ideas and pictures, the audience doesn't need to see my outline any more than they need to see the two-by-four studs supporting the sheetrock wall in my living room. The contractor who framed my house occasionally reminded me and some of the volunteer help (well, mainly me!), "We're not building a piano." In other words, we want a sturdy frame, but it doesn't have to be a polished work of art. It will not be visible when we're all done. When I preach, I may or may not say the statement exactly as I have it worded in my first point. The key is, by the time I'm done with the first main point, the idea it expresses will have formed in the hearer's mind, or I will have related the section of the story it describes.

Related to this is a second tip: View main points as endings, not beginnings. I used to struggle constantly with outlining story sermons. The reason, I eventually discovered, is that while stories work inductively, outlines work deductively. Jon Franklin explains the difference between an outline of a story or drama and the typical "English Teacher's Revenge" (ETR) outline:

> The statements in the ETR outlines represent topic sentences and therefore specify what comes at the *beginning* of the section they are supposed to

---

3. McDougall, "Central Ideas, Outlines, and Titles," 234.

represent. The first sentence in the outline expresses the thought that opens the piece. That's because in "logical" writing the writer states his premise first, then develops it.

In storytelling, on the other hand, the dramatic action that makes your point comes at the *end* of each section, where climaxes belong. That means your statements represent endings, not beginnings.[4]

Typically, a preacher will move out of an introduction and state the first main point. After stating the main point, the preacher will move to subpoint A, then to subpoint B, and so on. However, in the outline of a story sermon, the preacher will often move out of the introduction into subpoint A, then to subpoint B, and then through further subpoints. Only at the end of the subpoints does the idea in the first main point emerge. When you prepare your outline, you should indicate which main points will be developed inductively. Simply put "develop inductively"—italicized in parentheses—after the statement of the main point.

A third tip is to state your outline points in full sentences. Haddon Robinson explains the rationale for this practice: "Keep in mind that each point in the outline represents an idea, and thus should be a grammatically complete sentence. When only words and phrases stand as points, they deceive us because they are incomplete and vague. Partial statements allow thought to slip through our minds like a greased football."[5] Writing an outline is a way of thinking. You will short-circuit the thinking process if you do not write out your points in complete sentences.

Fourth, think in terms of "moves" instead of points. A movement is a section of your sermon in which a particular element of the narrative—a certain scene, a conversation, or a theological idea—forms in the minds of your listeners. As David Buttrick once said, "homiletic thinking is always *a thinking of theology toward images.*"[6] So, when you prepare your outline, think in terms of plotting out the movements in the preaching of the story: First, I need to tell them this. Second, I need to tell them this. Next, I plan to tell them this.

Fifth, aim for two to four main points. Your points reflect the major movements in your sermon, and you can only do so much in thirty minutes

---

4. Franklin, *Writing for Story*, 117–18.
5. Robinson, *Biblical Preaching*, 94.
6. Buttrick, *Homiletic*, 29 (emphasis original).

or so. A lot of Old Testament narrative sermons I preach have two points. As you might suppose, these two points reflect the crisis and the resolution. You can have more main points, of course, but I suggest never exceeding four. If you have more than four main points, chances are that the structure of your sermon is too complex. The way to reduce the number of points is not to get rid of any but simply to combine them.

Finally, include your big idea in the outline. I prefer to state it as one of the main points, though some preachers and teachers of preachers prefer to put it in the introduction (if the sermon is deductive) or in the conclusion (if the sermon is inductive). However, since the big idea is a prominent part of the sermon, I prefer to make it prominent in my outline. In most narratives, the big idea emerges at the end. So my final main point will typically be my big idea—whether the main point covers the final section of the text or whether I devote a final main point to the big idea after I have worked through the text. I do not lose any sleep over which way to go. Make your outline as simple as possible.

Preparing Your Sermon Outline

To build your sermon outline, go back to your exegetical outline and review the flow of the story. Perhaps you will simply reword the points of your exegetical outline to turn it into a sermon outline. However, while you will generally follow the same set of tracks as the storyteller, you might decide to rearrange some of the details for rhetorical effect. Or, you might decide to group some of the main points together, depending on where you want the emphasis to lie. Let's take a look at how to create an outline for a sermon on Judges 17–18. Here is the exegetical outline developed earlier:

I. Micah builds an idol and appoints a priest for his "house of God" (17:1–13)

II. The Danites decide to seize the distant city of Laish instead of taking over the inheritance assigned to them (18:1–10)

III. The Danites take Micah's idol and priest on their way to capturing Laish, leaving Micah with nothing (18:11–26)

IV. The Danites capture Laish and establish the city of Dan, worshiping Micah's idol until the land ends up in captivity (18:27–31)

I could build my sermon outline on this exegetical outline and then create a fifth point that contains the big idea. However, this exceeds the "four-point limit" I am trying to follow. I decided to go with a two-point outline for the sake of simplicity and clarity.[7] Remember, my goal is not for my listeners to see or remember my outline. It is simply a guide to know what ideas I need to convey clearly and emphatically.

> I. Micah and the Danites turn from God to idols (17:1–18:17) [*develop inductively*]
>   A. Micah makes an idol and builds an unauthorized religious system (17:1–13)
>   B. The Danites seize the distant city of Laish instead of taking over the inheritance assigned to them (18:1–10)
>   C. The Danites take Micah's idol and priest on their way to capturing Laish (18:11–17)
> II. As a result, Micah and the Danites did not experience the presence of God (18:18–31) [*develop inductively*]
>   A. Micah ended up with nothing after the Danites took his idols and priests (18:18–26)
>   B. The Danites eventually ended up in captivity after conquering Laish (18:27–30)
>   C. Ironically, the presence of God was available at "the house of God" in Shiloh all the time Micah's idol was in use (18:31)
>   D. (Big Idea) *When we turn from God to idols, we miss out on the presence of God*

Notice that the main points zero in on the crisis and resolution of the story. Then, the subpoints reflect the main scenes in the story. Both the main points and first level of subpoints convey the key ideas that my listeners need to grasp as I retell the story. Again, I will not state these verbatim. I will not say, "My first point is that Micah and the Danites turn from God to idols." Rather, the first point expresses the idea I want to communicate as I retell this section of the narrative.

---

7. For a full sermon outline of Judg. 17–18, including the introduction and conclusion as well as a further level of subpoints, see appendix A.

Frankly, outlining can be maddening. For example, should I have devoted a third main point to my big idea rather than including it as the final subpoint under main point II? I could have done so, but I decided not to because I did not need to devote a significant amount of time in the sermon to developing it. This will be clear from the sermon manuscript on Judges 17–18 that appears in appendix A. I have learned not to obsess over decisions like this. Instead, I aim for simplicity and clarity. My outline needs to provide good directions—simple enough to follow, yet detailed enough to capture the substance of the sermon.

There is another issue to consider when creating a sermon outline, and that is whether to state the main points as theological ideas rather than a summary of the main events in the story. In my above example, my main points simply describe the main events in the story. Below is an example of the main points stated as theological ideas that relate to God's people today.

I. We are prone to turn from God to idols (17:1–18:17)
II. (*Big Idea*) *When we turn from God to idols, we miss out on the presence of God*

In this scenario, I would still develop both main points inductively. I would do so by working through the various scenes in the narrative as reflected by the subpoints.

The danger of this approach is that it can convey theological messages that a narrative does not necessarily communicate. Or at least it confuses application with theology. In my example, I am quite confident that point II captures the main theological message of the narrative. That is why I have identified it as the narrative's big idea. Point I, however, is more of an application statement. It is basically saying that what happened to Micah and the Danites still happens to us today. Like Micah and the Danites, we are prone to wander and fall into idolatry.

Here is another example from Exodus 15:22–17:7. This sermon outline reflects an inductive-deductive approach. The big idea emerges halfway through the sermon. This is clear because there is no notation to develop point II inductively, as there is for point I. Once the big idea is presented, the remainder of the sermon attempts to validate it by answering the second functional question, Is it really true?

I. God's people easily slip from praise into complaining when they face trials and inconveniences [*develop inductively*]
   A. Israel complains over a lack of water (15:22–27; 17:1–7)
   B. Israel complains over a lack of food (16:1–36)
   C. You, too, may find yourself complaining shortly after God comes through for you
II. *(Big idea) Complaining is the worst way for God's people to respond when they face trials and inconveniences*
   A. When you complain, you call God's integrity into question (15:24; 16:3, 7–8; 17:7)
   B. When you complain, you create a climate for disobedience (16:20–28)
   C. When you complain, you fail a test God wants you to pass (15:25b–26; 16:4; 17:2)

This sermon tackles three complaining stories all at once. Notice that the two major moves or points state timeless theological principles extracted from the stories. The first move in the sermon advances the idea that God's people easily slip from praise into a complaining mode when they face trials and inconveniences. Subpoints A and B recap the stories of Israel's fall from praise into a complaining mode. Subpoint C then moves into the twenty-first century and makes it clear that people today act the same way. Once again, the first main point serves as an ending, not a beginning. The idea stated in Roman numeral I fully emerges only after the sermon moves from the ancient Israelites to twenty-first-century believers.

At this place in the sermon, I will go ahead and disclose the big idea as it appears in Roman numeral II. This is a different tactic. Rather than serving as an ending, my second main point serves as a beginning. I will start with it because I want to raise the second functional question, Is it really true? Can I really believe it? As the outline shows, the remainder of the sermon is validation. It involves going back through the story and noting details or statements that verify and support the idea. Notice, too, that I have stated the subpoints as timeless principles. However, it would not be wrong to leave them in the past. For example, subpoint A could read, "When the Israelites complained, they called God's integrity into question." Preachers have to make this decision at every point in the sermon. At what moment do you abstract from then to now? Whenever possible, I try to turn statements into theological ideas if that's where I plan to arrive anyway. However, as noted above, I am cautious about trying to turn every scene in a narrative into the theological idea.

While an outline is not a sermon, the outline you create allows you to see on paper the shape your sermon will take. It allows you to track the sermon's basic movements in thought and to evaluate how well your sermon will flow like a story. If you like the flow of thought, you can use your outline as the framework on which to build your actual sermon.

13

Mastering the Storyteller's Craft

The same story can either bore or thrill an audience. What makes the difference is the storyteller. Preachers who hope to communicate stories with flair must master the storyteller's craft. The time has come to fill in the sermon outline. As Haddon Robinson puts it, it's time to make dry bones live.

As a preacher, your task is to preach a sermon, not an outline. An outline is not a sermon; it resembles a skeleton without flesh. How do you go about putting flesh on the skeleton? More important, how do you go about putting flesh on the skeleton to make the final product attractive rather than bland?

Preparing a Sermon Manuscript

The most reliable tool for filling in your sermon outline is a manuscript. Write out your sermon word for word. You don't need to memorize it. Preferably, you will not even take the manuscript with you to the pulpit. Haddon Robinson explains:

> Agonize with thought and words at your desk, and what you write will be internalized. . . . When you step into the pulpit, your written text [sermon manuscript] will have done its work to shape your use of language. Much of the wording will come back to you as you preach, but not all. In the

heat of your delivery, your sentence structure will change, new phrases will occur to you, and your speech will sparkle like spontaneous conversation. Your manuscript, therefore, contributes to the thought and wording of your sermon, but it does not determine it.[1]

The purpose of the sermon manuscript is to assist you in your thinking. Writing is a way of thinking. You are trying to capture on paper what will come out of your mouth when you preach the Old Testament narrative you have prepared. The trick is to write in an oral style. That is, what you produce should resemble a transcript of your sermon as the audience hears it. Try to write as if you are speaking. This means the sentence fragments that angered your English teacher are okay. Contractions aren't a problem.

With outline in hand, you're ready to write your oral transcript. But what goes into the mix? How do you flesh out your sermon outline?

Telling the Story Well

Preachers usually flesh out their sermon outlines by adding a variety of supporting materials that attempt to explain, prove, or apply their ideas. Some typical devices a preacher may use include restatement, explanation, definition, statistics, quotations, storytelling, and illustrations.

In a sermon on an Old Testament narrative, the preacher's primary tactic will be telling the story well. To be more precise, the preacher's primary tactic will be *retelling* the story well. The authors of Old Testament stories tell them in a rather spare, lean style. You won't find any throwaway lines. Every detail serves a purpose. Meir Sternberg points out that elaborate descriptions "perform no other role than realistic fullness."[2] In Old Testament narrative, other concerns overshadow the need for realistic fullness. However, a modern preacher may need to pursue realistic fullness to connect with a modern audience. Preachers need to engage listeners with sensory details. Jeffrey Arthurs offers wise counsel: "Keep the plot moving forward steadily. Don't let it stall with unnecessary digressions for lengthy explanation or illustration. On the other hand, suspending the plot with *purposeful* support material can enhance the tension of the message."[3]

---

1. Robinson, *Biblical Preaching*, 186.
2. Sternberg, *Poetics of Biblical Narrative*, 329.
3. Arthurs, *Preaching with Variety*, 91 (emphasis original).

The trick is to strike a balance between economy and detail. The preacher's retelling of the story must bring the story to life. This means placing sensory details at strategic places in the narrative. It also means avoiding excess. The temptation is to add too many details and descriptions—to pursue elegance rather than simplicity. Ernest Hemingway models the balance between economy and detail in his classic novel *A Farewell to Arms*. At the end of chapter 9, Hemingway describes the ambulance ride of Frederic Henry, a wounded American soldier who is en route to a field hospital during World War I. Another wounded soldier lies on a stretcher above him.

> I felt something dripping. At first it dripped slowly and regularly, then it pattered into a stream. . . . The stream kept on. In the dark I could not see where it came from the canvas overhead. I tried to move sideways so that it did not fall on me. Where it had run down under my shirt it was warm and sticky. I was cold and my leg hurt so that it made me sick. After a while the stream from the stretcher above lessened and started to drip again and I heard and felt the canvas above move as the man on the stretcher settled more comfortably.
> "How is he?" the Englishman called back. "We're almost up." "He's dead I think," I said.
> The drops fell very slowly as they fall from an icicle after the sun has gone. It was cold in the car in the night as the road climbed.[4]

A statement Hemingway once made about prose also applies to retelling Bible stories: "Prose is architecture, not interior decoration."[5] While modern readers are used to fuller descriptions than Bible stories contain, they do not demand as many details as one might expect. Writer Oakley Hall observes that modern fiction can omit more details than the fiction of a century ago: "More economy is necessary because the reader's threshold of irrelevancy is lower. Part of the irrelevant is what is obvious, or what the reader can supply out of his own imagination, experience, or past reading."[6]

Reading well-crafted stories can enhance a preacher's storytelling skills. In addition to reading classics by Ernest Hemingway or Charlotte Brontë,

---

4. Hemingway, *Farewell to Arms*, 61.
5. Hemingway, *Death in the Afternoon*, 153.
6. Hall, *Art and Craft of Novel Writing*, 117.

preachers would do well to read the best contemporary storytellers. Notice how they use words and craft phrases. I still dip into Garrison Keillor's *Lake Wobegon Days* occasionally—for his storytelling as well as his humor and insight into how people think and act.

Read Creative Descriptions of Old Testament Stories, Characters, and Culture

A good place for preachers to start is to read creative descriptions of Old Testament characters, stories, and culture. Preachers can learn from these and even adapt them as they craft images that bring the stories of the Old Testament to life. Eugene Peterson models the kind of storytelling that preachers should pursue when he describes David's meeting with Saul in the wilderness cave near En-Gedi:

> David and a few of his men are hidden in a cave cut in the cliffs above the Dead Sea. The day is hot and the cave is cool. They're deep in the cave, resting. Suddenly there's a shadow across the mouth of the cave; they're astonished to see that it's King Saul. They didn't know that he was that close in his pursuit. Saul enters the cave but doesn't see them: fresh from the hard glare of desert sun, his eyes aren't adjusted to the darkness and don't pick out the shadowy figures in the recesses of the cave. Besides, he isn't looking for them at that moment; he has entered the cave to respond to the call of nature. He turns his back to them.[7]

Paul Maier's documentary novels *Pontius Pilate* and *The Flames of Rome* provide a good starting point. Even though these novels relate New Testament events, they model the kind of storytelling that sticks to the facts while painting a vivid picture. In the preface to *Pontius Pilate*, Maier assures his readers that unlike a work of historical fiction, his documentary novel takes no liberties with the facts.[8] He uses them as discovered, without alteration. He simply fills in the gaps. While preachers should use their imaginations when retelling stories, they should also allow the rigorous exegesis they have done to keep their imaginations in check.

James Michener's tome, *The Source*, sweeps back and forth between the fictional account of an archaeological excavation in western Galilee and

---

7. Peterson, *Leap over a Wall*, 76.
8. Maier, *Pontius Pilate*, 7.

the ancient stories behind the artifacts it uncovers. The first third of the book, covering archaeological levels XV–XI, supplies vivid images from Jewish history through 605 BC, particularly the daily routines of family life, farming, and Canaanite religious practice.[9] Michener's depiction of a Canaanite child sacrifice ritual is particularly stunning.[10] Notice how Michener describes the scene when an Israelite farmer, Urbaal, and his wife, Timna, receive the news that their six-month-old son has been chosen to be sacrificed:

> When Urbaal reached home he received the ugly news that Timna had feared. The priests of Melak had returned to deliver their decision: "The stars indicate that we shall be attacked from the north. By a host larger than before. It is therefore essential to take steps and we shall have a burning of first sons tomorrow." With a red dye obtained from the seashore they stained the wrists of Urbaal's son and then directed the farmer to halt the screaming of his wife. Proving by their implacable detachment that there could be no appeal from their decision, they stalked from the house and proceeded to seven others, where they similarly stained the wrists of children from the leading families of Makor.[11]

Over the years, several writers have told Old Testament stories with flair. Expositors who preach from Judges or the David stories may find a couple books by John Hercus to be useful. The titles are *God Is God: Samson and Other Case Histories from the Book of Judges* and *David*. Hercus's style is almost sermonic. His descriptions of characters and scenes bring them to life, although his use of colloquial language and homespun expressions may seem a bit dated and overdone to some preachers. The following sample is from the story of Ehud:

> The Moabite servants bowed and silently slipped out of the room. Only Eglon, huge mountainous Eglon still reclining back in his padded chair, and Ehud, left-handed Ehud kneeling on his left knee with that so-businesslike little dagger still strapped to his right thigh, remaining.
>
> And the distance is still not quite right. It will take both a lunge and a step to reach Eglon with the sword. About two seconds too much time is needed, it's just not right, even now!

---

9. Michener, *Source*, 11–373.
10. Michener, *Source*, 132–42.
11. Michener, *Source*, 134.

And Ehud hasn't moved. Not a fraction of an inch. His voice is still a hoarse whisper, as with downcast eyes he speaks. "Yes sir, it's from God. I had to come and tell you."

"Speak up, man! I can't properly hear you. Tell me, what is it the gods want me to know?"

Was it greed? Was it conceit? Was it something more than greed, something greater than conceit? Was it perhaps fear, the fear man always has when finally confronted by his God? Was it this that swept this caution aside? Perhaps that is the real answer, perhaps that properly explains why his two hands gripped the arms of his chair so strongly, why there was that sudden heave as he raised his whole lumbering bulk on to feet that could just barely carry him—and there he was, half-standing, just above Ehud, just that half-pace closer that Ehud needed.

A sudden flash, a slight hiss of breath as the Benjamite springs, a single muffled gasp from the stricken king, and it's over. Eglon is dead. Collapsed in a ghastly mountain of fat-enveloped flesh. . . . The dagger has disappeared completely into the great belly of the Moabite king, the flesh has closed over the blade and haft alike. Eglon now has it! Only the small trickle of blood and the large stream of bowel contents give out the secret at all. That and the stench that now no nostril could mistake. Eglon is dead.[12]

A more recent attempt to retell the stories of Scripture appears in *The Book of God* by Walter Wangerin Jr. Wangerin succeeds at capturing the passion, color, and grit of the Bible's stories as he narrates them. His volume follows the storyline of the Bible, and he dramatizes most of the major Old Testament narratives in the process. For example, here is Wangerin's depiction of the fall of Jericho in Joshua 6:

On this day, Israel circled Jericho not once, but seven times, from dawn to late afternoon. Suddenly, in the midst of their seventh passage, the sound of the ram's horns changed. It rose to the shrieks of eagles. And all the voices, all the throats of Israel opened. Ten thousand warriors turned inward, roaring, and charged the city. The city walls themselves began to shudder. The king felt a terrible agitation in the stones beneath his feet. His archers leaped up. Spearmen reached for spears. Women brought smudgepots to ignite the oil in sheets of fire. But just as Israel entered the range of Jericho's arrows, the city walls rose three feet into the air, bellowed like a living thing,

---

12. Hercus, *God Is God*, 39–40.

cracked at every join and mortar, then collapsed—a great crush of stones on all the people below.

The king of Jericho tumbled down into his dying city. The burning oil spilled inward. Fire and timber and rock fell with him. And the final vision vouchsafed unto the king was a piece of wall which neither crumbled nor burned, a slim finger of stone with one window two stories up from which hung a scarlet cord.

In his last instant of life all the world seemed to the king a bitter joke—for why should that one live at last and not another? The window belonged to an outcast! A whore named Rahab.[13]

In *Peculiar Treasures: A Biblical Who's Who*, Frederick Buechner offers brief, witty character sketches that will pique the imaginations of preachers who want to breathe color into Bible characters. For example, Buechner portrays the story of Naaman in 2 Kings 5 like this:

Naaman was a five-star general in the Syrian army and also a leper. His wife had working for her a little Jewish slave-girl who mentioned one day that there was a prophet named Elisha back home who could cure leprosy as easily as a toad cures warts. So Naaman took off for Israel with a letter of introduction from the king and a suitcase full of cash and asked Elisha to do his stuff.

Elisha told him to go dunk in the Jordan seven times, and after some initial comments to the effect that there were rivers back in Syria that made the Jordan look like a cow track, Naaman went and did what he was told. When he came out, he could have passed for an ad for Palmolive soap. Naaman was so grateful that he converted on the spot and reached into his suitcase for an inch of fifties, but Elisha said he was a prophet of Yahweh, not a dermatologist, and refused to take a cent.[14]

In *Leap over a Wall: Earthy Spirituality for Everyday Christians*, Eugene Peterson offers reflections on the life of David. Peterson's primary interest is spiritual formation, but his reflections will stir the imaginations of preachers who want to tell the stories well. Peterson is a first-rate wordsmith, as demonstrated by his description of Shammah in the story of David's anointing from 1 Samuel 16: "Shammah was a mincing

---

13. Wangerin, *Book of God*, 134.
14. Buechner, *Peculiar Treasures*, 112–13.

little sophisticate in Calvin Klein jeans and alligator cowboy boots. He hated living in backwater Bethlehem. He could hardly get across the street without getting cow flop on his boots. Mingling with all these common people, their vulgar games and coarse entertainment, was torture for him. He didn't know what Samuel was up to, but it looked as if it could be a ticket to a finer life—a life of culture and taste. But Samuel dismissed him with one shake of the head."[15]

The previous examples raise a question: should preachers use colloquial language, particularly the kind that imports modern images into the story? Preachers may take this liberty as long as their exegesis informs and limits it and as long as they do not overuse it. Like overdone humor, excessive use of colloquial language and modern images will come across as corny, to use a colloquial term. Preachers bring the story to life when they describe Boaz praising Ruth for choosing him instead of chasing all the young bucks wearing Wranglers.[16] Placing the statement in modern terms helps readers to grasp more fully what Boaz was saying. It does not mislead or confuse hearers; they recognize what the preacher is trying to do.

Do Ample Historical-Cultural Research

Painting scenes like the ones above requires ample historical-cultural research in Bible dictionaries, Bible encyclopedias, Bible atlases, and archaeology books. Such research supplies concrete details and keeps one's imagination in line with the biblical text. For example, half an hour of research on the Jordan River valley can lead to the following portrayal of the scene in Joshua 3:

> When the first rays of the sun peeked over the mountain plateau and lit up the Jordan valley, the air was already sticky with humidity. It was springtime in this geological gash in the cellar of the earth, a sunken valley between two fault lines, at this place about one thousand feet below sea level. Thousands and thousands of Israelites were getting ready to enter the Promised Land. But crossing the valley at this time of year is virtually impossible. A river runs through it. Not Old Man River, which just keeps meandering and rolling along. But Angry Old Man River. The Jordan isn't a terribly wide river. But in the springtime, the snow runoff sends it snarling and raging

15. Peterson, *Leap over a Wall*, 15.
16. This image is adapted from Buechner, *Peculiar Treasures*, 148–49.

down the Jordan Valley Rift. It's a swollen, chocolate brown mess, tearing off chunks of cliff as it twists and turns and spits and thrashes. But Israel is going to have to cross it to get the land God promised.

Follow the Accepted Elements of Style

Storytellers in our culture have developed a style that draws hearers or readers into the story. While some matters boil down to preference, preachers should follow the basic rules. Telling a story is an art form, so rules need to be bent at times. Nevertheless, preachers should master the rules before bending them.

1. *Use concrete, specific words.* Feature writer Jon Franklin says, "The key to word choice, as well as to the inherent power of active images, is specificity."[17] What preaching professor Wayne McDill observes about preaching in general is especially true of preaching in Old Testament narrative literature: "If the sermon doesn't have the particulars, with specifics like broccoli and cheesecake, it seems abstract and dull. It is too heavy with generals. These rather generic attempts at development are often announced with preacher talk like 'We live in a world that . . .' Or 'Oftentimes . . .' Or 'Many times.' What follows is usually a bland, flat generalization instead of a specific, concrete particular which makes the concept come alive."[18]

Generalities and clichés fail to grab the listener's interest. So start by enlisting strong verbs. Instead of saying, "David goes to the front of the cave," try "David creeps to the front of the cave." Choosing verbs like "stifled" instead of "held back" or "slugged" or "jabbed" in place of "hit" may make the difference between an engaging story and a bland one. Sometimes a thesaurus will get you out of a verbal rut, but be careful to choose an appropriate word. Specific nouns help too. Instead of trying to boost a noun like "rock" with a generic modifier like "big," use a word like "boulder." Instead of "flowers" choose the appropriate designation like "daisies" or "lilies" or "roses." Rather than "unpleasant smell," try "stench." Instead of "food," use "corn bread" or "figs" or "grapes." "Alarm" or "terror" works better than "great fear."

2. *Avoid excessive modifiers.* Some communicators use adjectives and adverbs to try to pick up the slack left by weak verbs and nouns. However, modifiers tend to litter the story. Ernest Hemingway learned to distrust

---

17. Franklin, *Writing for Story*, 181.
18. McDill, *12 Essential Skills*, 225–26.

adjectives, and Voltaire considered them the enemies of the noun. Later in his life, Carl Sandburg wrote, "I am more suspicious of adjectives than at any other time in all my born days."[19] Adjectives like "fine," "bad," "good," "big," and "nice" fail because they are too general. Notice how excessive modifiers clutter the following description of the prostitute Rahab.

> One of the many dwellings attached to Jericho's inside wall was the home of a prostitute. She really excelled at her shady profession. She could easily turn on the charm, cunningly flash a grand smile, and smooth-talk vulnerable men with her words. But she was very shrewd and extremely calculating, and she could skillfully read the lustful desires of most men who knocked quietly on her door. Some of them desperately wanted her services as a prostitute. Others merely sought lodging. She offered very cheap lodging. It was a strategic part of her business strategy. She knew that most men who merely wanted lodging couldn't resist her delightful charm and would end up paying the price for an hour or two of physical pleasure.

Removing excess adverbs and adjectives accomplishes for the above paragraph what losing twenty or thirty pounds does for an overweight body. Notice how striking out certain modifiers tightens up the description.

> One of the ~~many~~ dwellings attached to Jericho's inside wall was the home of a prostitute. She ~~really~~ excelled at her ~~shady~~ profession. She could ~~easily~~ turn on the charm, ~~cunningly~~ flash a grand smile, and smooth-talk ~~vulnerable~~ men with her words. But she was ~~very~~ shrewd and ~~extremely~~ calculating, and she could ~~skillfully~~ read the ~~lustful~~ desires of most men who knocked ~~quietly~~ on her door. Some of them ~~desperately~~ wanted her services as a prostitute. Others merely sought lodging. She offered ~~very~~ cheap lodging. It was ~~a strategic~~ part of her business strategy. She knew that most men who merely wanted lodging couldn't resist her ~~delightful~~ charm and would end up paying the price for an hour or two of ~~physical~~ pleasure.

The adjectives "lustful," "strategic," and "delightful" get the axe because they are redundant. Other adjectives, such as "many," "shady," "vulnerable," and "physical," add details that the hearers' imaginations will supply. Adverbs like "really" and "very" are lame. However, some modifiers remain. An adjective like "most" remains to clarify that not all men who

---

19. Sandburg, *Complete Poems*, xxix.

knocked on Rahab's door wanted sexual favors. The adverb "merely" makes the same point. The adjective "inside" is necessary to specify location. While a speaker could dispense with the modifier "grand," it seems to evoke a more precise picture of Rahab's smile. Notice how the adjectives "shrewd" and "calculating" follow the pronoun "she." Writer Oakley Hall claims that since a sentence is linear, moving from left to right, modifiers work best when they occur on the right—after the noun or verb. Notice how well the description flows after shedding its verbal flab.

> One of the dwellings attached to Jericho's inside wall was the home of a prostitute. She excelled at her profession. She could turn on the charm, flash a grand smile, and smooth-talk men with her words. But she was shrewd and calculating, and she could read the desires of most men who knocked on her door. Some of them wanted her services as a prostitute. Others merely sought lodging. She offered cheap lodging. It was part of her business strategy. She knew that most men who merely wanted lodging couldn't resist her charm and would end up paying the price for an hour or two of pleasure.

Concise always wins the day. Keep your sentences short. Weed out the clutter. Aim for lean prose. But be careful. As the previous sentences betray, your descriptions will appear choppy if you don't sprinkle in a longer sentence among the shorter ones.

3. *Eliminate the deadeners*. Like rainfall on a campfire, certain elements douse the flicker of life in a story. For instance, the passive voice sucks out the vigor. A passive verb receives the action and consists of "is," "was," "were," or "has been" plus the past participle of the verb. Note the two passive verb forms in the following sentence: Goliath's forehead *was struck* by a stone that *had been hurled* from David's sling. Using active verb forms provides more zip. An active verb describes the action that the subject is performing. The following sentence uses active verbs to visualize David's conquest of Goliath: David *hurled* a stone from his sling and *struck* Goliath's forehead.

Furthermore, the term "there" deadens prose and can bog down the story. Notice the following examples. The use of "there" weakens the first one. The second one corrects the problem.

- There was something ironic about Sisera's instructions to Jael.
- Sisera's instructions to Jael dripped with irony.

Of course, a preacher could break the rule and use a "there was" construction when the intent is to linger on a particular point. Also, the term "that" frequently resembles a piece of deadwood. Notice how the term "that" can be chopped from the first sentence with no loss of meaning. (And yes, I used a passive verb in the previous sentence! Sometimes it is necessary.)

- Naomi hoped that her two daughters-in-law would remain in Moab.
- Naomi hoped her two daughters-in-law would remain in Moab.

4. Refrain from being too clever. Too many creative words and descriptions have the same effect as pouring too much maple syrup on pancakes. The temptation is to use overly sensational descriptions. In their quest to avoid stale words, some speakers opt for terms that try to do too much. While "Goliath said" is too lame, "Goliath bellowed" may be too sensational. Perhaps "Goliath shouted" makes the point most effectively. The word "shouted" is vivid, yet it doesn't take on a life of its own.

In a similar vein, Oakley Hall warns, "Varying speech tags is *not* a way to insure against monotony in long exchanges of dialog, and many a writer has made a fool of himself by being discontented with *said*." Consider Hall's example:

> "If you're wondering what's good, the chili's our specialty," she grinned.
> "That sounds good," I agreed. "But I've been longing for a good cup of homemade soup."
> "Oh, I wouldn't have the soup if I were you," she counseled. "The chili's better." "Okay, chili," I conceded.[20]

Speech tags like "grinned," counseled," and "conceded" are a bit excessive. Perhaps "agreed" works here for the sake of variety. Otherwise, "said" is sufficient everywhere else.

5. Show the reader rather than tell. Cause readers to conclude or feel something for themselves rather than telling them. For example, instead of saying, "Goliath was a huge man," or even "Goliath was an incredible hulk of a man," say, "When Goliath stood in a doorway, he filled the entire frame." Or you could say, "Goliath's bronze jacket tipped the

---

20. Hall, *Art and Craft of Novel Writing*, 105.

scales at about 125 pounds, and the tip on his spear weighed as much as a shotput." For another example, a preacher describing David's feelings in the guard tower waiting for a report on the battle against Absalom could say, "David was extremely nervous as he waited to hear what had become of his son. He was impatient as he waited with a city guard in the little guard room between the two city gates leading into Mahanaim." But the preacher will do better to show David's emotions by telling the story like this: "David paced and fumed as he waited in the little room between the two city gates leading into Mahanaim. Above him a guard scanned the landscape. David was like the girl or boy in the back seat of your SUV who keeps asking, 'Are we there yet?' David kept asking, 'Do you see anybody yet?' The guard kept scanning the countryside and hollering down, 'Nope. Nobody's coming.'"

By now, you may be thinking, "I'll never have enough time to compose a manuscript that tells the story well. I don't have hours to agonize over word choice and to trim the excess." Here is a solution. I suggest working with a key paragraph or two of your manuscript for each sermon. If you try to polish an entire manuscript, you will bite off more than you can chew. But you can devote thirty minutes to polishing three or four hundred words. If you work with a key section or two in each sermon, this will help you in the long run. You will hone your communication style. Writing will force you to develop concrete, specific images that will work themselves into your pulpit conversation. Your storytelling will become vivid, yet lean.

Images

Aside from retelling the story, preachers who preach Old Testament narrative texts will want to spend some time developing images. Pictures must form in the listeners' minds. People respond to the pictures that hang in the gallery of their minds. In addition to visualizing the action of the story itself, what else do you need to visualize for your listeners?

Explanatory Images

Some details in a story require explanation. Suppose you are preaching on Josiah's response to God's covenant in 2 Kings 23. In verse 10, you read that Josiah "desecrated Topheth, which was in the Valley of Ben Hinnom, so no one could use it to sacrifice their son or daughter in the fire to Molek." You assume correctly that the Canaanite custom of child sacrifice is foreign to your listeners. You need to explain it. Often, preachers will begin by saying, "In ancient Canaanite religion . . ." There is a more effective way, however. Paint the scene with your listeners in it. You could adapt James Michener's description quoted earlier in this chapter to form an image like this: "Imagine arriving home from a day's work in your olive groves and finding the priests of your village. They relate the ugly news that you and your spouse have feared: 'The stars indicate that we shall be attacked from the north. By a host larger than before. It is therefore essential to take steps and we shall have a burning of first sons tomorrow.' With a red dye obtained from the seashore they stain your infant's wrists and then direct you to halt your sobbing."

In a sermon on Joshua 6, you will probably need to explain a bit about siege warfare. You could introduce the information by saying, "Based on archaeological data, Bible scholars can accurately describe how the ancients conducted siege warfare." However, this sounds dull—if not downright boring. An image can convey the information in a more interesting way.

> The city of Jericho has shut its gates. You expect this, but it is not what you want to hear. It's tough to attack a fortified city with closed gates and people holed up inside. Guards wait in towers perched high on the walls, ready to shoot arrows, pour hot oil, and dump boulders on you if you get close to the gates. Since the gate system is potentially the weakest part of the wall, the entrance consists of a series of two or three gates. Punch through one, and you still have one or two left. So, you hope to get some battering rams close enough to start whacking at the wall. But punching a hole through a thick, stone wall can take weeks, even months. Scaling the wall is next to impossible. A flurry of arrows will kill you before you get too far.

In fact, I urge preachers never to say, "Let me give you some background to help you understand the story we're going to look at today." Instead, simply relate the background information as part of the story.

Application Images

Effective preachers also paint pictures of what the truth looks like fleshed out in a listener's life. I'll never forget attending the closing arguments of a murder trial in our community. A young man stood trial for deliberate homicide in the shooting death of a longtime friend. Both the prosecutor and the defense attorney told stories. Each attorney crafted a story of the defendant's involvement in the murder. Each attorney left out a lot of technical data—ballistic reports, crime lab analyses of bloodstains, and so on. Each attorney asked the jury to act on a particular story of the crime.

Preachers follow the same approach. They punctuate their storytelling with application images that either raise questions or offer solutions. The following application image from a sermon on Judges 4 helps the reader relate to Barak. The image shows what Barak's approach to his unique situation looks like when we face our own unique situations.

> It's easy to hesitate like Barak in the face of God's commands. God commanded Barak to lead the Israelite army against Jabin's army. For you, it might be God's call to proclaim the gospel and acknowledge Jesus before the people in your life. Yet, you are reluctant to speak up, knowing you will put your safety and comfort at risk. Or perhaps you struggle to discipline your children, to train them in the way of wisdom. You hesitate to set boundaries for their social media consumption. You lack the courage to say, "You may not download that app on your smartphone."

Illustrations, Quotations, and Factual Information

Sermons on Old Testament stories will not rely as heavily on illustrations, quotations, statistics, and similar types of factual information. Or, they will at least use such materials differently. The following are some examples of supporting materials that work when retelling Old Testament stories.

Illustrations

Regardless of the literary genre you are preaching, the illustrations you choose work most effectively when they come out of your own reading and your real-life experiences. Illustrations lifted out of illustration books usually sound stale.

In Old Testament narrative literature, the story carries its own weight. It does not need an illustration to add interest or stir emotion. However, an illustration can help a preacher explain, validate, or apply a concept. The trick is to keep the illustration as concise as possible so you don't bog down the progress of the story. For example, after reading or describing the military strategy God lays out in Joshua 6:2–5, I might say, "It does not take an expert on military battles to see how odd this strategy is. It's almost like a coach saying to his or her basketball team, 'Here is the game plan. I want you to go out and hold the ball for four quarters. Don't take any shots. Even if you have an open layup, don't take it. In the last seconds of the game, throw the ball up in the air, and it will end up going through the hoop and we'll win!' Seems crazy, doesn't it?"

Quotations

Generally, save quotations for the introduction or conclusion of a sermon. They don't interface well with the flow of the story. I recall a sermon on 2 Samuel 11–12 in which Haddon Robinson used a quote attributed to John Knox as he approached the sermon's end: "I will keep the ground that God has given me, and perhaps in his grace he will ignite me again. But ignite me or not, I will by his grace and his power, hold the ground." Robinson used this quote to advance the idea that men and women of God need to walk with God in their middle years when life flattens out.

Factual Information

While preachers must not allow their Old Testament narrative sermons to atrophy into exegetical lectures, audiences appreciate insight into the inner workings of the text. When I preach Genesis 22:1–19, I talk about how the tension builds in God's identification of Isaac (v. 2). In Joshua 3, I point out how the narrative slows to a crawl in verses 14–17. Usually, I choose one or two key grammatical features to mention. I do this succinctly, and I show the significance for experiencing the story. As mentioned earlier, don't use shop talk. Describe it in a way that an intelligent person without a background in biblical studies can grasp.

Historical-cultural information is necessary too. Listeners need to understand who the Philistines were, how ancient warfare happened, and so on. But remember, these are not the issues that keep people awake at night. You may need to explain them on your way to answering a question that does keep someone awake at night, but don't belabor the point. You may be fascinated by the Philistines, but many (most?) listeners are not.

What about commenting on individual words? Usually, this is unnecessary. When appropriate, though, do not bog down the advance of the story.

Nor should you squeeze words until they bleed. However, in the story of Ruth, as well as in the story of David and Mephibosheth in 2 Samuel 9, the term "loyal love" (*hesed*, חֶסֶד) plays a key role. There's reason, then, to discuss it. You will do your listeners a service if you point out that the term *voice* carries the narrative in 1 Samuel 15. Package your discussion, though, so it does not sound like a bland exegetical lecture. Use pictures and modern analogies to describe what the term means.

The goal in this step of sermon preparation is to fill in your sermon outline with the kind of supporting material that enables you to tell the story well. You finish the stage when you complete a manuscript for the body of your sermon. Now you are ready to prepare an introduction and conclusion. Logically, this step happens last. Of course, ideas for the introduction and conclusion often strike preachers earlier in the process, and you may occasionally prepare one or the other before your manuscript is finished. However, forming both an introduction and conclusion before you finish the body of the sermon makes no more sense than preparing an advertisement for a product that has not been fully developed. The next chapter will guide you through the process of creating an effective introduction and conclusion to your sermon.

14

Entering and Exiting

Below Tower Fall in Yellowstone National Park, Tower Creek empties into the Yellowstone River. The stretch of river above this confluence is one of my favorite places to fly-fish. It holds a healthy population of cutthroat trout. I love to catch them on dry flies—imitations that float on the surface. Some of these dry flies are as tiny as a kernel of corn. What I have learned over the years is that presentation is everything. If my fly disturbs the surface of the water rather than landing softly, the trout ignore it. Sometimes, they scatter. In fly-fishing, presentation is everything.

This same dynamic takes place when a preacher stands before a congregation. No matter how compelling an Old Testament narrative might be, listeners will check out if the entrance into the text is not appealing. The first few seconds are critical. Like a trout analyzing a fly, a listener takes only a short window of time to decide whether or not to accept the preacher's offering. That's why preaching professors often tell their students that the length of a sermon's introduction is disproportionate to its importance.

The most vulnerable, dangerous times for airline flights are the takeoffs and landings. Sermons from Old Testament narrative texts share the same points of vulnerability.

The Entrance

The effective sermon introduction will accomplish three things (see table 14.1). First, it gets people's attention. I once heard Haddon Robinson quip,

"When you stand up to preach, people are bored and expect you to make it worse." A good introduction must also surface a need. People listen to sermons because they want to learn how to deal with their money, their suffering, their anger, or their sexual urges. When you show them that the text you plan to preach deals with the concerns they face, they are ready to listen. Finally, an effective introduction orients people to the text or to the body of the sermon. It eases people into the Bible story you plan to tell.

Generally, expositors find the grist for sermon introductions in stories, illustrations, quotations, questions, poems, song lyrics, or personal experiences. In the introduction to a story sermon, however, there are some differences. Since you are already about to tell a story such as Deborah and Barak, Samson and Delilah, or Ruth and Naomi, you may make your sermon too "story-intensive" by introducing it with another story. You may do better with a pointed question like, "Why does God often give you more than you can handle? You ask him for your daily bread, and he seems to eat your lunch instead." You might provide a concrete example or two. Then you are ready to orient your listeners to a narrative that speaks to this problem.

Often, a "cold open" is an effective way of starting. Essentially, this means jumping right into the story with a carefully crafted description of a scene. You will need to visualize the scene for your listeners. A sermon on Joshua 2 might begin like this:

> It was late in the day when the knock came at the door. The afternoon sun lengthened the shadows of the men standing in the doorway. The prostitute adjusted her silver bracelets and the gold hair net that covered her braided hair. She had accented her upper eyelids with black eye paint, and her lower lids sported a narrow green streak. The smell of frankincense wafted up from a small incense burner. There were two men at the door. Short, bearded, they weren't from town. Their feet were covered with dust. Little did the prostitute know that her life would never be the same.

A cold open works especially well in a flashback sermon. The preacher opens the sermon by painting a vivid picture of a dramatic moment,

---

Table 14.1

Marks of an Effective Introduction

1. It commands the listener's attention.
2. It surfaces a need for the listener to listen.
3. It orients the listener to the text.

perhaps the climax, of the story. The preacher then retreats to the beginning and relates the scenes leading up to this climax or dramatic moment. Usually, the preacher stops short of sharing all the details or of fully resolving the dramatic moment. For example, Haddon Robinson once introduced a sermon on 2 Samuel 13–18 by quoting 2 Samuel 18:33: "The king was shaken. He went up to the room over the gateway and wept. As he went, he said: 'O my son Absalom! My son, my son Absalom! If only I had died instead of you—O Absalom, my son, my son!'" While this approach seems to give the answer away too quickly, it has the effect of raising a rather tension-filled question: How did David end up in this situation? Sure, we learn up front that Absalom dies. But how? Why? By whom? How come David could not prevent his son's death? These questions create a tension that carries the story. Once you've painted the picture of a dramatic moment in the story, you can go back and raise questions and help your listeners understand why this story is important and what message it provides.

In a first-person narrative, the preacher can start in one of two ways. One option is starting with a formal introduction. This introduction should be brief. Either you can do the introduction, or you can get someone else to do it. If someone else gives the introduction, then you can assume the role of the character from your very first word. If you give the introduction yourself, then you need to make a clear signal that you are assuming the role of a particular character. Both your words and your body language must signal this change. You might say, "If Samson showed up today to tell his story, it would sound something like this." Or, "Today, I want to tell you the story of Naomi and Ruth from the perspective of one of the elders of the city. Here is his account." Your body language should then reinforce this verbal signal. You may simply bow your head and remain in that posture for a couple of seconds. When you look up at the audience again, you look at them as David or Samson, not as Pastor Johnson.

When Daniel Buttry gives a brief introduction to his first-person sermons, he follows the introduction by taking a step back, pausing, and then stepping to the pulpit in the character of the biblical or historical figure.[1] Don Sunukjian negotiates the transition from introduction to monologue by briefly turning his back on the congregation. When he turns around

---

1. Buttry, *First-Person Preaching*, 22.

to face his audience, he assumes the character. To signal a change from introduction to monologue, you may move to another place on stage, or you may move from standing to sitting on a stool. In most cases, you will not want to adopt an accent or a different tone of voice—unless you have the skill and the preparation time to do so. Even then, it could come across as acting rather than preaching.

Another option is to begin immediately as a character and introduce yourself in a dimension of the character's life that you want to highlight.[2] For example, you might introduce a first-person narrative sermon on Samson from Samson's perspective by saying, "I never intended for my life to end the way it did. I was a tragic failure. My name is Samson." Or, "I always figured that the movie based on my life story would be called *The Natural*. But a more appropriate title would be *The Jerk*. My name is Samson."

A final issue to consider is how to incorporate a Scripture reading into your introduction. In some churches or church traditions, it is customary for the preacher or another reader to read the sermon text right before the sermon. This raises a couple of concerns. First, what if the narrative is long? Should you take the time to read the entire narrative if you are preaching Judges 17–18? Second, and perhaps more concerning, won't the Scripture reading give away the ending and kill the suspense? Neither concern should cause any stress. If you're dealing with a larger narrative, simply read a portion of it—particularly a tense, dramatic moment. Read something that will pique the interest of your listeners. As far as giving away the narrative's ending and killing the suspense, don't worry. Your listeners likely know (spoiler alert here) that David killed Goliath. Yet if you tell the story well, they will experience the same tension and relief when they hear the ending for the thirty-eighth time. This resembles what happens when you rewatch a favorite movie. You still experience the emotional journey no matter how many times you have watched it before.

The Exit

Like the final bars of a symphony, a conclusion attempts to arrive at a grand finish. Haddon Robinson says that the conclusion should bring the sermon to its burning focus. I sometimes use a flying metaphor; the

---

2. David M. Brown argues that "the most effective introduction of a narration is to begin in character" (*Dramatic Narrative in Preaching*, 40).

conclusion resembles landing a plane. Some conclusions resemble a passenger jet that keeps circling an airport in a holding pattern. The passengers will wonder if it will ever land.

To form conclusions, preachers usually draw from the same spring of material that feeds introductions: stories, illustrations, quotations, questions, poems, song lyrics, or personal experiences. Once again, using a story may not work effectively as it can steal the spotlight from the Bible story you have just preached. Something brief, such as a quotation or a line from a song, may complement the story more effectively. In some stories, application works best at the very end, after the full idea emerges. In this case, the preacher may need to sketch some application images or raise some concluding questions. Whenever possible, let your last line or two return to the story. You might save a key detail for the end, like Paul Borden does in his sermon on 2 Samuel 11–12. At the end he returns to Uriah, identifying him as the real hero of the story—the one who embodies the integrity David did not achieve. This is why I encourage preachers to listen to or read Paul Harvey's stories. He is a master of withholding a key detail—such as a person's full name or a chronological or geographical item—until the very end. The key is to not wander away from the story you've just preached.

When concluding a first-person narrative, should you conclude as the character relating the story, or should you break away from the character back to yourself? If you started the sermon as the character, breaking back to yourself may confuse the audience. Of course, if you started the sermon as yourself and then broke into character, it will be easier to break out of character at the end of the sermon. You must decide whether or not your character can relate some applicational material without undermining the realism you have achieved. If so, consider using your character to share it.

If you decide to break away from the character and back to yourself as the preacher, make this shift clear. Generally, break out of character the same way you broke into character. If you bowed your head for a few seconds, do that motion and then return the floor to yourself as the preacher. If you turned around with your back to the audience, repeat that gesture. When you turn back to face the audience, you will no longer be delivering an eyewitness account but speaking as yourself.

Of course, finishing as the main character and sitting down is highly effective. Someone else can offer a closing prayer or a few words of reflection if needed. However, if you have done your job well, a few words of reflection may be anticlimactic. Haddon Robinson closes his sermon on 2 Samuel 13–18 by returning to the pain-drenched words of 18:33 and adding a final remark. Beginning and ending with the same scene or words forms a satisfying union.

When developing a sermon manuscript, pay special attention to the introduction and conclusion. Initial words set the pace. They determine how the hearer will listen to the rest of the sermon. Last words get remembered first. So take time to polish both of these elements. Labor a little bit longer over word choice and phrasing. Entering and exiting well will enhance your story.

15

Delivering the Goods

Now it's time to deliver the goods. You've polished your sermon manuscript. You've pored over it and prayed over it. You've invested hours and days to get to this moment. You're ready to tell the story with conviction and style.

What to Forget

To get off to a good start, remember to forget your notes. That's right. Leave the manuscript in which you invested so many hours on your desk. The payoffs for preaching without notes are enormous compared to the advantages you think you have with notes. Notes are a security blanket; we're afraid we'll stumble or ramble without them. Communicating "eyeball to eyeball" is essential in a television age. Notes get in the way. The Bible story you tell will seem more alive and more personal when you leave home without them.

Of course, many fine preachers use notes or even full manuscripts when they preach. If preaching without notes does not work for you, that's alright. But consider giving it a try.

Your mind is more reliable than you realize. Try telling someone the story of your favorite childhood Christmas morning. You'll recall all of the sights and smells as well as the feelings of anticipation, euphoria, or disappointment. You'll remember details such as sizes, colors, and flavors.

You don't need an outline. You lived the situation, so all you have to do is reach back into the recesses of your mind to relive it. When you have the story inside of you, you don't need notes. If you ever listened to Bible teacher R. C. Sproul, you know that his presentations were chock-full of data. Yet Sproul preached and taught without notes, and he counseled preachers to follow suit: "We do this all the time when we're talking with each other. We don't have notes in front of us. We call upon our normal vocabulary patterns and our minds to think ahead of our mouths. Notes are a terrible barrier to communication."[1]

Perhaps you fear what happened to George W. Truett, pastor of the First Baptist Church in Dallas. After expounding for only seven minutes on "Ye are the light of the world," he said, "My little light went out."[2] But he recovered from the trauma to go on preaching without notes.

How do you learn to preach without notes? Just do it. There are no surefire formulas or steps; however, there are some things you can do (see table 15.1).

First, make sure to *organize* your sermon well. Haddon Robinson told his preaching classes, "A good sermon remembers itself." Writing out a word-for-word manuscript forces you to organize your sermon. Writing is a way of thinking.

Second, *internalize* your material. That is, go over it again and again. This is the meaning of the word *meditate*, which occurs in both Joshua 1:8 and Psalm 1:2 and is applied to the way people treat Scripture. Originally, *meditate* described the sound of an animal growling or moaning. Eventually, it was used to describe any repeated sound, including the sound of reading. Meditating on Scripture means reading over it again and again and again and again. You don't have to memorize your sermon manuscript. In fact, it's better if you don't try to do this. A memorized story is "as impotent as one that is read."[3] Besides, listeners don't know when you forget an image or misspeak. They do not

Table 15.1

Preparing to Preach without Notes

1. *Organize* your sermon well.
2. *Internalize* it, but don't try to memorize it.
3. *Pray* through it.
4. *Rehearse* it.

---

1. Duduit, "Theology and Preaching in the 90s," 23.
2. Fant, "Memory," 330.
3. D. Brown, *Dramatic Narrative in Preaching*, 41.

have your manuscript in front of them.[4] To internalize your manuscript, review it over and over again. Getting your manuscript done a few days before you preach gives you an edge—you can read through it every night before you turn in for bed.

Third, *pray* through your manuscript. Turn the major moves of your sermon into prayer requests. Ask God to help you communicate each section clearly and, if necessary, to help you say something differently.

Finally, *rehearse* your delivery. Take your manuscript with you into the empty worship center where you will preach. Start by reading a section through. Then, set aside the manuscript and deliver the section without it. If you slip, you can refer to the manuscript and find out what you forgot and perhaps why you forgot it. The closer you get to delivery day, run through the whole sermon without notes. If you stumble over the same area, you may need to work on a transition or revise a section that does not flow.

If you decide to use notes, I encourage you to use a simple, uncluttered outline rather than a detailed outline or a full manuscript. Usually, we forget the big elements of our sermon, not the little details.

Here is a final encouragement for those who want to try preaching without notes. You can always write the big idea at the top of the page in your Bible where you find your preaching text. You can even write one-word notes in the margins to serve as memory triggers. However, resist the temptation to cram the margin with notes. Of course, all of this assumes you preach from a copy of Scripture in book form. You can do something similar, though, if you access your text on an electronic device.

What to Wear and Wield

What about costumes and props? Should the preacher use these, particularly in a first-person narrative sermon? As noted earlier, prophets like Jeremiah and Ezekiel made use of both costuming and props, so there's no theological reason to avoid them. The question becomes a practical one: Will the use of a costume or a prop work for or against my communication of this sermon?

My personal preference is to avoid costuming. Jeffrey Arthurs cites at least two practical reasons to forego the use of costumes: "Costumes tend

---

4. D. Brown, *Dramatic Narrative in Preaching*, 41.

to communicate to the audience that the message is more entertainment than edification. When it comes to costuming, less is often more. That is, the more that audience members use their imaginations, the more they will participate in the sermon."[5]

On two separate occasions, I attended worship services in which Haddon Robinson and Don Sunukjian delivered first-person narrative sermons. Robinson preached part of the David story from David's perspective, while Sunukjian told the story of Esther from the viewpoint of one of the minor characters in the book.[6] Neither preacher wore costumes. Both delivered their sermons effectively.

On the other hand, friends have told me how effective it was when Paul Borden preached a first-person narrative from an Old Testament story and dressed the part of Jacob or Abraham. Each expositor will have to make the call. A costume is not necessary. If one is used, however, it should be more than a bathrobe and slippers. A preacher's resources, time, and skill will help determine whether or not to try any costuming.

As far as props, less is probably more. There's no substitute for painting a verbal picture. On occasion, though, a sword, animal jawbone, scroll, or piece of broken pottery might serve the telling. Props tend to attract attention and take on lives of their own, though, so be careful.

On Stage

You should think about the platform or stage on which you will deliver your sermon. In general, it is helpful to have a little more space than normal when you preach an Old Testament narrative. Storytellers tend to move around a bit. The area does not need to be large. But it needs to be free from clutter.

One issue in some settings is the presence of a pulpit. I appreciate what pulpits symbolize—the preaching of the Word of God. Yet I do not feel bound to them since they do not appear in Scripture. I remember the time when Ray Stedman preached at a church I pastored. Before his sermon, Ray moved out from behind the pulpit and stood in front of it. He joked about hiding behind what Spurgeon called a "coward's castle." Through

---

5. Arthurs, "Performing the Story," 35.
6. For a transcript of the first-person narrative on Esther, see Sunukjian, "Night in Persia," 69–88.

the years, I've watched preachers improve their communication by getting out from behind the pulpit. As Don Sunukjian tells his students, "There is no communication advantage to standing behind a box." If a pulpit is a permanent fixture in your worship setting, whether physically or emotionally, then figure out how you can stand beside it or in front of it when preaching a narrative.

Although preaching is not acting, it is helpful to move from one spot to another when there is a change of scene or geographic location in a narrative. For example, when preaching the story of Ruth, you may designate a spot on the stage for Moab and a spot on the stage for Bethlehem. As the narrative proceeds, you will change locations to coincide with changes of scene. It is fine if these spots are only a couple of steps apart. When recreating a conversation, you do not need to change your physical location for different speakers. This can be too abrupt visually if the characters are speaking brief lines back and forth, as in the exchange between Samuel and Saul in 1 Samuel 15:13–31. It can also be confusing to change locations for different speakers when you are already doing this to coincide with changes in scene or geography. Simply turn about forty-five degrees from center to the right for one character's speech. Then turn about forty-five degrees from center to the left for the other character's speech.

It is fine to speak (preach) as you move from one spot to another. However, do not pace. This creates a visual distraction. Deliver your words from a fixed point. Change that point as often as the story demands it, but don't wander back and forth as you talk.[7] At times, you may even want to use a stool, particularly if you plan to deliver part of the sermon standing and part of the sermon sitting. Also, if you are moving from one scene to another, it may work best to be silent. The combination of a verbal pause and a physical shift from one place to another will highlight the change.

Delivery

In any preaching event, how you use your voice is important. Vocal variety engages your listeners. This means varying your pitch (higher, lower),

---

7. For more elaborate details on staging, see Grant and Reed, *Telling Stories to Touch the Heart*, 68–70.

volume (louder, softer), rate (faster, slower)—and then including some well-placed pauses.[8] Use a combination of these elements to convey the emotion of what the characters say.

As a general rule, you're not being as dramatic as you think you are. For example, if you are moving from loud to soft, it may seem to you like the volume drops from level 9 to level 2. When your audience hears it, however, or when you listen to yourself on a recording, the volume level only drops from 6 to 4. The pause that seemed like four seconds to you only took one second. So don't be afraid to overexaggerate your contrasts.

When you deliver your story, use large gestures. Large gestures help preachers get rid of nervousness. They also add realism to your story. Storytelling lends itself to gesturing more than any other form of communication. Using your hands, you can toss wheat into the air with a pitchfork. You can draw a bowstring and shoot an arrow. You can point to Jerusalem or Bethlehem or a well or the field of Boaz. You can shield the sun from your eyes.

There are a couple of other things you can do to help your audience visualize the scene you're constructing. Remember to keep Jerusalem or Shechem at the same spot throughout the whole sermon. If you point to your left at the imaginary city of Jerusalem, you must always point to your left when indicating Jerusalem. If you point to your left the first two times and to your right the third time, you will create visual confusion. Furthermore, remember that your congregation sees everything backwards. When you draw a line from left to right, your audience sees a line being drawn from right to left. So, if you are trying to construct a timeline and talk about the past, you will want to start the line on the congregation's left, which happens to be your right.

Eye contact is also important. Haddon Robinson notes, "Almost without exception, a congregation will not listen attentively to speakers who do not look at them."[9] He counsels looking at and talking with one listener at a time for a second or two. Look that listener in the eye, then turn to someone else. The goal is not simply looking at listeners but talking with them.

However, storytelling is the one time a preacher may momentarily gaze over the audience and look into space. As Fred Craddock observes, "A

---

8. Robinson, *Biblical Preaching*, 161–63. He refers to these elements as pitch, punch, progress, and pause.
9. Robinson, *Biblical Preaching*, 158.

good storyteller seldom looks at anyone."[10] A preacher may want to look beyond the audience when relating a dialogue between two characters. In a first-person narrative, the preacher might look beyond the listeners when delivering the reminiscences or reflections of a character in the story. Essentially, you are looking beyond the audience to the scene you are imagining. The trick is to reestablish eye contact with your listeners as soon as you are finished. You cannot afford to spend your whole sermon staring off into space.

Finally, pay attention to timing and pause. Annette Simmons says, "The language of silence and timing can be more powerful than verbal language.... Pauses give your listener time to participate, think, and to process your story."[11] So consider a couple seconds of silence before you deliver a key line in your narrative. For example, toward the end of a sermon on Judges 17–18, I will talk about the consequences of idolatry for Micah and the Danites. Micah ended up with nothing. The Danites ended up in captivity. Then, I will tell my listeners that there is an even more devastating consequence that stands behind both emptiness and bondage. Then, I will point them to the last line of the narrative, in 18:31: "They continued to use the idol Micah had made, all the time the house of God was in Shiloh." After reading this line, I will pause two or three seconds to let it linger. Then, I will say, "Oh, what irony! What a damning statement!"

Like a Christmas present you ship from one state to another, the Old Testament story you plan to deliver must arrive intact at its destination or the sermon has failed. Remember, people's lives are at stake. Proclaiming a well-studied story in a well-prepared way will do what good stories intend to do: sneak past the listener's defenses to penetrate the heart.

---

10. Craddock, *Overhearing the Gospel*, 117.
11. Simmons, *Story Factor*, 100.

Appendix A

Sample Sermon on Judges 17–18

Foreword

What follows is a manuscript for a sermon I prepared and preached on Judges 17–18. It models the approach I have presented in this volume. Scripture passages appear in italics, and my statements of the sermon's big idea appear in bold. The title of the sermon is "Why It Pays to Avoid Idolatry."

If you are interested in additional examples, I contributed a sermon on Judges 3:12–30 titled "The Story of the Left-Handed Assassin and the Obese King" in *Models for Biblical Preaching: Expository Sermons from the Old Testament*, edited by Haddon W. Robinson and Patricia Batten.[1] For an example of a first-person narrative, see my sermon on the book of Ruth titled "An Ordinary Hero" in *It's All in How You Tell It: Preaching First-Person Expository Messages* by Haddon W. Robinson and Torrey W. Robinson.[2]

I developed the following sermon on Judges 17–18 as part of a series on the book of Judges. Yes, I had the audacity to preach a sermon series on the entire book of Judges. In fact, I did this twice, in two different churches where I served as a pastor. Following the manuscript, I have included an afterword that provides a brief analysis of the sermon. I placed numbers

---

1. Mathewson, "Story of the Left-Handed Assassin," 41–60.
2. Robinson and Robinson, *It's All in How You Tell It*, 79–87.

at the beginning of each paragraph in the manuscript so that I can refer to specific paragraphs in this analysis in the afterword.

Sermon Manuscript

1. The human heart is "a perpetual factory of idols." John Calvin made that claim, and he's right. We're always looking to idols to provide what only God can provide. Idols are simply substitutes for God. We look to them for pleasure or comfort or security. Kacey Musgraves's song, "Merry Go Round," reveals a few common idols and the power they wield over us. Each of us is hooked on something. For mama, it's Mary Kay. For brother, it's Mary Jane. For daddy, it's Mary two doors down.

2. The Scriptures warn us to keep ourselves from idols. But what is the danger? Why does it matter if we pour our lives into selling cosmetics? Or if we find a bit of escape or relief by smoking weed? Or if we find a bit of pleasure in fantasizing about the neighbor a couple houses down from ours? Today we come to Judges 17–18, a narrative that shows us why it pays to keep ourselves from idols. Please find Judges 17–18 in your Bible or on your Bible app.

3. The message of the book of Judges is that God's people self-destruct when they adopt the values of their culture instead of obeying God. And one of those sources of self-destruction is idolatry. Yes, idolatry is a heart problem, but our culture's value system feeds it. So then, what happens when you turn from God to idols as the people of Israel did? God's vision for his people, according to Judges 5:31, is that they become like the sun when it rises in its strength. What does idolatry do to that vision? That's what we're going to learn from this story.

4. When I start reading Judges 17–18 I am reminded of a "What's wrong with this picture?" exercise—like the ones that used to appear in the *Highlights* magazine that I subscribed to as a boy. Each issue had a picture that compelled you, if you were alert to the details, to say, "Hey, that's wrong! There's a bicycle in the tree. The dog is wearing sunglasses. And there is a duck watching television on the roof of the house!" Judges 17–18 is a sophisticated story, designed to elicit the same kind of response. The narrator presumes that we know the law God gave his people through Moses, particularly the book of Deuteronomy. Thus, the narrator does not need to keep saying, "This is wrong, and so is that." We are expected

to identify what is wrong with the picture. So let's look at the story and spot the problems—and why they are problems.

5. The story begins with a man named "Micah." His name means, "Who is like Yahweh?" The name is a claim that nothing or no one compares with Yahweh, the God of Israel. There is no one like him, no one else worthy of worship. Unfortunately, though, Micah does not live like that is true. He does not live up to his name. The story begins like this: *Now a man named Micah from the hill country of Ephraim said to his mother, "The eleven hundred shekels of silver that were taken from you and about which I heard you utter a curse—I have that silver with me; I took it." Then his mother said, "The* Lord *bless you, my son!" When he returned the eleven hundred shekels of silver to his mother, she said, "I solemnly consecrate my silver to the* Lord *for my son to make an image overlaid with silver. I will give it back to you." So after he returned the silver to his mother, she took two hundred shekels of silver and gave them to a silversmith, who used them to make the idol. And it was put in Micah's house.*

6. Wow. It doesn't take us long to spot a problem, does it? Micah confesses that he stole some money from his mother. It's good that he confessed, although you have to wonder about his motives. He seems concerned about the curse his mother uttered. His mother, though, pronounces God's blessing on him, and then the two of them make some horrible decisions. Micah's mother dedicates the stolen silver he returned to the Lord—Yahweh—in order for Micah to make an image. What?! This blatantly defies one of the "ten words" God gave his people. "You shall not make for yourself an image"—or an "idol." That's what God commands in Deuteronomy 5:8.

7. But the situation gets worse. Verse 5 of chapter 17 tells us, *Now this man Micah had a shrine, and he made an ephod and some household gods and installed one of his sons as his priest.* Micah had his own place of worship. The word "shrine" in verse 5 is actually "house of God" or "house of gods." The word for God is plural here, either a plural of respect that refers to the God of Israel or else a reference to several gods—and the latter seems to be the case here. Micah had his own "house of gods." According to Deuteronomy 12:4–7, there was to be one central place of worship in Israel for the worship of the Lord God—the one who alone is God. But Micah defies that. And he also makes an ephod and some

household gods. There's another violation of the "no idols" command. And then he installed one of his sons as his priest. Once again, we are supposed to cry out, "Hey, that's not right!" Numbers 3:9–10 makes it clear that only Aaron's descendants were to serve as priests.

8. Now we come to the refrain, in verse 6, that echoes throughout chapters 17–21: *In those days Israel had no king; everyone did as they saw fit.* There was no physical king, but more importantly, there was no spiritual king. The people did not recognize the reign of Yahweh their God. And so they did whatever was right in their own eyes. That's our culture today. In the United States, our national anthem is really the late Frank Sinatra's classic, "I Did It My Way." The point, then, is that Micah and his family are not exceptions. Everyone else in Israel was living godless lives as well. And we see this in the next scene.

9. In verses 7–9, we meet a new character: *A young Levite from Bethlehem in Judah, who had been living within the clan of Judah, left that town in search of some other place to stay. On his way he came to Micah's house in the hill country of Ephraim. Micah asked him, "Where are you from?" "I'm a Levite from Bethlehem in Judah," he said, "and I'm looking for a place to stay."* At first reading, there doesn't appear to be anything wrong here. But then you remember how Levites were supposed to live and serve in particular towns—Levitical towns. We learn that in Joshua 21:9–16. So again, there's something wrong with this picture. Here is a Levite who comes from the wrong town—Bethlehem was not a Levitical town—and is wandering aimlessly.

10. And yet, look how Micah responds. Verses 10–14 continue the story: *Then Micah said to him, "Live with me and be my father and priest, and I'll give you ten shekels of silver a year, your clothes and your food." So the Levite agreed to live with him, and the young man became like one of his sons to him. Then Micah installed the Levite, and the young man became his priest and lived in his house. And Micah said, "Now I know that the* LORD *will be good to me, since this Levite has become my priest."* This is crazy! Micah asks this young priest to be both a spiritual father to him and a priest. Yet Micah becomes like a father to his spiritual father. This is the "Build-A-Bear" approach to religion. You pick and choose the elements you want. Micah builds his own religion, and then he has the audacity to assume that it will guarantee God's blessing. Astonishing!

11. Our story takes another interesting twist as it continues. In the next scene, we meet another character—not an individual, but an entire tribe—the tribe of Dan. The opening words of chapter 18 suggest that the situation is not going to improve: *In those days Israel had no king.* And that's what we discover as the narrative continues. Verses 1–2 of chapter 18 report: *And in those days the tribe of the Danites was seeking a place of their own where they might settle, because they had not yet come into an inheritance among the tribes of Israel. So the Danites sent five of their leading men from Zorah and Eshtaol to spy out the land and explore it. These men represented all the Danites. They told them, "Go, explore the land." So they entered the hill country of Ephraim and came to the house of Micah, where they spent the night.* Alright, let's continue our "what's wrong with this picture?" exercise. Here is a tribe that had already received an allotment of land from God. You can read about it in Joshua 19:41–48. Yet because they failed to possess this territory as God had called them to do, they look elsewhere. So this is an unauthorized spy mission—a violation of what God had commanded them to do.

12. In verse 3, the narrator pauses the action briefly to share an important detail: *When they were near Micah's house, they recognized the voice of the young Levite.* This doesn't mean they recognized him as someone they knew personally. It means they recognized his accent. He was an Israelite, not a local. Verse 3 continues: *so they turned in there and asked him, "Who brought you here? What are you doing in this place? Why are you here?"*

13. The following discussion in verses 4–5 of chapter 18 is fascinating: *He told them what Micah had done for him, and said, "He has hired me and I am his priest." Then they said to him, "Please inquire of God to learn whether our journey will be successful."* I'd suggest that the Danites' reference to "God" rather than using the personal name "Yahweh" betrays their situation. They are not acting according to Yahweh's instructions. Now they want an answer, and Micah's priest gives it to them. According to verse 6, *The priest answered them, "Go in peace. Your journey has the LORD's approval."* That's stunning. Micah's priest tells them that their journey, though clearly unauthorized by Yahweh and in violation of his commands, has Yahweh's approval!

14. Thus, the Danite spies continue their mission. Verses 7–13 report: *So the five men left and came to Laish, where they saw that the people were*

living in safety, like the Sidonians, at peace and secure. And since their land lacked nothing, they were prosperous. Also, they lived a long way from the Sidonians and had no relationship with anyone else. When they returned to Zorah and Eshtaol, their fellow Danites asked them, "How did you find things?" They answered, "Come on, let's attack them! We have seen the land, and it is very good. Aren't you going to do something? Don't hesitate to go there and take it over. When you get there, you will find an unsuspecting people and a spacious land that God has put into your hands, a land that lacks nothing whatever." Then six hundred men of the Danites, armed for battle, set out from Zorah and Eshtaol. On their way they set up camp near Kiriath Jearim in Judah. This is why the place west of Kiriath Jearim is called Mahaneh Dan to this day. From there they went on to the hill country of Ephraim and came to Micah's house.

15. Now things really start to get interesting! Beginning in verse 14, we learn what happens once the armed forces arrive at Micah's house: *Then the five men who had spied out the land of Laish said to their fellow Danites, "Do you know that one of these houses has an ephod, some household gods and an image overlaid with silver? Now you know what to do." So they turned in there and went to the house of the young Levite at Micah's place and greeted him. The six hundred Danites, armed for battle, stood at the entrance of the gate. The five men who had spied out the land went inside and took the idol, the ephod and the household gods while the priest and the six hundred armed men stood at the entrance of the gate. When the five men went into Micah's house and took the idol, the ephod and the household gods, the priest said to them, "What are you doing?" They answered him, "Be quiet! Don't say a word. Come with us, and be our father and priest. Isn't it better that you serve a tribe and clan in Israel as priest rather than just one man's household?" The priest was very pleased. He took the ephod, the household gods and the idol and went along with the people. Putting their little children, their livestock and their possessions in front of them, they turned away and left.* Once again, we're left shaking our heads. The Danites have broken another one of the ten commandments: "You shall not steal"—Deuteronomy 5:19. And how about the priest? Did you catch his sudden change in attitude? What an opportunist. One moment he questions what they are doing. But when he finds out that he has an opportunity to advance his career—to step into a bigger, better position of influence—he is very pleased. So much

for trusting in God's promise in Numbers 18:20–24 that the LORD would be the priests' inheritance.

16. What do you suppose Micah will do when he discovers that all his religious objects have been stolen and his priest is gone? Verses 22–26 tell us what happens: *When they had gone some distance from Micah's house, the men who lived near Micah were called together and overtook the Danites. As they shouted after them, the Danites turned and said to Micah, "What's the matter with you that you called out your men to fight?" He replied, "You took the gods I made, and my priest, and went away. What else do I have? How can you ask, 'What's the matter with you?'" The Danites answered, "Don't argue with us, or some of the men may get angry and attack you, and you and your family will lose your lives." So the Danites went their way, and Micah, seeing that they were too strong for him, turned around and went back home.* What a pathetic figure. Micah has lost everything.

17. Now the story hurries to its ending. Verses 27–28 report: *Then they took what Micah had made, and his priest, and went on to Laish, against a people at peace and secure. They attacked them with the sword and burned down their city. There was no one to rescue them because they lived a long way from Sidon and had no relationship with anyone else. The city was in a valley near Beth Rehob.* Here's one more violation of God's law. The Danites take a peaceful city by violence. Deuteronomy 20:10–15 is clear that the people of Israel were to offer terms of peace to faraway cities.

18. Then the story ends like this, beginning in the middle of verse 28 through verse 31: *The Danites rebuilt the city and settled there. They named it Dan after their ancestor Dan, who was born to Israel—though the city used to be called Laish. There the Danites set up for themselves the idol, and Jonathan son of Gershom, the son of Moses, and his sons were priests for the tribe of Dan until the time of the captivity of the land. They continued to use the idol Micah had made, all the time the house of God was in Shiloh.* Perhaps the final blow is that when the Danites built a new city and named it Dan, they set up the idol Micah had made. And in an astonishing twist, we learn the name and family background of Micah's priest, the wandering Levite. He is Jonathan, a descendent of Moses. So the wandering Levite becomes the first in a line of priests in Dan whose family line goes back to Moses.

19. So what is the outcome of all of this? It kind of looks like the Danites lived happily ever after, right? Maybe idolatry isn't so serious after all. Well, not so fast. When you listen closely to this story, you realize that idols never deliver. That it really does pay to keep yourself from idols. Micah and the Danites both turned from God to idols. What did it get them? Micah ended up with nothing. At the end of the story he is a pathetic figure who is unable to hang on to his gods and priest. They did nothing for him. And that's what idolatry does. It leaves you empty, with nothing. No security. No hope. No future. But it gets even worse. If you think that the Danites lived happily ever after, look again at the ending of the story. Notice the little line at the end of verse 30: *until the time of the captivity of the land.* Yes, the Northern Kingdom eventually ends up being taken into captivity by the mighty, brutal Assyrian empire in 722 BC. The Old Testament makes it quite clear that it is the result of its idolatry. Read 1 and 2 Kings. Turning to idols, then, leaves you with nothing and lands you in bondage.

20. Now remember that an idol is simply a substitute for God. Sure, it can be a statue of a Greek or Hindu god or goddess. But for most of us, our idols are the good things that we turn into God things. I do not have figurines or little statues of gods or goddesses on the mantle of my fireplace. Yet the photos of my son in his football uniform or the photo of my grandkids reveal a potential source of idolatry. To be sure, my family members and their pursuits are God's good gifts. However, we can take God's good gifts and look to them for what only God can provide. That's why the apostle Paul, in Colossians 3:5, equates greed with idolatry. Some idols, though, are harder to identify. If I am constantly posting my accomplishments on social media, there is a good chance that I struggle with the idol of status. I am looking to the recognition and affirmation of others for my significance—rather than looking to my identity in Christ. If I manipulate or domineer others, and insist on getting my way, then my idol is being in control. Friends, when you have an idol problem, you don't stop believing in God, but you diminish God to a good luck charm rather than a sovereign king. That's what Micah and the Danites did. And what was the payoff? Emptiness and bondage. Whatever you look to besides God to rescue you from hopelessness or helplessness will either leave you empty or enslaved.

21. However, there is an even more devastating consequence that stands behind both emptiness and bondage. It appears in the last line of the

narrative, at the end of verse 31: *They continued to use the idol Micah had made, all the time the house of God was in Shiloh.* Oh, what irony! What a damning statement! All the while that idolatry was happening in Dan, the presence of God was available. Early in the narrative, in 17:5, we learned that Micah had a "house of gods." Now, the narrator reminds us that all this time, and even after the Danites plundered Micah's "house of gods" and set up his priest and his idol in their new city, THE house of God was in Shiloh. And that house of God was the place where God revealed his presence to his people—through the tabernacle.

22. Friends, **when we turn from God to idols, we miss out on the presence of God.** That's the ultimate payoff of idolatry. What a tragedy! You see, the Bible is the story of God reestablishing the gift of his presence. God, the Creator, is also the Redeemer. The Scriptures tell the story of God redeeming us from sin and restoring us to life in his presence. This is the beauty of the gospel. First Peter 3:18 says that the gift of the gospel of Jesus Christ is God himself: *For Christ also suffered once for sins, the righteous for the unrighteous, to bring you to God.* Through the death and resurrection of King Jesus, we can experience life in God's presence—now and forever. And because Jesus is God come in human flesh, there is no greater pursuit in life than our quest to know Jesus. That's why the apostle Paul speaks of the "surpassing worth of knowing Christ Jesus my Lord" in Philippians 3:8. Do you see why idolatry is so tragic? **When we turn from God to idols, we miss out on the presence of God.**

23. C. S. Lewis wrote this in his essay "The Weight of Glory": "We are half-hearted creatures, fooling about with drink and sex and ambition when infinite joy is offered us. We are far too easily pleased."[3] That's why the apostle John says at the end of his letter we identify as 1 John, "Dear children, keep yourselves from idols" (5:21). That's striking because he didn't say a thing about idolatry in his letter. Yet he knew that idolatry could keep his readers from the fellowship with God that he talked about in his letter. **When we turn from God to idols, we miss out on the presence of God.**

24. Look at the final statement of the narrative one more time: "all the time the house of God was in Shiloh." That's an indictment, for sure. And yet, it's also a reminder of God's great grace. Even during the darkest

---

3. Lewis, *Weight of Glory*, 26.

times, his presence is available. And his presence is available to us in Jesus—Immanuel, God with us. It's in his presence that we find complete joy. So may we respond to Judges 17–18 by praying and living out the words of an Irish hymn written more than a thousand years ago:

> Riches I heed not, nor man's empty praise.
> Thou mine inheritance, now and always.
> Thou and Thou only, be first in my heart.
> High king of heaven, my treasure Thou art.

Afterword

This sermon starts off in the twenty-first century AD before traveling back to the twenty-first century BC. Well, technically, the sermon begins in the sixteenth century with the John Calvin quote! But the introduction uses the language from a popular country song to create interest and raise a need. This need prepares listeners for the big idea, which will come at the end of the sermon, but it does not give the big idea away. Then it orients listeners to the text. Notice the brevity of the introduction (paragraphs 1–3). This is especially important with a longer narrative like Judges 17–18.

I was tempted to spend more time locating Judges 17–18 within the flow of the book of Judges. I wanted to talk about how it is the first part of the double conclusion that mirrors the double introduction. As I noted at the end of chapter 7, Judges 17–18 deals with the problem of idols, while chapters 19–21 focus on the problem of the war of destruction. However, the narrative is long enough that I could not afford to get bogged down in a longer introduction. So I left out this aspect of the literary setting, or context, and briefly discussed the message of the book (paragraph 3).

Although this is a long narrative, I opted for reading every verse in the narrative. I also worked my retelling of the story around the reading of the text. Doing this requires effective transition statements. These statements do not need to be long or elaborate, but they need to be specific. For example, I set up verse 3 (see paragraph 12) by saying, "In verse 3, the narrator pauses the action briefly to share an important detail." This is more effective than saying, "Now we come to verse 3." Similarly, when I arrived at verse 14 (see paragraph 15), I did not say, "Alright, now let's look at verse 14." Instead, I said, "Now things really start to get interesting!

Sample Sermon on Judges 17–18

Beginning in verse 14, we learn what happens once the armed forces arrive at Micah's house." There's nothing particularly dazzling about that statement. Yet it maintains the "story feel" of the sermon. Sometimes a question sets up the next section of the narrative. For example, I introduced verses 22–26 (see paragraph 16) by saying, "What do you suppose Micah will do when he discovers that all his religious objects have been stolen and his priest is gone?" A question like this creates suspense.

Notice that the sermon does not contain any lengthy illustrations. However, it does use brief images as analogies. The narrative expects us to spot "What's wrong with this picture?" just like the pictures in *Highlights* magazine (paragraph 4). Our culture's commitment to doing what is right in its own eyes is expressed by Frank Sinatra's song, "I Did It My Way" (paragraph 8). Micah's construction of his own religion is basically a "Build-A-Bear" approach (paragraph 10). Later in the sermon, I talk about how I do not have figurines or little statues of gods or goddesses on my fireplace mantle; but I do have photos of my son in his football uniform and photos of my grandkids (paragraph 20). I did not take time to elaborate on any of these images. I mention them briefly. Yet they provide vivid analogies or examples.

This sermon is clearly inductive because the big idea does not emerge until the end of the sermon. I stated it three times (see the sentences in bold in paragraphs 22 and 23). However, I worked it into the discussion without ever saying, "Here is the big idea of the text." Narrative is subtle, so there's usually no reason to point out what our big idea is. Simply repeat or restate it a few times, and listeners will remember it if it truly captures the heart of the narrative. Listeners were prepared for this big idea, I believe, by the questions I raised at the beginning of the sermon (see paragraph 3). What happens when you turn from God to idols as the people of Israel did? What does idolatry do to God's vision for his people? Later in the sermon, I begin to transition toward the big idea by reraising the question in a couple of different forms. I asked, "So what is the outcome of all of this?" (paragraph 19). Then, when I pointed out how Micah and the Danites had an idol problem that resulted in them treating God like a good luck charm, I asked, "What was the payoff?" (paragraph 20). Then, after identifying how Micah experienced emptiness and the Danites experienced bondage, I pointed out that there is an "even more devastating consequence" behind both consequences (paragraph 21).

Then, the first time I stated the big idea, I followed it by saying, "That's the ultimate payoff of idolatry" (paragraph 22). I suppose I could have referred to "the question that I raised at the beginning of the story." But since narrative works with subtlety, I try to do the same in my preaching.

Finally, the conclusion is brief, yet it punctuates the theological message of the narrative (see paragraphs 23 and 24). The conclusion begins with a quote from a C. S. Lewis essay, "The Weight of Glory," and ends with a stanza from the hymn, "Be Thou My Vision."

As far as the sermon's structure, it follows the contours of the narrative. Thus, it depends on the flow of the story, not on a logical argument. Listeners will certainly not leave with an outline. But there is an outline that stands behind this sermon—one that ensures the sermon develops with order and progress.

Introduction
    A. We are tempted to turn to idols as substitutes for God
    B. Judges 17–18 shows us why it pays to avoid idolatry
  I. Micah and the Danites turn from God to idols (17:1–18:17) [*develop inductively*]
    A. Micah makes an idol and builds an unauthorized religious system (17:1–13)
      1. Micah makes an idol in violation of Deuteronomy 5:8 (17:1–4)
      2. Micah sets up a shrine in violation of Deuteronomy 12:4–7 (17:5a)
      3. Micah installs one of his sons as priest in violation of Exodus 29:9 (17:5b)
      4. A refrain summarizes the spirit of the times (17:6)
      5. A young Levite from Bethlehem (not a Levitical town!) is wandering aimlessly in violation of Joshua 21:9–16 (17:7–9)
      6. Micah asks this young priest to be his spiritual father and priest (17:10–12)
      7. Micah assumes the religious structure he has created will guarantee God's blessing in contrast to Micah 6:1–8 (17:13)
    B. The Danites seize the distant city of Laish instead of taking over the inheritance assigned to them (18:1–10)

1. The Danites fail to possess their own territory, so they engage in an unauthorized spy mission—all contrary to Joshua 19:41–48 (18:1–3)
      2. The Danites seek God's blessing and then pursue an act that violates his instructions (18:5–10)
   C. The Danites take Micah's idol and priest on their way to capturing Laish—a violation of Deuteronomy 5:19 (18:11–17)
II. As a result, Micah and the Danites do not experience the presence of God (18:18–31) [*develop inductively*]
   A. Micah ends up with nothing after the Danites take his idols and priests (18:18–26)
   B. The Danites eventually end up in captivity after conquering Laish (18:27–30)
   C. Ironically, the presence of God is available at "the house of God" in Shiloh all the time Micah's idol is in use (18:31)
   D. (Big Idea) *When we turn from God to idols, we miss out on the presence of God*
      1. This is tragic because the Bible is the story of God reestablishing the gift of his presence
      2. As C. S. Lewis says in "The Weight of Glory," we are far too easily pleased

Conclusion
   A. The final statement is a reminder of God's grace as well as an indictment (18:31)
   B. A stanza of an Irish hymn ("Be Thou My Vision") provides an appropriate response to Judges 17–18

Appendix B

Using Hebrew in Narrative Exegesis

The Hebrew language may have been a foe during your seminary training. But it is a trusted friend when it comes to the exegesis of Old Testament narrative texts.

If you have never learned Biblical Hebrew and do not intend to learn it now, feel free to skip this appendix. While knowing Hebrew gives preachers an edge, you can still do solid exegetical work in Old Testament narrative literature without it. However, you might skim this chapter simply to understand what studies in the Hebrew text can contribute, or to gain some perspective on the discussions you encounter in the more in-depth commentaries. You might even decide it's worth learning Biblical Hebrew (and it is!). There are some outstanding elearning resources available (see below), and more seminaries teach beginning Hebrew in an online format.

If your Biblical Hebrew skills have waned or are on life support, there is still hope. There are so many new resources and Bible software programs that can help you re-engage with the language—even if you have long forgotten what a *dagesh forte* or a jussive verb is. This appendix may encourage you to get your Hebrew skills back to working order.

If you still do exegetical work in the Hebrew Bible at any level, then you know that the easiest portions of the Hebrew Bible to read are the narratives. The syntax is not complex. In fact, you probably started reading the text with portions of Genesis or with the book of Ruth. You also know that you do not have to operate at the skill level of your seminary Hebrew professors in order to benefit from it.

Getting (or Keeping) Your Hebrew up to Speed

The best way to get your Hebrew up to speed and to keep it there is to read the Hebrew Bible daily. I am a busy pastor, and I still spend a minimum of ten minutes a day in my Hebrew Bible and ten minutes a day in my Greek New Testament. What J. Gresham Machen said about reading the Greek Testament applies to the Hebrew Bible as well: "Ten minutes a day is of vastly more value than seventy minutes once a week."[1] So start by reading for ten minutes a day. Initially, you might only cover a verse or two a day. You can increase the amount as your proficiency grows. Use a Bible software program like *Logos Bible Software* to identify unfamiliar words or forms. This is as quick as placing your cursor on a word that is unfamiliar to you. You might want to purchase *Biblia Hebraica Stuttgartensia: A Reader's Edition* by Donald Vance, George Athas, and Yael Avrahami. I have enjoyed using this when I'm simply reading the Hebrew Bible. Also, find a reading partner. Two or three are better than one. For several years, when I served as a pastor in Montana, I met every other week with a pastor-friend, Dave Hansen, to read theology and the Hebrew Bible. We plodded together through the book of Judges and several psalms. This provided the structure and accountability needed for us to keep up our Hebrew language skills.

A second way to get or to keep your Hebrew up to speed is to work through an introductory Hebrew grammar. You might go with the one you used as a seminary student. However, if your seminary training has become more distant in your rearview mirror, I recommend purchasing a more recent grammar. I'm partial to *Learning Biblical Hebrew* by Karl V. Kutz and Rebekah L. Josberger or *Basics of Biblical Hebrew Grammar* by Gary D. Pratico and Miles V. Van Pelt. You can purchase extensive elearning resources to go with the latter volume. Take a chapter a week and do the exercises. Relearn basic vocabulary. I have used Hebrew vocabulary apps on my smartphone to review the words that occur one hundred or

---

1. Machen, afterword to *Minister and His Greek New Testament*, 146.

more times in the Hebrew Bible. If you are in the market for an intermediate Hebrew grammar that you can use for reference, I highly recommend *A Biblical Hebrew Reference Grammar* by Christo H. J. van der Merwe, Jacobus A. Naudé, and Jan H. Kroeze. Gary A. Long's *Grammatical Concepts 101 for Biblical Hebrew* is also helpful. Another way to brush up on developments in the use of Hebrew in exegesis is *Advances in the Study of Biblical Hebrew and Aramaic* by Benjamin J. Noonan.

If you need more encouragement or additional strategies to relearn or strengthen your knowledge of Biblical Hebrew, I highly recommend *Hebrew For Life: Strategies for Learning, Retaining, and Reviving Biblical Hebrew* by Adam J. Howell, Benjamin L. Merkle, and Robert L. Plummer.

Is it too much to ask someone who plans to invest his or her life in teaching a particular document to learn the language in which that document was written? My plea is, take the time to learn or relearn Hebrew. The investment will enrich your preaching of Old Testament narratives. Let me show you how.

The Wonderful World of Discourse Analysis

Over the years, literary scholars have helped us recover the way to read Old Testament narrative with sensitivity to its literary artistry. At the same time, Old Testament scholars working in the field of discourse analysis, or text linguistics, have helped us look beyond the grammar of individual clauses to see how clauses are connected to form larger discourse units.[2] Discourse analysis is a subdiscipline of general linguistics. Walter Bodine explains the larger discipline: "Linguistics is the study of language as language, in contrast to the study of any specific language. The term 'general linguistics' comprehends all of the varied theoretical positions of linguists."[3] As related to biblical studies, general linguistics would include aspects such as phonology (the sound system of a language), morphology (the study of forms or the smallest meaningful units of a language),

---

2. For simplicity, I will use the expression "discourse analysis" rather than "text linguistics" because I tend to use them interchangeably. Bodine observes, "What has been called 'discourse analysis' in the United States has more often been known as 'text linguistics' in Europe" (Bodine, *Discourse Analysis*, 2).

3. Bodine, "Linguistics and Biblical Studies," 327.

syntax (the study of the structure of such units as phrases, clauses, and larger combinations), semantics (the study of the expression of meaning in language), discourse analysis (the linguistic study of units that are larger than the sentence), historical/comparative linguistics (the study of language development over time and the systematic comparison of related languages), and graphemics (the study of writing systems).[4]

Table B.1

Notations Used in Discourse Analysis

qatal	perfect
yiqtol	imperfect
qetol	imperative
qotel	participle
wayyiqtol	preterite or imperfect with *waw* consecutive
weqatal	*waw* (w) plus perfect
NC	verbless noun (nominal) clause
w	marks the presence of a *waw* (w)
0	marks the absence of a *waw* (w)
x	indicates pre-verb material; something else in the clause "fronts" the verb

As a subdiscipline of general linguistics, discourse analysis focuses on blocks larger than the sentence, traditionally the largest unit of syntactical analysis.[5] Some of the earliest Old Testament scholars to work with discourse analysis were associated with the Summer Institute of Linguistics (SIL), the school behind the Wycliffe Bible Translators. They worked primarily from a functionalist approach to linguistics.

Admittedly, the world of discourse analysis and its larger discipline, linguistics, can lead you deep into the weeds with its complexity. However, its most basic insights are utterly helpful. The volume I referenced above by Benjamin J. Noonan, *Advances in the Study of Biblical Hebrew and Aramaic*, contains a concise discussion of the major approaches to linguistics, as well as a chapter on discourse analysis.[6]

---

4. Bodine, *Discourse Analysis*, 3–4.
5. Bodine, *Discourse Analysis*, 1–5. See also Bodine, "Linguistics and Biblical Studies," 330. Evangelicals have written two readable introductions to general linguistics for Bible students: Cotterell and Turner, *Linguistics and Biblical Interpretation*; and Silva, *God, Language, and Scripture*.
6. Noonan, *Advances*, 35–69, 145–80.

Discourse analysts work their way through a text clause by clause, observing the verb forms and their position in each clause. This is the key to understanding how clauses work together to form a larger discourse. To engage in this kind of analysis, exegetes must brush up on the notations that describe verbal forms and their positioning in a clause (see table B.1).

For example, a construction such as וְהִיא שָׁלְחָה (Gen. 38:25) is described as *w* + x + *qatal*. This notes that a perfect *(qatal)* verb is preceded by something, in this case a pronoun. The *w* marks the presence of *waw* (וֹ) before the pronoun. However, if the construction lacked the *waw* (וֹ) and read as הִיא שָׁלְחָה, then the notation appears as 0 + x + *qatal*. A form like וְשִׁחֵת (Gen. 38:9) is simply described as *w* + *qatal* or else as *weqatal*.[7]

So what's the payoff? Basically, discourse analysis will yield two results. First, it will help interpreters discover which clauses in the story carry the main storyline and which clauses contain background information that is subsidiary to the main line. Second, it will help interpreters discover which sections of the text are "marked" or emphasized.

Verbal Forms and Narrative Sequence

Paying attention to verbal forms can help us track the main storyline of a narrative. Essentially, narrative texts consist of narrated discourse (nonquotational clauses) and direct speech (quotational clauses). The narrated discourse sections divide into foreground and background (see table B.2). Some clauses provide foreground—that is, "the main flow of thought of a text."[8] Other clauses provide background—that is, "any peripheral information that does not move the main flow of thought forward."[9]

Table B.2

A Clause Taxonomy for Biblical Hebrew Narrative

1. Narrated discourse (nonquotational clauses)
    a. Continuation (foreground)
    b. Pause (background)
2. Direct speech (quotational clauses)

---

7. For the full range of possibilities, see Den Exter Blokland, "Clause-Analysis," 87–89.
8. Patton, Putnam, and Van Pelt, *Basics of Hebrew Discourse*, 43.
9. Patton, Putnam, and Van Pelt, *Basics of Hebrew Discourse*, 43.

Continuation (Foreground)

Generally, Hebrew Bible scholars recognize that *wayyiqtol* verbs introduce the "principal events of the narrative story (foreground of the narration)."[10] Earlier studies suggested that *wayyiqtol* clauses indicated temporal succession. That is, they presented "chronologically successive events."[11] However, more recent studies argue that *wayyiqtol* forms simply signify continuation, whether they refer to "logically and/or temporally consecutive actions" (often) or even to "background or descriptive information *within* a narrative" (seldom).[12]

Pause (Background)

Clauses with other verb forms pause the narrative, indicating background or a subsidiary line in the narrative. Patton, Putnam, and Van Pelt correctly observe: "Since narrative is carried forward by the continuative form *wayyiqtol*, any departure from the *wayyiqtol* merits close attention."[13] Bryan Rocine provides a helpful illustration of the difference between the main line and the secondary line of a story. Think of the narrative as a video. "The mainline forms keep the video playing. The off-the-line [background] forms slow or even freeze the video for commentary, often at the points of greatest emphasis."[14] David Dawson concurs, noting that "material in non-mainline clauses adds to the narrative, not by moving it forward, but by contributing background information and creating a setting for the narrative."[15] Below, I have briefly discussed some of the common ways that a narrator pauses his account.

---

10. Van der Merwe, Naudé, and Kroeze, *Biblical Hebrew Reference Grammar*, 189.

11. Bergen, "Evil Spirits and Eccentric Grammar," 325. John H. Sailhamer describes *wayyiqtol* verbal patterns as providing "the effect of sequence in time" (*Pentateuch as Narrative*, 13). See also Niccacci, "Analysis of Biblical Narrative," 176–79.

12. Van der Merwe, Naudé, and Kroeze, *Biblical Hebrew Reference Grammar*, 189, 191. Elizabeth Robar proposes "that *wayyiqtol* does not mark sequentiality/succession, nor does it mark foregrounding, but it does mark something closely related: it has to do with schematic continuity." She defines this as "the conceptual (and almost always structural) bond between all the material held together within a single paragraph" (*Verb and the Paragraph*, 77). Noting her concerns, I still find the distinction between "foreground" and "background" helpful in narrative analysis—even though "continuation" may be more accurate or precise than "foreground." Another alternative is to speak of "mainline" and "secondary line" (or "subsidiary line") clauses. Even Patton, Putnam, and Van Pelt retain the "foreground/background" distinction, though they refer to *wayyiqtol* verbs as a continuative form that sometimes continues background (*Basics of Hebrew Discourse*, 43, 66–67).

13. Patton, Putnam, and Van Pelt, *Basics of Hebrew Discourse*, 73.

14. Rocine, *Learning Biblical Hebrew*, 53.

15. Dawson, *Text-Linguistics and Biblical Hebrew*, 126. Dawson likens mainline clauses to "bones" and off-line [background] clauses to "joints."

X + Qatal

One of the most common interruptions of a *wayyiqtol* sequence is by a *qatal* verb preceded by a *waw* (ו) and then another element—either a subject, an object, or an adverb. Hebrew linguists refer to this construction as *waw* + x + *qatal* (or simply as x + *qatal*). Keep in mind that *wayyiqtol* verbs are always clause-initial. That is, nothing else precedes them. They stand first in a clause. Most Hebrew Bible scholars argue that the normal pattern in a clause is verb-subject-object (V-S-O), although this has been challenged recently by Robert Holmstedt.[16] If the normal pattern is V-S-O, when the verb in Biblical Hebrew is preceded by any other constituent (noun, adverb, etc.), marked word order occurs.[17] So the presence of a subject, object, or adverb between the *waw* and the *qatal* verb is another clue that the narrator has "paused" the narration to make a comment. Some linguists refer to this as "topicalization"—a focus-shifting function.[18] An x + *yiqtol* (imperfect) clause functions in a similar way, yet it describes habitual actions.[19] Similarly, an x + *qotel* (participle) expresses continuous actions or habitual events.[20]

Nominal Verbless Clauses

Nominal verbless clauses also move the storyline from foreground to background. According to Longacre, nominal verbless clauses provide information about the narrative's setting. He explains, "Such clauses offer necessary detail as to participants, props, and circumstances without which a story cannot be adequately staged—or restaged at crucial junctions—and without which the reader might not understand what is reported as transpiring."[21] Similarly, van Wolde claims their function is "the presentation of *background* information in which a situation, circumstance, or

---

16. Barry L. Bandstra explains, "Biblical Hebrew is a verb-first language. When an explicit subject is present, the expected and most frequent order of constituents in narrative verbal clauses is V-S-O. When the subject is implicit in the verbal form, the order is V-O" (Bandstra, "Word Order and Emphasis," 115). For an overview of the current debate, including Robert Holmstedt's challenges to the V-S-O view, see Noonan, *Advances*, 181–93.
17. Van der Merwe, "Discourse Linguistics and Biblical Hebrew Grammar," 43n34. Cf. van der Merwe, Naudé, and Kroeze, *Biblical Hebrew Reference Grammar*, 61; Patton, Putnam, and Van Pelt, *Basics of Hebrew Discourse*, 88.
18. Rocine, *Learning Biblical Hebrew*, 73.
19. Van der Merwe, Naudé, and Kroeze, *Biblical Hebrew Reference Grammar*, 162.
20. Van der Merwe, Naudé, and Kroeze, *Biblical Hebrew Reference Grammar*, 187.
21. Longacre, "Discourse Perspective on the Hebrew Verb," 179.

event is depicted that occurs simultaneously with the sequence of actions expressed in the preceding foreground clause."[22]

Weqatal

A *weqatal* form also moves the storyline from foreground to background information.[23] Van der Merwe, Naudé, and Kroeze point out that "the most typical semantic value of *wəqātal* in narration is iterative-habitual actions in the past."[24] For example, Genesis 29:3 uses four *weqatal* forms to describe the four steps that shepherds would typically take to water flocks from a well. This sets up the account of Jacob's significant deed for Rachel of single-handedly removing the rock from the well—a task normally completed when several shepherds are present.[25] Second, "an isolated *weqatal* in the narrative framework marks a climactic or at least a pivotal event."[26] For example, in Judges 3:20–23, a long string of *wayyiqtol* forms describes Ehud's assassination of King Eglon. However, the final act of bolting the door is reported with a *weqatal* form. Longacre takes this as a case of special marking.[27] Rocine considers an isolated *weqatal* a "surrogate mainline" since it advances the action like a *wayyiqtol* form does.[28] Longacre also argues that the *weqatal* form of the verb *hayah* (וְהָיָה) marks significant background or important events to follow.[29] For example, the action of the "battle" between David and Goliath in 1 Samuel 17:48–49 unfolds through a series of *wayyiqtol* forms. However, the first clause begins with וְהָיָה.[30] The clause indicates that the Philistine took the initiative to attack David.

---

22. Van Wolde, "Verbless Clause," 130.

23. Van der Merwe, Naudé, and Kroeze, *Biblical Hebrew Reference Grammar*, 196.

24. Van der Merwe, Naudé, and Kroeze, *Biblical Hebrew Reference Grammar*, 196. See also Longacre, "*Weqatal* Forms in Biblical Hebrew Prose," 57, 95; Patton, Putnam, and Van Pelt, *Basics of Hebrew Discourse*, 74–75.

25. For several additional examples and a fuller discussion of the Genesis 29:3 example, see Longacre, "*Weqatal* Forms in Biblical Hebrew Prose," 57–66.

26. Longacre "*Weqatal* Forms in Biblical Hebrew Prose," 71, 95. Tal Goldfajn argues, "Wayyiqtol and weqatal seem to be saying 'after that' where 'that' refers back to the last event narrated. In the case of the weqatal form it is mainly an 'after that' of future events . . . while the 'after that' of the wayyiqtol form refers to past events" (*Word Order and Time*, 143).

27. For a fuller discussion of this example and several others, see Longacre "*Weqatal* Forms in Biblical Hebrew Prose," 71–84.

28. Rocine, *Learning Biblical Hebrew*, 212–13.

29. Longacre "*Weqatal* Forms in Biblical Hebrew Prose," 84.

30. For further examples, see Longacre "*Weqatal* Forms in Biblical Hebrew Prose," 84–91.

Most English versions (NIV, NKJV, NASB) translate it as a temporal clause.

Wayehi (וַיְהִי)

The *wayyiqtol* form וַיְהִי (from the root היה, "be, happen") often functions as a discourse marker, signaling that an event or scene follows the preceding event or scene (see below under "Discourse Markers"). The timing of the scene or event is specified by the temporal expression following וַיְהִי.[31] For example, 2 Samuel 11:14 says: רֶפֶס דָּוִד בַּתִּכְיוֹ רֶקְבָב יְהָיוֹ בָּאֶל־יוֹא. Both the NIV and ESV leave וַיְהִי untranslated: "In the morning David wrote a letter to Joab." The KJV translates it as, "And it came to pass in the morning, that David wrote a letter to Joab." Occasionally, וַיְהִי simply functions as a *wayyiqtol* verb form, meaning "was, came, became."[32]

Clauses Beginning with a Conjunction or Relative Pronoun

Forms such as כִּי (causal conjunction), כַּאֲשֶׁר (comparative conjunction), and אֲשֶׁר (relative pronoun) are grammatically subordinate to the main clause that precedes them. Because *wayyiqtol* forms are clause initial, any conjunctions or relative pronouns must be followed by *qatal* forms.[33] By virtue of their function and the verb form they contain, such clauses supply backgrounded rather than foregrounded information. Niccacci comments: "Main and dependent sentences are identified not only by the absence or presence, respectively, of subordinating conjunctions such as *ki*, *'asher*, *lᵉma'an*, etc. They are also identified by the place of the finite verb: first place in main sentences, second place in subordinate sentences. When subordinating conjunctions are present, the subordination is both grammatical and syntactic; otherwise, it is syntactic only but no less real."[34]

Direct Speech

While the quotation formulas (used to introduce direct speech) in *wayyiqtol* forms advance the main line of the narrative, the actual quotation

---

31. Van der Merwe, Naudé, and Kroeze, *Biblical Hebrew Reference Grammar*, 429.
32. Van der Merwe, Naudé, and Kroeze, *Biblical Hebrew Reference Grammar*, 429. Patton, Putnam, and Van Pelt suggest four categories of common discourse functions (*Basics of Hebrew Discourse*, 71–73).
33. Rocine, *Learning Biblical Hebrew*, 68.
34. Niccacci, "Basic Facts and Theory," 198.

does not advance it "no matter how long and complex the direct speech is."[35] These quotations are "embedded" in the storyline.

What about doing discourse analysis with direct (embedded) speech? Unless a quotation consists of several sentences, discourse analysis becomes the kind of microanalysis that may not help preachers. Bandstra notes that "compared to narrative discourse, it [spoken discourse] allows greater flexibility. Nonverbal clauses are more frequent, as well as single words or fragmentary dialogue."[36] Therefore, the flexibility of direct speech makes it harder to pin down conclusions.

However, for those interpreters who are interested, Niccacci argues that the main line of communication in a direct speech is initiated by *qatal* forms (0 + *qatal*) for past action, simple nominal clauses for present, and x + *yiqtol* forms (followed by *weqatal* forms) for future action.[37] Subsidiary lines of communication that break into the main line of direct speech are indicated by the same forms that break into the main line of narrative or nonquotational material: x + *qatal* for the past, simple nominal clauses for the present, and x + *yiqtol* for the future. Of course, direct speech often utilizes imperative forms since characters frequently give directives to other characters.

To look at this from another angle, chains of *weqatal* forms in direct speech function like chains of *wayyiqtol* forms in narrative (nonquotational) materials. They continue the main line of the narrative.[38] For example, David's declaration to Goliath in 1 Samuel 17:46 begins with an x + *yiqtol* form and then proceeds with a series of *weqatal* forms: "This day Yahweh will deliver [x + *yiqtol*] you into my hand, and I will strike [*weqatal*] you and remove [*weqatal*] your head from you. And I will give [*weqatal*] the dead bodies of the army of the Philistines this day to the birds of the sky and the wild beasts of the earth, and all the earth will know [*weqatal*] that there is a God in Israel."[39]

---

35. Niccacci, "Analysis of Biblical Narrative," 180. For a thorough study of the "quotative frame"—that is, the report that introduces the quotation—see Miller, *Representation of Speech*. For a more concise discussion, see Miller, "Introducing Direct Discourse," 199–241.

36. Bandstra, "Word Order and Emphasis," 119.

37. For this analysis, see Niccacci, "Analysis of Biblical Narrative," 176–77. See also Niccacci, "Basic Facts and Theory," 182–87.

38. Niccacci, "Analysis of Biblical Narrative," 178. See also Patton, Putnam, and Van Pelt, *Basics of Hebrew Discourse*, 77–78.

39. Author's translation. The verb forms are underlined for convenience. The initial x + *yiqtol* form consists of the verb יְסַגֶּרְךָ fronted by the temporal construction הַיּוֹם הַזֶּה.

Bryan Rocine helpfully classifies the type of material in direct speech into four categories: predictive narrative, instructional discourse, hortatory discourse, and historical narrative.[40] Then, throughout his grammar, he describes how each of the four types distinguishes between mainline and off-the-line clauses. He notes that while historical narrative can be found inside direct speech, it acts a bit differently in this setting.[41]

Marked Text

In addition to helping interpreters distinguish between continuation (foreground) and pause (background), discourse analysis also helps interpreters spot sections of marked or emphasized text. Robert Bergen offers a helpful explanation:

> Since written language is a medium for the transference of facts, ideas, beliefs, and attitudes, it follows that a writer will drop some hints within a text to assist the reader in the task of figuring out which parts are more important than others. In other words, language texts are both semantically and grammatically contoured. The creator of a text *intends* some of the materials to be interpreted as more important than others.
>
> One means that authors often use to mark semantically noteworthy materials is with statistically rare . . . features, such as rare spellings, odd lexical items, irregular clause structures, and other higher-level deviations from established norms within a given genre. . . . Writers often encode one portion of a text as more important than others through the use of these statistically unusual features, so by identifying them a text analyst may predict with some degree of accuracy those portions of a text that the writer intended to be most important. Portions of a text identifiable by this means are considered to be "grammatically marked."[42]

Joshua 3:14–17 provides a prime example of how a cluster of non-*wayyiqtol* verbs can slow the pace of a narrative. After an initial וַיְהִי to mark the beginning of the episode (another וַיְהִי form begins a new episode in 4:1), the non-*wayyiqtol* verbs in the next six clauses pause the action until a *wayyiqtol* form (וַיַּעַמְדוּ) finally appears at the beginning of verse 16.

---

40. Rocine, *Learning Biblical Hebrew*, 62–63.
41. Rocine, *Learning Biblical Hebrew*, 62–63.
42. Bergen, "Evil Spirits and Eccentric Grammar," 321–22.

Winther-Nielsen describes the effect of the "miraculous syntax" of the episode: "Several temporal descriptive clauses *in slow motion* describe how the waters suddenly stopped when the feet of the priests were dipped into the water."[43] "And after this major event [indicated by the *wayyiqtol* form וַיַּעַמְדוּ], the story stops completely."[44] Further backgrounded clauses then furnish additional specifics. Finally, another *wayyiqtol* form appears in verse 17 and it, too, is followed by further backgrounded clauses that reiterate what has already been narrated. David Howard makes a similar analysis about the effect of the syntax in 3:14–17 on the pace of the narrative:

> Here the narrative slows to a crawl, so that the reader can savor the wonder of the miracle and view it from as many different perspectives as possible. The author, by writing in this way, affirms God's greatness and power and intervention on his people's behalf. The point is not so much that the people were able to cross over the Jordan, but the *manner* in which they were able to cross: by a glorious and mighty miracle of God.[45]

Discourse Markers

Interpreters will also want to note the various discourse markers that appear in both narrated discourse (nonquotational clauses) and direct speech (quotational clauses). Technically, the category "discourse marker" does not refer to a grammatical word class. It refers instead to the function that various word classes—like conjunctions, adverbs, and even verbs—fulfill in a text or discourse.[46] Discourse markers typically show the relationship between clauses.

Here are a few examples of discourse markers that play a prominent role in Hebrew narrative.[47] As previously noted, וַיְהִי often signals the beginning of a new narrative and a shift of time—whether at the beginning of a narrative or within it. The infinitive construct form לֵאמֹר, sometimes translated as "saying," introduces reported speech.[48] The particle form וְהִנֵּה often denotes surprise (mirativity, to use a linguistic term) on the part of a character when

---

43. Winther-Nielsen, "Miraculous Grammar," 308 (emphasis added).
44. Winther-Nielsen, "Miraculous Grammar," 310.
45. Howard, *Joshua*, 129.
46. Van der Merwe, Naudé, and Kroeze, *Biblical Hebrew Reference Grammar*, 382.
47. For a complete list of discourse markers and a helpful discussion, see Patton, Putnam, and Van Pelt, *Basics of Hebrew Discourse*, 51–60.
48. Van der Merwe, Naudé, and Kroeze, *Biblical Hebrew Reference Grammar*, 176–77.

a change of movement or scene is involved.⁴⁹ More recent English versions leave it untranslated, while older versions often render it as "behold" or "and behold." For example, here is the NASB translation of Genesis 37:29: "Now Reuben returned to the pit, *and behold* [וְהִנֵּה], Joseph was not in the pit; so he tore his garments." What Reuben discovered clearly surprised him. Recent translations like the NIV, ESV, and CSB opt for translating וְהִנֵּה in Genesis 37:29 as "and saw that." Unfortunately, this does not convey the surprise indicated by this particle form. It is worth noting that since it stands at the head of a clause, it always introduces a non-*wayyiqtol* clause. Thus, it creates a pause in the narrative. The relative particle אֲשֶׁר is another common discourse marker that usually introduces either a relative clause—one that modifies a subject, object, or adjunct—or a complement clause after verbs of perception or speech.⁵⁰ Finally, the conjunction כִּי has at least two main purposes in the nonquotational clauses in a narrative. First, it introduces a cause or causal grounds for the main clause that precedes it.⁵¹ For example, in Judges 18:1, כִּי introduces a clause that explains why the Danites were seeking a place to settle: they had not yet taken possession of an inheritance. Second, after verbs of perception such as "see" (ראה), "know" (ידע), "hear" (שמע), or "remember" (זכר), כִּי introduces what a character realizes or understands—not simply what they physically saw or heard or thought. As Yael Avrahami notes, "the expression 'to see that' (ראה כי) indicates an evaluation of the situation, and not just sight or consciousness."⁵²

Working with the Data

How can interpreters collect and utilize the data discussed above in their exegesis of Old Testament narrative texts? Here is an overview of the process I suggest. The first step is to go through the narrative and identify the verb form of each narrated discourse (nonquotational) clause—whether *wayyiqtol*, *qatal*, etc. Some clauses, of course, will be nominal verbless

---

49. Van der Merwe, Naudé, and Kroeze, *Biblical Hebrew Reference Grammar*, 412–13. In some instances, the situation observed is not surprising but is simply a confirmation of what is expected.
50. See van der Merwe, Naudé, and Kroeze, *Biblical Hebrew Reference Grammar*, 304–6.
51. See van der Merwe, Naudé, and Kroeze, *Biblical Hebrew Reference Grammar*, 434.
52. Yael Avrahami, *Senses of Scripture*, 168. Patton, Putnam, and Van Pelt refer to this discourse function as "expansion" since "the כִּי clause fills out what was said or seen or known" (*Basics of Hebrew Discourse*, 55). However, it is better to describe the function as "realization" since there are ראה כי ("saw that") constructions in the Hebrew Bible where physical perception (seeing) is not involved! See Gen. 38:14; 42:1–2; Exod. 32:1.

clauses. Remember that narrative texts contain both narrated discourse (nonquotational clauses) and direct speech (quotational clauses). In order to track the flow of the narrative, we are looking only at the verb forms (or lack of them) in the narrated discourse. Later, we can look at the verb forms in direct speech if necessary. This approach essentially separates the narrated discourse clauses into continuation clauses (foreground) and pause clauses (background). The second step is to create a "discourse layout" that provides a visual analysis of how the story flows from clause to clause. This layout will show where the narrative pauses, as well as how much direct speech is embedded into the narrative.[53]

Step 1: Verb Form Identification

One way to record and identify the verb forms in narrated discourse clauses is to mark them with colors as you read through the Hebrew text.[54] You can use colored pencils to underline verbs in a print edition. Or, if you copy and paste the Hebrew text from a Bible software program into a word processing document (such as Microsoft Word), you can use a font color feature. Table B.3 shows the color scheme I use for verb form identification.

Table B.3

A Color Scheme for Verb Identification

Wayyiqtol = Green
Qatal = Orange
Weqatal = Red
Yiqtol = Yellow
Infinitive = Blue
Participle = Purple

This is well worth the time, and it allows you to experience the joy of discovery as you work through the text.

However, there is another way to accomplish this, and it is lightning quick! Logos Bible Software will do this for you instantly if you learn to use its "visual filter" feature. It will take you a few minutes to set up the visual filter (once you learn how to do it). Then, when you apply the filter to a particular edition of the Hebrew Bible, any passage you open will instantly color code each verb according to the color scheme you establish in the visual filter. Even better,

---

53. This is a modification of the approach suggested in Chisholm, *From Exegesis to Exposition*, 135–42.

54. In the first edition of this book I suggested preparing a "Verb Form and Placement" chart to track all the verbs used in a narrative. This chart had fields for the reference (chapter and verse), the Hebrew verb itself, any pre-verb material (in the case of non-*wayyiqtol* forms), and description (whether *wayyiqtol*, x + *qatal*, *weqatal*, etc.). However, this approach was rather tedious compared to the options I am presenting here. Obviously, there are various ways you can develop to track verb identification data.

you can use these visual filters with any English translations that have been morphologically tagged—such as the ESV or the NASB 1995! This makes the information accessible to preachers or Bible students who do not know Hebrew. They can distinguish between continuation (foreground) and pause (background) simply by looking at the colors of the verbs.

Step 2: Discourse Layout

Once you have worked through the narrative and identified the verb forms in narrated discourse clauses, it is time to prepare a discourse layout, which breaks down the narrative into clauses. Simply copy the text from a Bible software program into your word processor. If you are copying text from Logos Bible Software, your verbs will appear in colors—if you created a color scheme using the visual filter feature. If you are copying the biblical text from another source, then you can change the font color of each verb in your word processor. Another alternative is simply to underline all of the verbs. This works better with English text. I suggest that you reserve colors and underlining only for verbs in the narrated discourse (nonquotational) clauses. If you import text with colored verbs from Logos Bible Software, you can easily eliminate the colors in the direct speech clauses by highlighting each direct speech clause and changing all the text to the default color (usually black).

Next, break the narrative down into clauses. Each clause goes on a separate line. Keep the continuation (foreground) clauses—the ones with a *wayyiqtol* verb—at the margin. Then, indent both the pause (background) clauses and the direct speech clauses. If your layout is in Hebrew, I suggest highlighting the pause (background) clauses in gray so that they stand out and are distinct from the direct speech clauses. I also put two asterisks (**) at the beginning and end of each block of direct speech. You can do the same if your layout is in English, although I prefer to put the pause (background) clauses in bold and the direct speech clauses in italics. If you create your layout in English, I also suggest putting a notation in brackets at the end of the pause (background) clauses to indicate whether the verb is a *qatal, weqatal, yiqtol,* infinitive, or participle.

The following discourse layouts for Genesis 38 and Joshua 1 will serve as examples of both the layout and then the insights that they yield.

Genesis 38

For Genesis 38, I have provided two examples of discourse layouts. The first is a layout of the entire chapter in Hebrew (discourse B.1), followed by a layout in English, using the ESV text (discourse B.2).

Discourse Layout B.1

Genesis 38 (Hebrew)

¹וַיְהִי֙ בָּעֵ֣ת הַהִ֔וא
וַיֵּ֥רֶד יְהוּדָ֖ה מֵאֵ֣ת אֶחָ֑יו
וַיֵּ֛ט עַד־אִ֥ישׁ עֲדֻלָּמִ֖י וּשְׁמ֥וֹ חִירָֽה׃
²וַיַּרְא־שָׁ֧ם יְהוּדָ֛ה בַּת־אִ֥ישׁ כְּנַעֲנִ֖י וּשְׁמ֣וֹ שׁ֑וּעַ
וַיִּקָּחֶ֖הָ
וַיָּבֹ֥א אֵלֶֽיהָ׃
³וַתַּ֖הַר
וַתֵּ֣לֶד בֵּ֑ן
וַיִּקְרָ֥א אֶת־שְׁמ֖וֹ עֵֽר׃
⁴וַתַּ֥הַר ע֖וֹד
וַתֵּ֣לֶד בֵּ֑ן
וַתִּקְרָ֥א אֶת־שְׁמ֖וֹ אוֹנָֽן׃
⁵וַתֹּ֤סֶף עוֹד֙
וַתֵּ֣לֶד בֵּ֔ן
וַתִּקְרָ֥א אֶת־שְׁמ֖וֹ שֵׁלָ֑ה
וְהָיָ֥ה בִכְזִ֖יב בְּלִדְתָּ֥הּ אֹתֽוֹ׃
⁶וַיִּקַּ֧ח יְהוּדָ֛ה אִשָּׁ֖ה לְעֵ֣ר בְּכוֹר֑וֹ וּשְׁמָ֖הּ תָּמָֽר׃
⁷וַיְהִ֗י
עֵ֚ר בְּכ֣וֹר יְהוּדָ֔ה רַ֖ע בְּעֵינֵ֣י יְהוָ֑ה
וַיְמִתֵ֖הוּ יְהוָֽה׃
⁸וַיֹּ֤אמֶר יְהוּדָה֙ לְאוֹנָ֔ן
בֹּ֛א אֶל־אֵ֥שֶׁת אָחִ֖יךָ וְיַבֵּ֣ם אֹתָ֑הּ וְהָקֵ֥ם זֶ֖רַע לְאָחִֽיךָ׃
⁹וַיֵּ֣דַע אוֹנָ֔ן כִּ֛י לֹּ֥א ל֖וֹ יִהְיֶ֣ה הַזָּ֑רַע
וְהָיָ֞ה אִם־בָּ֨א אֶל־אֵ֤שֶׁת אָחִיו֙
וְשִׁחֵ֣ת אַ֔רְצָה
לְבִלְתִּ֥י נְתָן־זֶ֖רַע לְאָחִֽיו׃
¹⁰וַיֵּ֛רַע בְּעֵינֵ֥י יְהוָ֖ה אֲשֶׁ֣ר עָשָׂ֑ה
וַיָּ֖מֶת גַּם־אֹתֽוֹ׃
¹¹וַיֹּ֣אמֶר יְהוּדָה֩ לְתָמָ֨ר
שְׁבִ֧י אַלְמָנָ֣ה בֵית־אָבִ֗יךְ עַד־יִגְדַּל֙ שֵׁלָ֣ה בְנִ֔י
כִּ֣י אָמַ֔ר

208   Appendix B

Using Hebrew in Narrative Exegesis

פֶּן־יָמוּת גַּם־הוּא כְּאֶחָיו
וַתֵּלֶךְ תָּמָר
וַתֵּשֶׁב בֵּית אָבִיהָ:
12 וַיִּרְבּוּ הַיָּמִים
וַתָּמָת בַּת־שׁוּעַ אֵשֶׁת־יְהוּדָה
וַיִּנָּחֶם יְהוּדָה
וַיַּעַל עַל־גֹּזֲזֵי צֹאנוֹ הוּא וְחִירָה רֵעֵהוּ הָעֲדֻלָּמִי תִּמְנָתָה:
13 וַיֻּגַּד לְתָמָר לֵאמֹר
הִנֵּה חָמִיךְ עֹלֶה תִמְנָתָה לָגֹז צֹאנוֹ:
14 וַתָּסַר בִּגְדֵי אַלְמְנוּתָהּ מֵעָלֶיהָ
וַתְּכַס בַּצָּעִיף
וַתִּתְעַלָּף
וַתֵּשֶׁב בְּפֶתַח עֵינַיִם אֲשֶׁר עַל־דֶּרֶךְ תִּמְנָתָה
כִּי רָאֲתָה כִּי־גָדַל שֵׁלָה
וְהִוא לֹא־נִתְּנָה לוֹ לְאִשָּׁה:
15 וַיִּרְאֶהָ יְהוּדָה
וַיַּחְשְׁבֶהָ לְזוֹנָה
כִּי כִסְּתָה פָּנֶיהָ:
16 וַיֵּט אֵלֶיהָ אֶל־הַדֶּרֶךְ
וַיֹּאמֶר
הָבָה־נָּא אָבוֹא אֵלַיִךְ
כִּי לֹא יָדַע כִּי כַלָּתוֹ הִוא
וַתֹּאמֶר
מַה־תִּתֶּן־לִי כִּי תָבוֹא אֵלָי:
17 וַיֹּאמֶר
אָנֹכִי אֲשַׁלַּח גְּדִי־עִזִּים מִן־הַצֹּאן
וַתֹּאמֶר
אִם־תִּתֵּן עֵרָבוֹן עַד שָׁלְחֶךָ:
18 וַיֹּאמֶר
מָה הָעֵרָבוֹן אֲשֶׁר אֶתֶּן־לָךְ
וַתֹּאמֶר
חֹתָמְךָ וּפְתִילֶךָ וּמַטְּךָ אֲשֶׁר בְּיָדֶךָ
וַיִּתֶּן־לָהּ
וַיָּבֹא אֵלֶיהָ
וַתַּהַר לוֹ:
19 וַתָּקָם
וַתֵּלֶךְ
וַתָּסַר צְעִיפָהּ מֵעָלֶיהָ
וַתִּלְבַּשׁ בִּגְדֵי אַלְמְנוּתָהּ:
20 וַיִּשְׁלַח יְהוּדָה אֶת־גְּדִי הָעִזִּים בְּיַד רֵעֵהוּ הָעֲדֻלָּמִי לָקַחַת הָעֵרָבוֹן מִיַּד הָאִשָּׁה

וְלֹא מְצָאָהּ:
²¹וַיִּשְׁאַל אֶת־אַנְשֵׁי מְקֹמָהּ לֵאמֹר
אַיֵּה הַקְּדֵשָׁה הִוא בָעֵינַיִם עַל־הַדָּרֶךְ
וַיֹּאמְרוּ
לֹא־הָיְתָה בָזֶה קְדֵשָׁה:
²²וַיָּשָׁב אֶל־יְהוּדָה
וַיֹּאמֶר
לֹא מְצָאתִיהָ וְגַם אַנְשֵׁי הַמָּקוֹם אָמְרוּ לֹא־הָיְתָה בָזֶה קְדֵשָׁה:
²³וַיֹּאמֶר יְהוּדָה
תִּקַּח־לָהּ פֶּן נִהְיֶה לָבוּז הִנֵּה שָׁלַחְתִּי הַגְּדִי הַזֶּה וְאַתָּה לֹא מְצָאתָהּ:
²⁴וַיְהִי| כְּמִשְׁלֹשׁ חֳדָשִׁים
וַיֻּגַּד לִיהוּדָה לֵאמֹר
זָנְתָה תָּמָר כַּלָּתֶךָ וְגַם הִנֵּה הָרָה לִזְנוּנִים
וַיֹּאמֶר יְהוּדָה
הוֹצִיאוּהָ וְתִשָּׂרֵף:
²⁵הִוא מוּצֵאת
וְהִיא שָׁלְחָה אֶל־חָמִיהָ לֵאמֹר
לְאִישׁ אֲשֶׁר־אֵלֶּה לּוֹ אָנֹכִי הָרָה
וַתֹּאמֶר
הַכֶּר־נָא לְמִי הַחֹתֶמֶת וְהַפְּתִילִים וְהַמַּטֶּה הָאֵלֶּה:
²⁶וַיַּכֵּר יְהוּדָה
וַיֹּאמֶר
צָדְקָה מִמֶּנִּי כִּי־עַל־כֵּן לֹא־נְתַתִּיהָ לְשֵׁלָה בְנִי
וְלֹא־יָסַף עוֹד לְדַעְתָּהּ:
²⁷וַיְהִי בְּעֵת לִדְתָּהּ
וְהִנֵּה תְאוֹמִים בְּבִטְנָהּ:
²⁸וַיְהִי בְלִדְתָּהּ
וַיִּתֶּן־יָד
וַתִּקַּח הַמְיַלֶּדֶת
וַתִּקְשֹׁר עַל־יָדוֹ שָׁנִי לֵאמֹר
זֶה יָצָא רִאשֹׁנָה:
²⁹וַיְהִי| כְּמֵשִׁיב יָדוֹ
וְהִנֵּה יָצָא אָחִיו
וַתֹּאמֶר
מַה־פָּרַצְתָּ עָלֶיךָ פָּרֶץ
וַיִּקְרָא שְׁמוֹ פָּרֶץ:
³⁰וְאַחַר יָצָא אָחִיו אֲשֶׁר עַל־יָדוֹ הַשָּׁנִי
וַיִּקְרָא שְׁמוֹ זָרַח:

Using Hebrew in Narrative Exegesis

| Discourse Layout B.2 |

Genesis 38 (ESV)

¹It <u>happened</u> at that time
that Judah <u>went down</u> from his brothers
and <u>turned aside</u> to a certain Adullamite, whose name was Hirah.[a]
²There Judah <u>saw</u> the daughter of a certain Canaanite whose name was Shua.
He <u>took</u> her
and <u>went in</u> to her,
³and she <u>conceived</u>
and <u>bore</u> a son,
and he <u>called</u> his name Er.
⁴She <u>conceived</u> again
and <u>bore</u> a son,
and she <u>called</u> his name Onan.
⁵Yet again she <u>bore</u> a son,
and she <u>called</u> his name Shelah.
    Judah was in Chezib when she bore him. [weqatal + infinitive construct]
⁶And Judah <u>took</u> a wife for Er his firstborn, and her name was Tamar.
⁷But [it <u>happened</u> that]
    Er, Judah's firstborn, was wicked in the sight of the LORD, [nominal cls]
and the LORD <u>put him to death</u>.
⁸Then Judah <u>said</u> to Onan,
    "Go in to your brother's wife and perform the duty of a brother-in-law to her,
    and raise up offspring for your brother."
⁹But Onan <u>knew</u>
    that the offspring <u>would not be</u> his. [yiqtol]
    So [it <u>happened</u> that] [weqatal of "to be"]
    whenever he <u>went in</u> to his brother's wife [qatal]
    he <u>would waste</u> the semen on the ground, [weqatal]
    so as not <u>to give</u> offspring to his brother. [infinitive]
¹⁰And what he did <u>was wicked</u> in the sight of the LORD,
and he <u>put him to death</u> also.
¹¹Then Judah <u>said</u> to Tamar his daughter-in-law,
    "Remain a widow in your father's house, till Shelah my son grows up"—
    for he <u>feared</u>[b] [qatal]
    that he would die, like his brothers.
So Tamar <u>went</u>
and <u>remained</u> in her father's house.

---

[a] Technically, "whose name was Hirah" could be indented on a separate line because it is a nominal verbless cause. However, the pause is so slight I have chosen to keep it with the preceding clause. I have followed this practice every time a character is named throughout this narrative.

[b] The term here is actually "said" (אמר), and the italicized line that follows is direct speech.

¹²In the course of time [lit. "the days <u>became many</u>"]
the wife of Judah, Shua's daughter, <u>died</u>.
When Judah <u>was comforted</u>,
he <u>went up</u> to Timnah to his sheepshearers, he and his friend Hirah the Adullamite.
¹³And when Tamar <u>was told</u>,ᶜ
    "Your father-in-law is going up to Timnah to shear his sheep,"
¹⁴she <u>took off</u> her widow's garments
and <u>covered</u> herself with a veil,
<u>wrapping</u>ᵈ herself up,
and <u>sat</u> at the entrance to Enaim, which is on the road to Timnah.
    For she <u>saw</u> that Shelah was <u>grown up</u>, [*qatal; qatal*]
    and she <u>had not been given</u> to him in marriage. [*qatal*]
¹⁵When Judah saw her,
he <u>thought</u> she was a prostitute,
    for she had covered her face. [*qatal*]
¹⁶He <u>turned</u> to her at the roadside
and <u>said</u>,
    "Come, let me come in to you,"
    for he did not know that she was his daughter-in-law. [*qatal*]
She <u>said</u>,
    "What will you give me, that you may come in to me?"
¹⁷He <u>answered</u>,
    "I will send you a young goat from the flock."
And she <u>said</u>,
    "If you give me a pledge, until you send it—"
¹⁸He <u>said</u>,
    "What pledge shall I give you?"
She <u>replied</u>,
    "Your signet and your cord and your staff that is in your hand."
So he <u>gave</u> them to her
and <u>went in</u> to her,
and she <u>conceived</u> by him.
¹⁹Then she <u>arose</u>
and <u>went away</u>,
and <u>taking off</u> her veil she put on the garments of her widowhood.
²⁰When Judah <u>sent</u> the young goat by his friend the Adullamite
    to <u>take back</u> the pledge from the woman's hand,ᵉ
he did not <u>find</u> her.ᶠ

ᶜ Here, the verb "told" is actually followed by "saying" (לֵאמֹר), which the ESV leaves untranslated since it functions as a marker of direct speech. This is also the case in verses 21, 24, 25, and 28.

ᵈ Here, and at a few other places in the narrative, the ESV translates *wayyiqtol* forms as participles. This is fine because it makes for a less choppy English translation. However, by keeping these clauses at the left margin, it is clear that the verb is a *wayyiqtol*.

ᵉ The verb "to take back" is an infinitive. Since it completes the main clause, I have not put it in bold print.

ᶠ Even though this clause contains a *qatal*, it does so because the verb is negated. Thus, the verb still continues the action (foreground).

²¹And he <u>asked</u> the men of the place,
   "Where is the cult prostitute who was at Enaim at the roadside?"
And they <u>said</u>,
   "No cult prostitute has been here."
²²So he <u>returned</u> to Judah
and <u>said</u>,
   "I have not found her. Also, the men of the place said, 'No cult prostitute has been here.'"
²³And Judah <u>replied</u>,
   "Let her keep the things as her own, or we shall be laughed at. You see, I sent this young goat, and you did not find her."
²⁴[It <u>happened that</u>] About three months later
Judah <u>was told</u>,
   "Tamar your daughter-in-law has been immoral. Moreover, she is pregnant by immorality."
And Judah <u>said</u>,
   "Bring her out, and let her be burned."
   ²⁵**As she was being brought out,** [participle]
   she sent word to her father-in-law, [*qatal*]
   "By the man to whom these belong, I am pregnant."
And she <u>said</u>,
   "Please identify whose these are, the signet and the cord and the staff."
²⁶Then Judah <u>identified</u> them
and <u>said</u>,
   "She is more righteous than I, since I did not give her to my son Shelah."
And he <u>did not know</u> her again.
²⁷[It <u>happened that</u>] When the time of her labor <u>came</u>,⁹
   there were twins in her womb. [*hinneh* ("behold") + nominal clause]
²⁸And [it <u>happened that</u>] when she was <u>in labor</u>,
one <u>put out</u> a hand,
and the midwife <u>took</u>
and <u>tied</u> a scarlet thread on his hand, <u>saying,</u>
   "This one came out first."
²⁹But [it <u>happened that</u>] as he <u>drew back</u> his hand,
   behold, his brother came out. [*qatal*]
And she <u>said</u>,
   "What a breach you have made for yourself!"
Therefore his name <u>was called</u> Perez.
   ³⁰**Afterward his brother came out with the scarlet thread on his hand,** [*qatal*]
and his name <u>was called</u> Zerah.

---

⁹ Once again, an infinitive form completes the clause; so I have let it remain as part of the main clause. This also occurs in verse 28.

Exactly how does a discourse layout help an interpreter? It makes it easy to spot where various forms interrupt the string of *wayyiqtol* forms and where the story moves from continuation (foreground) to pause (background).

Genesis 38 unfolds with a series of *wayyiqtol* forms. Sixteen occur in sequence—including an initial וַיְהִי—until the first "pause" occurs at the end of verse five. A *weqatal* form of the verb *hayah* (וְהָיָה) pauses the narrative to provide background information: Judah was at Chezib when she bore Shelah. Notice that an infinitive construct conveys the act of giving birth in this "paused" clause. Then, a *wayyiqtol* form in verse six continues the narrative, reporting that Judah took a wife for his firstborn son, Er. However, a verbless nominal clause in verse 6 pauses the action again briefly to give us the name of Er's wife: Tamar.[55]

Another significant pause in the narrative occurs in verse 9. First, the conjunction כִּי introduces a clause containing an imperfect verb fronted by both the negative particle לֹא and the preposition with suffix לֹו, emphasizing that the offspring resulting from a union between Onan and Tamar would not be considered an heir of Onan's. The next clause begins with another וְהָיָה form, introducing three more clauses that supply another key piece of background information: Onan refused to impregnate Tamar.[56]

In verse 11, a *qatal* verb preceded by כִּי provides the motive for Judah's instructions to Tamar to remain a widow in her father's house until Shelah, Judah's son, was old enough to marry her.

There is another significant pause in the narrative in verse 14. There, the prior string of *wayyiqtol* forms is interrupted by a causal כִּי clause, which explains why she took off her clothes of mourning and disguised herself with a veil. Three *qatal* forms provide the explanation: she <u>saw</u> that even though Shelah <u>was grown</u>, she <u>was not given</u> to Shelah as a wife. This information also sets the stage for what happens next in the narrative.

In verse 16, the narrative is paused briefly to reveal the motive for Judah's bold request to have sex with Tamar. A causal כִּי plus a *qatal* verb informs the reader that Judah did not know that this disguised woman was his daughter-in-law.

---

55. The verb וַיְהִי at the beginning of Gen. 38:7 simply functions as a *wayyiqtol* verb, meaning "was." Thus the translation is, "But Er, Judah's firstborn, was wicked in the sight of the Lord."

56. The relative clause in v. 10, אֲשֶׁר עָשָׂה, simply serves as the subject of the *wayyiqtol* verb at the beginning of the clause: "And what he did was wicked in the sight of the Lord."

Using Hebrew in Narrative Exegesis 215

The next significant variation from *wayyiqtol* clauses occurs in verse 25.[57] After Judah's declaration in verse 24 that Tamar should be brought out and burned for her alleged immorality, two paused clauses slow down the narrative and set up Tamar's response to her father-in-law. The first, using a *qotel* (participle), emphasizes the time ("As she was being brought out"). The second, using a *qatal* form, emphasizes her act of sending a couple items to her father-in-law that lead to her exoneration.

In verse 27, the narrator draws attention to the concluding scene by highlighting the shift in time (וַיְהִי plus an infinitive) as well as the surprise (indicated by וְהִנֵּה plus a nominal verbless clause) that there were twins in her womb! Verses 28 and 29 both begin as well with וַיְהִי plus an infinitive to denote shifts in time—when Tamar gave birth (28) and when the son who appeared to be coming out first drew back his hand (29). The drawing back of this twin's hand leads to a surprising outcome, indicated by וְהִנֵּה plus *qatal*: his brother came out! A final *qatal* form in verse 30 pauses the narrative to remind us that after his birth, the other twin, who had the scarlet thred on his hand, finally came out.

Joshua 1

Here are discourse layouts for Joshua 1 (see discourses B.3 and B.4). Both the Hebrew and English (ESV) layouts cover the entire chapter.

Discourse Layout B.3

Joshua 1 (Hebrew)

¹וַיְהִ֗י אַחֲרֵ֛י מ֥וֹת מֹשֶׁ֖ה עֶ֣בֶד יְהוָ֑ה
וַיֹּ֤אמֶר יְהוָה֙ אֶל־יְהוֹשֻׁ֣עַ בִּן־נ֔וּן מְשָׁרֵ֥ת מֹשֶׁ֖ה לֵאמֹֽר׃

²מֹשֶׁ֥ה עַבְדִּ֖י מֵ֑ת וְעַתָּה֩ ק֨וּם עֲבֹ֜ר אֶת־הַיַּרְדֵּ֣ן הַזֶּ֗ה אַתָּה֙ וְכָל־הָעָ֣ם הַזֶּ֔ה אֶל־הָאָ֕רֶץ אֲשֶׁ֧ר אָנֹכִ֛י נֹתֵ֥ן לָהֶ֖ם לִבְנֵ֥י יִשְׂרָאֵֽל׃ ³כָּל־מָק֗וֹם אֲשֶׁ֨ר תִּדְרֹ֧ךְ כַּֽף־רַגְלְכֶ֛ם בּ֖וֹ לָכֶ֣ם נְתַתִּ֑יו כַּאֲשֶׁ֥ר דִּבַּ֖רְתִּי אֶל־מֹשֶֽׁה׃ ⁴מֵהַמִּדְבָּר֩ וְהַלְּבָנ֨וֹן הַזֶּ֜ה וְֽעַד־הַנָּהָ֧ר הַגָּד֣וֹל נְהַר־פְּרָ֗ת כֹּ֚ל אֶ֣רֶץ הַֽחִתִּ֔ים וְעַד־הַיָּ֥ם הַגָּד֖וֹל מְב֣וֹא הַשָּׁ֑מֶשׁ יִֽהְיֶ֖ה גְּבוּלְכֶֽם׃ ⁵לֹֽא־יִתְיַצֵּ֥ב אִישׁ֙ לְפָנֶ֔יךָ כֹּ֖ל יְמֵ֣י חַיֶּ֑יךָ כַּאֲשֶׁ֨ר הָיִ֤יתִי עִם־מֹשֶׁה֙ אֶהְיֶ֣ה עִמָּ֔ךְ לֹ֥א אַרְפְּךָ֖ וְלֹ֥א אֶעֶזְבֶֽךָּ׃ ⁶חֲזַ֖ק וֶאֱמָ֑ץ כִּ֣י אַתָּ֗ה תַּנְחִיל֙ אֶת־הָעָ֣ם הַזֶּ֔ה אֶת־הָאָ֕רֶץ אֲשֶׁר־נִשְׁבַּ֥עְתִּי לַאֲבוֹתָ֖ם לָתֵ֥ת לָהֶֽם׃ ⁷רַ֣ק חֲזַ֣ק וֶֽאֱמַץ֮ מְאֹד֒ לִשְׁמֹ֤ר

---

57. Note that the negated *qatal* verbs in vv. 20 and 26 simply function like *wayyiqtol* forms and continue the main storyline. The use of *qatal* forms is necessary since *wayyiqtol* forms cannot be negated.

לַעֲשׂוֹת כְּכָל־הַתּוֹרָ֗ה אֲשֶׁ֤ר צִוְּךָ֙ מֹשֶׁ֣ה עַבְדִּ֔י אַל־תָּס֥וּר מִמֶּ֖נּוּ יָמִ֣ין וּשְׂמֹ֑אול
לְמַ֣עַן תַּשְׂכִּ֔יל בְּכֹ֖ל אֲשֶׁ֥ר תֵּלֵֽךְ׃ ⁸לֹֽא־יָמ֡וּשׁ סֵפֶר֩ הַתּוֹרָ֨ה הַזֶּ֜ה מִפִּ֗יךָ וְהָגִ֤יתָ בּוֹ֙
יוֹמָ֣ם וָלַ֔יְלָה לְמַ֙עַן֙ תִּשְׁמֹ֣ר לַעֲשׂ֔וֹת כְּכָל־הַכָּת֖וּב בּ֑וֹ כִּי־אָ֛ז תַּצְלִ֥יחַ אֶת־דְּרָכֶ֖ךָ
וְאָ֥ז תַּשְׂכִּֽיל׃ ⁹הֲל֤וֹא צִוִּיתִ֙יךָ֙ חֲזַ֣ק וֶאֱמָ֔ץ אַֽל־תַּעֲרֹ֖ץ וְאַל־תֵּחָ֑ת כִּ֤י עִמְּךָ֙ יְהוָ֣ה
אֱלֹהֶ֔יךָ בְּכֹ֖ל אֲשֶׁ֥ר תֵּלֵֽךְ׃ פ**

¹⁰וַיְצַ֣ו יְהוֹשֻׁ֔עַ אֶת־שֹׁטְרֵ֥י הָעָ֖ם לֵאמֹֽר׃

**¹¹עִבְר֣וּ ׀ בְּקֶ֣רֶב הַֽמַּחֲנֶ֗ה וְצַוּ֤וּ אֶת־הָעָם֙ לֵאמֹ֔ר הָכִ֥ינוּ לָכֶ֖ם צֵידָ֑ה כִּ֞י בְּע֣וֹד ׀
שְׁלֹ֣שֶׁת יָמִ֗ים אַתֶּם֙ עֹבְרִים֙ אֶת־הַיַּרְדֵּ֣ן הַזֶּ֔ה לָבוֹא֙ לָרֶ֣שֶׁת אֶת־הָאָ֔רֶץ אֲשֶׁר֙
יְהוָ֣ה אֱלֹֽהֵיכֶ֔ם נֹתֵ֥ן לָכֶ֖ם לְרִשְׁתָּֽהּ׃ ס**

¹²וְלָרֽאוּבֵנִי֙ וְלַגָּדִ֔י וְלַחֲצִ֖י שֵׁ֣בֶט הַֽמְנַשֶּׁ֑ה אָמַ֥ר יְהוֹשֻׁ֖עַ לֵאמֹֽר׃

**¹³זָכוֹר֙ אֶת־הַדָּבָ֔ר אֲשֶׁ֨ר צִוָּ֥ה אֶתְכֶ֛ם מֹשֶׁ֥ה עֶֽבֶד־יְהוָ֖ה לֵאמֹ֑ר יְהוָ֤ה אֱלֹֽהֵיכֶם֙
מֵנִ֣יחַ לָכֶ֔ם וְנָתַ֥ן לָכֶ֖ם אֶת־הָאָ֥רֶץ הַזֹּֽאת׃ ¹⁴נְשֵׁיכֶ֣ם טַפְּכֶם֮ וּמִקְנֵיכֶם֒ יֵשְׁב֣וּ בָּאָ֔רֶץ
אֲשֶׁ֨ר נָתַ֥ן לָכֶ֛ם מֹשֶׁ֖ה בְּעֵ֣בֶר הַיַּרְדֵּ֑ן וְאַתֶּם֩ תַּעַבְר֨וּ חֲמֻשִׁ֜ים לִפְנֵ֣י אֲחֵיכֶ֗ם כֹּ֚ל
גִּבּוֹרֵ֣י הַחַ֔יִל וַעֲזַרְתֶּ֖ם אוֹתָֽם׃ ¹⁵עַ֠ד אֲשֶׁר־יָנִ֨יחַ יְהוָ֥ה ׀ לַאֲחֵיכֶם֮ כָּכֶם֒ וְיָרְשׁ֣וּ
גַם־הֵ֔מָּה אֶת־הָאָ֕רֶץ אֲשֶׁר־יְהוָ֥ה אֱלֹֽהֵיכֶ֖ם נֹתֵ֣ן לָהֶ֑ם וְשַׁבְתֶּ֞ם לְאֶ֤רֶץ יְרֻשַּׁתְכֶם֙
וִֽירִשְׁתֶּ֣ם אוֹתָ֔הּ אֲשֶׁ֣ר ׀ נָתַ֣ן לָכֶ֗ם מֹשֶׁ֛ה עֶ֥בֶד יְהוָ֖ה בְּעֵ֥בֶר הַיַּרְדֵּ֖ן מִזְרַ֥ח
הַשָּֽׁמֶשׁ׃**

¹⁶וַיַּעֲנ֔וּ אֶת־יְהוֹשֻׁ֖עַ לֵאמֹ֑ר

**כֹּ֤ל אֲשֶׁר־צִוִּיתָ֙נוּ֙ נַֽעֲשֶׂ֔ה וְאֶֽל־כָּל־אֲשֶׁ֥ר תִּשְׁלָחֵ֖נוּ נֵלֵֽךְ׃ ¹⁷כְּכֹ֤ל אֲשֶׁר־שָׁמַ֙עְנוּ֙
אֶל־מֹשֶׁ֔ה כֵּ֖ן נִשְׁמַ֣ע אֵלֶ֑יךָ רַ֠ק יִֽהְיֶ֞ה יְהוָ֤ה אֱלֹהֶ֙יךָ֙ עִמָּ֔ךְ כַּאֲשֶׁ֥ר הָיָ֖ה עִם־
מֹשֶֽׁה׃ ¹⁸כָּל־אִ֞ישׁ אֲשֶׁר־יַמְרֶ֣ה אֶת־פִּ֗יךָ וְלֹֽא־יִשְׁמַ֧ע אֶת־דְּבָרֶ֛יךָ לְכֹ֥ל אֲשֶׁר־
תְּצַוֶּ֖נּוּ יוּמָ֑ת רַ֖ק חֲזַ֥ק וֶאֱמָֽץ׃ פ**

Discourse Layout B.4

Joshua 1 (ESV)

¹[It <u>happened that</u>] After the death of Moses the servant of the Lord,
the Lord <u>said</u> to Joshua the son of Nun, Moses' assistant,

²"Moses my servant is dead. Now therefore arise, go over this Jordan, you and
all this people, into the land that I am giving to them, to the people of Israel.
³Every place that the sole of your foot will tread upon I have given to you, just
as I promised to Moses. ⁴From the wilderness and this Lebanon as far as the
great river, the river Euphrates, all the land of the Hittites to the Great Sea
toward the going down of the sun shall be your territory. ⁵No man shall be able
to stand before you all the days of your life. Just as I was with Moses, so I will

Using Hebrew in Narrative Exegesis

be with you. I will not leave you or forsake you. ⁶Be strong and courageous, for you shall cause this people to inherit the land that I swore to their fathers to give them. ⁷Only be strong and very courageous, being careful to do according to all the law that Moses my servant commanded you. Do not turn from it to the right hand or to the left, that you may have good success wherever you go. ⁸This Book of the Law shall not depart from your mouth, but you shall meditate on it day and night, so that you may be careful to do according to all that is written in it. For then you will make your way prosperous, and then you will have good success. ⁹Have I not commanded you? Be strong and courageous. Do not be frightened, and do not be dismayed, for the LORD your God is with you wherever you go."

¹⁰And Joshua <u>commanded</u> the officers of the people,

¹¹"Pass through the midst of the camp and command the people, 'Prepare your provisions, for within three days you are to pass over this Jordan to go in to take possession of the land that the LORD your God is giving you to possess.'"

¹²**And to the Reubenites, the Gadites, and the half-tribe of Manasseh Joshua <u>said</u>**, [*qatal*]

¹³"Remember the word that Moses the servant of the LORD commanded you, saying, 'The LORD your God is providing you a place of rest and will give you this land.' ¹⁴Your wives, your little ones, and your livestock shall remain in the land that Moses gave you beyond the Jordan, but all the men of valor among you shall pass over armed before your brothers and shall help them, ¹⁵until the LORD gives rest to your brothers as he has to you, and they also take possession of the land that the LORD your God is giving them. Then you shall return to the land of your possession and shall possess it, the land that Moses the servant of the LORD gave you beyond the Jordan toward the sunrise."

¹⁶And they <u>answered</u> Joshua,

"All that you have commanded us we will do, and wherever you send us we will go. ¹⁷Just as we obeyed Moses in all things, so we will obey you. Only may the LORD your God be with you, as he was with Moses! ¹⁸Whoever rebels against your commandment and disobeys your words, whatever you command him, shall be put to death. Only be strong and courageous."

Basically, Joshua 1 consists of four speeches. After an initial וַיְהִי form, a pattern develops. A *wayyiqtol* form followed by the infinitive form לֵאמֹר precedes the direct speech embedded into the narrative. This pattern occurs at three of four points where nonquotational material introduces direct speech (quotational material). The clear variation is in the announcement of the third speech in verse 12a, where a perfect verb preceded by three prepositional phrases (each preceded by a *waw*) occurs instead of a *wayyiqtol* form. This construction is still followed by לֵאמֹר. While this marks or highlights the recipients of the address (the Reubenites, the Gadites, and the half-tribe of Manasseh) it also marks this speech as subsidiary to the main storyline. This does not imply that the speech is less important. Rather, it distinguishes the section in 1:12–15 from 1:16–18. The "answer" in verse 16, then, comes in response to Joshua's "order" to the whole nation in 1:10–11, not simply the words to the Transjordan tribes in 1:12–15.

The Way Forward

The whole point of discourse analysis is not to lead you into the weeds where you get lost. Rather, it is designed to show you how the writer put a text together. Discourse analysis looks at the overall structure—the macrostructure—of a narrative. You can develop your own methods, just as I did, for recording the data you observe. Keep it as simple as possible, or you'll stop doing it. When done properly, discourse analysis will confirm (or challenge) the conclusions you reached when analyzing the action, characters, talking, and setting of a narrative.

If you want to learn more about discourse analysis in Old Testament narratives, you will benefit from a source to which I have referred several times: *Basics of Hebrew Discourse: A Guide to Working with Hebrew Prose and Poetry* by Matthew H. Patton, Frederic Clarke Putnam, and Miles V. Van Pelt. Part 1 deals with Hebrew prose, including narrative. Another helpful resource is Gary A. Long's *Grammatical Concepts 101 for Biblical Hebrew*. The final section of the book focuses on discourse analysis. Reading the appropriate sections in these two volumes will help interpreters understand the various issues related to discourse analysis. In addition, Benjamin J. Noonan's chapter on discourse analysis in *Advances in the Study of Biblical Hebrew and Aramaic* will shed light on how various linguistic theories lead to different approaches to discourse analysis. An older work by Robert B. Chisholm Jr. is still quite useful. His volume, *From Exegesis to Exposition: A Practical Guide to Using Biblical Hebrew*, contains helpful chapters on the basic structure of Hebrew narrative (and poetry) as well as narrative (and poetry) as literature. Finally, Jason DeRouchie has helpful chapters titled "Clause and Text Grammar" and "Argument-Tracing" in *How to Understand and Apply the Old Testament*. However, he does not show how this applies to a narrative text—only to speeches within a narrative.

Appendix C

Commentaries for Narrative Exegesis

Commentaries provide an important source of help for interpreters of Old Testament narrative literature. When it comes to selecting commentaries on Old Testament narrative books, Tremper Longman offers solid advice in his *Old Testament Commentary Survey*.[1] This resource is updated every few years. The *Denver Journal*, an online journal published by Denver Seminary, contains an "Annotated Old Testament Bibliography," which provides commentary recommendations and is updated annually.[2]

In the following pages, I have provided a handful of commentaries for each Old Testament book from Genesis through Esther according to the English Bible's order of books. The list of suggestions includes Leviticus, Numbers, and Deuteronomy. Even though these books consist primarily of legal literature or discourse, they contain some narratives. Besides, they make up part of the narrative about the origins of Israel as the people of God.

The more I do exegesis for preaching, the more I limit my commentary work primarily to two or three of the best. I like a couple of strong exegetical commentaries, as well as a couple of more concise ones—particularly

---

1. Longman, *Old Testament Commentary Survey*, 1–153.
2. Go to https://denverseminary.edu/ and click on "Resources" to access the *Denver Journal*.

those that summarize the narrative well and reflect on how it fits into the larger storyline of the Bible. This is the grid I have used to make suggestions below. Of course, do not limit yourself to my recommendations. That's especially true because my list will be out-of-date as soon as this volume hits the market. I'm grateful for the publication of more helpful commentaries on Old Testament narrative books than we had a couple decades ago.

Before I turn to the individual books themselves, I want to recommend a resource that I believe anyone who preaches from the Old Testament—and especially its narrative sections—should purchase. It is *The Hebrew Bible: A Translation and Commentary* by Robert Alter. His concise comments on the text reflect the approach he espouses in his classic, *The Art of Biblical Narrative*. If you want to explore exegetical insights from the patristic or Reformation eras, I recommend the Ancient Christian Commentary on Scripture series as well as the Reformation Commentary on Scripture series—both published by Zondervan. Now, here are recommendations for individual books.

Genesis

Perhaps the best place to start is Bruce Waltke's volume, *Genesis: A Commentary*, or Gordon Wenham's two volumes in the Word Biblical Commentary. Both Waltke and Wenham are sensitive to the literary and theological dimensions of the text. Allen Ross's volume *Creation and Blessing* builds on his conviction that "the biblical narratives . . . are far more than illustrative stories. They are highly developed and complex narratives that form theological treatises."[3] Ross provides an expository (central) idea and an expository outline for sixty-four preaching/teaching units in Genesis. These outlines consist of theological statements that are grounded in a sound literary analysis of the text. This is an excellent resource, although Ross sometimes makes theological statements where the text is only relating background information. J. P. Fokkelman's *Narrative Art in Genesis* is worth consulting, even though it covers only two small units (11:1–9; 28:10–22) and three extended complexes of stories in the Jacob cycle (25–28; 29–31; and 32–35). Writing before literary analysis of

---

3. Ross, *Creation and Blessing*, 13.

biblical texts was in vogue, Jewish scholar Umberto Cassuto offers some excellent literary insights in his two volumes on Genesis. Although written from a more critical perspective, Walter Brueggemann's volume in the Interpetation series has some brilliant theological observations.

Exodus

It is hard to beat T. Desmond Alexander's in the Apollos Old Testament Commentary as the "go to" commentary for Exodus. Douglas Stuart's volume in the New American Commentary is solid as well. Brevard Childs wrote a more critical volume in the Old Testament Library series. While Childs does not deny the presence of sources behind the text, he is most interested in the text in its final form and presents a literary analysis for each unit. Terence Fretheim's volume in the Interpretation series provides some stellar theological insights. Umberto Cassuto's commentary on Exodus, like his work on Genesis, shows sensitivity to the literary artistry of the text.

Leviticus

There are very few narratives in Leviticus (e.g., 10:1–20; 24:10–23). Gordon Wenham handles them well in his volume in the New International Commentary on the Old Testament. Mark Rooker's volume in the New American Commentary is also worth consulting. Another good resource is *Leviticus, Numbers* by Roy Gane in The NIV Application Commentary. The commentary by Richard Hess in *The Expositor's Bible Commentary* (vol. 1) is excellent as well. It may not be advisable to purchase Jacob Milgrom's three volumes in the Anchor Yale Bible Commentary for the handful of narratives you'll find in Leviticus, yet this work is a classic.

Numbers

The book of Numbers contains more narrative texts than you might suspect. One commentary that handles the literary shape of the book and its narratives effectively is Ronald B. Allen's commentary in *The Expositor's Bible Commentary* (vol. 2). Gordon Wenham's brief volume on Numbers in the Tyndale Old Testament Commentary series is also helpful. If you have Roy Gane's commentary on Leviticus and Numbers (see above under "Leviticus"), you'll certainly want to consult it too. Once again, Jacob Milgrom has provided a masterpiece in his JPS Torah Commentary on Numbers.

Deuteronomy

While Deuteronomy possesses more narrative sections than Leviticus, legal materials dominate the fifth and final book in the Torah (Pentateuch). Daniel Block's volume in The NIV Application Commentary is outstanding. Peter Craigie handles the narrative sections well in *The Book of Deuteronomy*, a volume in the New International Commentary on the Old Testament series. For a shorter but helpful treatment, consult Christopher Wright's volume in the Understanding the Bible Commentary Series.[4]

Joshua

David Howard handles the narratives in Joshua superbly in his volume in the New American Commentary series. So does Robert Hubbard's volume in The NIV Application Commentary. I really like the recent work by Lissa Wray Beal in The Story of God Bible Commentary. Richard Hess has a fine volume in the Tyndale Old Testament Commentary Series. Finally, Robert Polzin has offered an interesting literary study of Joshua in his volume *Moses and the Deuteronomist*.

Judges

For years there were no great options for commentaries on the book of Judges. Then Daniel Block published an outstanding volume in the New American Commentary series. It is a great place to begin. K. Lawson Younger's volume in The NIV Application Commentary is excellent as well. Barry Webb's contribution in the New International Commentary on the Old Testament is a masterpiece. So is Mary Evan's volume, *Judges*

---

4. The volumes in the Understanding the Bible Commentary Series (BakerBooks) were originally published in the New International Biblical Commentary (Hendrickson).

and Ruth, in the Tyndale Old Testament Commentary series. I also admire *A Commentary on Judges and Ruth* by Robert Chisholm Jr. in the Kregel Exegetical Library. I profited as well by reading David J. H. Beldman's commentary on Judges in The Two Horizons Old Testament Commentary. For another helpful literary study of Judges, see Robert Polzin's volume *Moses and the Deuteronomist*. So much for limiting myself to two or three commentaries on this book!

Ruth

The leader in the field of commentaries on Ruth is the volume by Robert Hubbard in the New International Commentary on the Old Testament series. Daniel Block has an excellent volume on Ruth in the Zondervan Exegetical Commentary on the Old Testament series. The volumes mentioned above under Judges by Mary Evans, Daniel Block, K. Lawson Younger, and Robert Chisholm are in the "can't miss" category as well. Interpreters will find helpful insights in D. F. Rauber's brief essay on the book of Ruth in *Literary Interpretations of Biblical Narratives*.

Samuel

The price of J. P. Fokkelman's four-volume work *Narrative Art and Poetry in the Books of Samuel* may give you sticker shock. However, Fokkelman's brilliant literary analyses make it worth every dollar. Robert Bergen's work in the New American Commentary series is a fine contribution from an evangelical who has done extensive work in the field of discourse analysis. Perhaps the definitive commentary at this moment is David Tsumura's two volumes in the New International Commentary. He provides a lot of helpful insights based on discourse analysis. For more brief, yet solid treatments of 1 and 2 Samuel, consult Mary Evans in the Understanding the Bible Commentary Series and Robert Chisholm Jr. in the Teach the Text Commentary Series. Walter Brueggemann's commentary in the Interpretation series is one of the more creative analyses that pays attention to the literature of the text. Also, Eugene Peterson's *Leap over a Wall: Earthy Spirituality for Everyday Christians*, while not a commentary per se, provides a superb retelling of and reflection on the David stories. Robert Polzin has offered an insightful literary study of the books of Samuel in his volumes *Samuel and the Deuteronomist* (1 Samuel) and *David and the Deuteronomist* (2 Samuel). Bill Arnold does an admirable job in his volume in The NIV Application Commentary Series too.

Kings

Lissa Wray Beal's volume in the Apollos Old Testament Commentary is, in my opinion, the best all-around commentary on Kings at this moment. She has a profound insight into the literary features, the structure, and the theological message of the text. A shorter, but equally outstanding volume is by Iain Provan in the Understanding the Bible Commentary Series. Walter Brueggemann, as you might expect, offers keen literary and theological insights in his volume in the Smith & Helwys Bible Commentary. So does Terence Fretheim in *First and Second Kings* in the Westminster Bible Companion series. Paul House contributed a solid volume on Kings to the New American Commentary. Finally, Peter Leithart has written one of the better commentaries from the theological interpretation of Scripture school, and it appears in the Brazos Theological Commentary on the Bible.

Chronicles

Roddy Braun and Raymond Dillard have provided helpful commentaries on 1 and 2 Chronicles in the Word Biblical Commentary series. J. A. Thompson's volume in the New American Commentary series offers, at times, some good literary insights. Eugene Merrill's volume, *A Commentary on 1 and 2 Chronicles*, in the Kregel Exegetical Library is worth consulting. So is Andrew Hill's volume in The NIV Application Commentary. Peter Leithart's volume in the Brazos Theological Commentary on the Bible is helpful from a theological interpretation of Scripture perspective.

Ezra-Nehemiah

The clear leader in commentaries on Ezra-Nehemiah is the volume in the Word Biblical Commentary series by H. G. M. Williamson, a specialist in postexilic literature. Another outstanding volume on these books is by Donna Petter and Thomas Petter in The NIV Application Commentary. The

Interpretation volume by Mark Throntveit, as you might expect, is helpful with the literary features and theological message of Ezra-Nehemiah.

Esther

The best commentary by far on the book of Esther is The NIV Application Commentary volume by Karen Jobes. If you decide to consult only one commentary on Esther, this is it. Adele Berlin's volume in the JPS Bible Commentary is a masterpiece even though evangelicals will dispute some of her conclusions about the purpose of the book. For more concise, yet helpful treatments of Esther, see Elaine Phillips in The Expositor's Bible Commentary (vol. 4) or Debra Reid in the Tyndale Old Testament Commentary.

Bibliography

Alcántara, Jared. *The Practices of Christian Preaching: Essentials for Effective Proclamation.* Grand Rapids: Baker Academic, 2019.

Alexander, T. Desmond. *The City of God and the Goal of Creation.* Wheaton: Crossway, 2018.

———. *Exodus.* Apollos Old Testament Commentary 2, edited by David W. Baker and Gordon J. Wenham. Downers Grove, IL: InterVarsity, 2017.

———. *From Eden to the New Jerusalem: An Introduction to Biblical Theology.* Grand Rapids: Kregel Academic, 2008.

Allen, Ronald B. "Numbers." In *The Expositor's Bible Commentary*, rev. ed., edited by Tremper Longman III and David E. Garland, 2:23–456. Grand Rapids: Zondervan, 2012.

Alter, Robert. *The Art of Biblical Narrative.* New York: Basic Books, 1981.

Alter, Robert, and Frank Kermode, eds. *The Literary Guide to the Bible.* Cambridge, MA: Harvard University Press, 1987.

Amit, Yairah. *Reading Biblical Narratives: Literary Criticism and the Hebrew Bible.* Minneapolis: Fortress, 2001.

Arnold, Bill T. *1 and 2 Samuel.* The NIV Application Commentary. Grand Rapids: Zondervan, 2003.

Arthurs, Jeffrey D. "Performing the Story." *Preaching* 12 (March–April 1997): 30–35.

———. *Preaching with Variety: How to Re-create the Dynamics of Biblical Genres.* Grand Rapids: Kregel, 2007.

Auerbach, Erich. *Mimesis.* Translated by Willard Trask. New York: Doubleday, 1953.

Aurandt, Paul. *Destiny.* New York: Bantam Books, 1983.

———. *More of Paul Harvey's The Rest of the Story.* New York: Bantam Books, 1980.

———. *Paul Harvey's The Rest of the Story.* New York: Bantam Books, 1977.

Avishur, Yitzhak. *Studies in Biblical Narrative: Style, Structure, and the Ancient Near Eastern Literary Background*. Tel Aviv-Jaffa, Israel: Archaeological Center Publication, 1999.

Avrahami, Yael. *The Senses of Scripture: Sensory Perception in the Hebrew Bible*. Library of Hebrew Bible / Old Testament Studies 545. New York: Bloomsbury T&T Clark, 2012.

Bandstra, Barry L. "Word Order and Emphasis in Biblical Hebrew Narrative." In *Linguistics and Biblical Hebrew*, edited by Walter R. Bodine, 109–23. Winona Lake, IN: Eisenbrauns, 1992.

Bar-Efrat, Shimon. *Narrative Art in the Bible*. Sheffield, UK: Almond, 1989.

Beal, Lissa M. Wray. *1 and 2 Kings*. Apollos Old Testament Commentary 9, edited by David W. Baker and Gordon J. Wenham. Downers Grove, IL: InterVarsity, 2014.

———. *Joshua*. The Story of God Bible Commentary, edited by Tremper Longman III and Scot McKnight. Grand Rapids: Zondervan Academic, 2019.

Beale, G. K. *The Temple and the Church's Mission: A Biblical Theology of the Dwelling Place of God*. New Studies in Biblical Theology 17. Downers Grove, IL: InterVarsity, 2004.

Beale, G. K., and Mitchell Kim. *God Dwells among Us: Expanding Eden to the Ends of the Earth*. Downers Grove, IL: InterVarsity, 2014.

Beck, John A. *God as Storyteller: Seeking Meaning in Biblical Narrative*. St. Louis: Chalice, 2008.

Beldman, David J. H. *Judges*. The Two Horizons Old Testament Commentary. Grand Rapids: Eerdmans, 2020.

Bergen, Robert, ed. *Biblical Hebrew and Discourse Linguistics*. Dallas: Summer Institute of Linguistics; Winona Lake, IN: Eisenbrauns, 1994.

———. "Evil Spirits and Eccentric Grammar: A Study of the Relationship between Text and Meaning in Hebrew Narrative." In Bergen, *Biblical Hebrew and Discourse Linguistics*, 320–35.

———. *1, 2 Samuel*. New American Commentary 7, edited by E. Ray Clendenen. Nashville: Broadman & Holman, 1996.

Berlin, Adele. *Esther*. The JPS Torah Commentary. Philadelphia: The Jewish Publication Society, 2001.

———. *Poetics and Interpretation of Biblical Narrative*. Sheffield, UK: Almond, 1983.

Block, Daniel I. *Deuteronomy*. The NIV Application Commentary. Grand Rapids: Zondervan, 2012.

———. *Judges, Ruth*. New American Commentary 6, edited by E. Ray Clendenen. Nashville: Broadman & Holman, 1999.

———. *Ruth: The King Is Coming*. Zondervan Exegetical Commentary on the Old Testament. Grand Rapids: Zondervan, 2015.

Bibliography

Bodine, Walter R., ed. *Discourse Analysis of Biblical Literature: What It Is and What It Offers*. Society of Biblical Literature Semeia Studies. Atlanta: Scholars Press, 1995.

———, ed. *Linguistics and Biblical Hebrew*. Winona Lake, IN: Eisenbrauns, 1992.

———. "Linguistics and Biblical Studies." In *The Anchor Bible Dictionary*, edited by David Noel Freedman, 4:327–33. New York: Doubleday, 1992.

Borden, Paul. "Is There Really One Big Idea in That Story?" In *The Big Idea of Biblical Preaching*, edited by Keith Willhite and Scott M. Gibson, 67–80. Grand Rapids: Baker, 1998.

Borden, Paul, and Steven D. Mathewson. "The Big Idea of Narrative Preaching." In *The Art and Craft of Biblical Preaching*, edited by Craig Brian Larson and Haddon Robinson, 271–80. Grand Rapids: Zondervan, 2005.

Braun, Roddy. *1 Chronicles*. Word Biblical Commentary 14. Waco: Word, 1986.

Brooks, Phillips. *Lectures on Preaching*. New York: Dutton, 1877.

Brown, David M. *Dramatic Narrative in Preaching*. Valley Forge, PA: Judson, 1981.

Brown, Jeannine K. *The Gospels as Stories: A Narrative Approach to Matthew, Mark, Luke, and John*. Grand Rapids: Baker Academic, 2020.

Brueggemann, Walter. *1 and 2 Kings*. Smyth & Helwys Bible Commentary. Macon, GA: Smyth & Helwys, 2000.

———. *First and Second Samuel*. Interpretation: A Bible Commentary for Teaching and Preaching, edited by James L. Mays. Louisville: John Knox, 1990.

———. *Genesis*. Interpretation: A Bible Commentary for Teaching and Preaching, edited by James L. Mays. Louisville: John Knox, 1982.

Buechner, Frederick. *Peculiar Treasures: A Biblical Who's Who*. New York: Harper & Row, 1979.

Buttrick, David. *Homiletic: Moves and Structures*. Philadelphia: Fortress, 1987.

Buttry, Daniel L. *First-Person Preaching: Bringing New Life to Biblical Stories*. Valley Forge, PA: Judson, 1998.

Carson, D. A. "Systematic Theology and Biblical Theology." In *New Dictionary of Biblical Theology*, edited by T. Desmond Alexander, Brian Rosner, D. A. Carson, Graeme Goldsworthy, 89–104. Downers Grove, IL: InterVarsity, 2000.

Cassuto, Umberto. *Commentary on Exodus*. Translated by Israel Abrahams. Jerusalem: Magnes Press, Hebrew University, 1967.

———. *Commentary on Genesis*. 2 vols. Translated by Israel Abrahams. Jerusalem: Magnes Press, Hebrew University, 1964.

Chapell, Bryan. *Christ-Centered Preaching: Redeeming the Expository Sermon*. 3rd ed. Grand Rapids: Baker Academic, 2018.

———. "Redemptive-Historic View." In *Homiletics and Hermeneutics: Four Views on Preaching Today*, edited by Scott M. Gibson and Matthew D. Kim, 1–29. Grand Rapids: Baker Academic, 2018.

Childs, Brevard S. *The Book of Exodus*. Old Testament Library. Philadelphia: Fortress, 1974.

Chisholm, Robert B., Jr. *A Commentary on Judges and Ruth*. Kregel Exegetical Library. Grand Rapids: Kregel Academic, 2013.

———. *1 & 2 Samuel*. Teach the Text Commentary Series. Grand Rapids: Zondervan, 2013.

———. *From Exegesis to Exposition: A Practical Guide to Using Biblical Hebrew*. Grand Rapids: Baker, 1998.

Coles, Robert. *The Call of Stories: Teaching and the Moral Imagination*. Boston: Houghton Mifflin, 1989.

Cotterell, Peter, and Max Turner. *Linguistics and Biblical Interpretation*. Downers Grove, IL: InterVarsity, 1989.

Craddock, Fred B. *As One without Authority*. Nashville: Abingdon, 1971.

———. *Overhearing the Gospel*. Nashville: Abingdon, 1978.

Craigie, Peter C. *The Book of Deuteronomy*. New International Commentary on the Old Testament. Grand Rapids: Eerdmans, 1976.

Culley, Robert C. *Themes and Variations: A Study of Action in Biblical Narrative*. Society of Biblical Literature Semeia Studies, edited by Edward L. Greenstein. Atlanta: Scholars Press, 1992.

Davis, Dale Ralph. *The Word Became Fresh: How to Preach from Old Testament Narrative Texts*. Fearn, UK: Christian Focus Publications, 2009.

Dawson, David Allen. *Text-Linguistics and Biblical Hebrew*. Sheffield, UK: Sheffield Academic Press, 1994.

Den Exter Blokland, A. F. "Clause-Analysis in Biblical Hebrew Narrative—An Explanation and a Manual for Compilation." *Trinity Journal* 11 (Spring 1990): 73–102.

Deuel, David C. "Expository Preaching from Old Testament Narrative." In *Rediscovering Expository Preaching*, edited by John MacArthur Jr., 273–87. Dallas: Word, 1992.

Dickson, Charles R. *From Story Interpretation to Sermon Crafting: A Structure-Repetition Approach for Exegesis and Sermon Crafting of Old Testament Narratives*. Eugene, OR: Wipf & Stock, 2011.

Dillard, Raymond B. *2 Chronicles*. Word Biblical Commentary 15. Waco: Word, 1987.

Doriani, Daniel M. *Putting the Truth to Work: The Theory and Practice of Biblical Application*. Phillipsburg, NJ: P & R Publishing, 2001.

Dorsey, David A. *The Literary Structure of the Old Testament: A Commentary on Genesis–Malachi*. Grand Rapids: Baker, 1999.

Dryden, J. De Waal. *A Hermeneutic of Wisdom: Recovering the Formative Agency of Scripture*. Grand Rapids: Baker Academic, 2018.

Duduit, Michael. "Theology and Preaching in the 90s: An Interview with R. C. Sproul." *Preaching* 9 (March–April 1994): 19–23.

Duvall, J. Scott, and J. Daniel Hays. *God's Relational Presence: The Cohesive Center of Biblical Theology*. Grand Rapids: Baker Academic, 2019.

Ellingsen, Mark. *The Integrity of Biblical Narrative: Story in Theology and Proclamation*. Eugene, OR: Wipf & Stock, 2002.

Evans, Mary J. *1 and 2 Samuel*. Understanding the Bible Commentary Series. Grand Rapids: Baker Books, 2000.

———. *Judges and Ruth*. Tyndale Old Testament Commentaries. Downers Grove, IL: IVP Academic, 2017.

Exum, J. Cheryl. *Tragedy and Biblical Narrative: Arrows of the Almighty*. Cambridge: Cambridge University Press, 1992.

Fant, Clyde E. "Memory." In *Concise Encyclopedia of Preaching*, edited by William H. Willimon and Richard Lischer, 330–32. Louisville: Westminster John Knox, 1995.

Fields, Weston W. *Sodom and Gomorrah: History and Motif in Biblical Narrative*. Journal for the Study of the Old Testament Supplement Series 231, edited by David J. A. Clines and Philip R. Davies. Sheffield, UK: Sheffield Academic Press, 1997.

Fokkelman, J. P. *Narrative Art and Poetry in the Books of Samuel: A Full Interpretation Based on Stylistic and Structural Analyses*. 4 vols. Assen, Netherlands: Van Gorcum, 1981–93.

———. *Narrative Art in Genesis: Specimens of Stylistic and Structural Analysis*. Amsterdam: Van Gorcum, 1975.

———. *Reading Biblical Narrative: An Introductory Guide*. Philadelphia: Westminster, 1999.

Franklin, Jon. *Writing for Story: Craft Secrets of Dramatic Nonfiction by a Two-Time Pulitzer Prize Winner*. New York: Plume/Penguin, 1986.

Frei, Hans W. *The Eclipse of Biblical Narrative*. New Haven: Yale University Press, 1974.

Fretheim, Terence E. *Exodus*. Interpretation: A Bible Commentary for Teaching and Preaching, edited by James L. Mays. Louisville: John Knox, 1991.

———. *First and Second Kings*. Westminster Bible Companion. Louisville: Westminster John Knox, 1999.

Gallo, Carmine. *Talk Like TED: The 9 Public-Speaking Secrets of the World's Top Minds*. New York: St. Martin's Griffin, 2014.

Gane, Roy. *Leviticus, Numbers*. The NIV Application Commentary. Grand Rapids: Zondervan, 2004.

Goldfajn, Tal. *Word Order and Time in Biblical Hebrew Narrative*. Oxford Theological Monographs. Oxford: Clarendon, 1998.

Goldsworthy, Graeme. *Gospel and Kingdom: A Christian's Guide to the Old Testament*. Minneapolis: Winston, 1981.

Grant, Reg, and John Reed. *Telling Stories to Touch the Heart*. Wheaton: Victor Books, 1990.

Greidanus, Sidney. *The Modern Preacher and the Ancient Text*. Grand Rapids: Eerdmans, 1988.

———. *Preaching Christ from the Old Testament*. Grand Rapids: Eerdmans, 1999.

———. *Sola Scriptura: Problems and Principles in Preaching Historical Texts*. Eugene, OR: Wipf & Stock, 2001.

Grisham, John. *The Testament*. New York: Island Books, 1999.

Gunn, David M., and Danna Nolan Fewell. *Narrative in the Hebrew Bible*. Oxford: Oxford University Press, 1993.

Hall, Oakley. *The Art and Craft of Novel Writing*. Cincinnati: Story, 1989.

Harwell, Blake. "Why Story." *Preaching* 13 (March–April 1998): 43–44.

Hasel, Gerhard. *Old Testament Theology: Basic Issues in the Current Debate*. 4th ed. Grand Rapids: Eerdmans, 1991.

Heath, Chip, and Dan Heath. *Made to Stick: Why Some Ideas Survive and Others Die*. New York: Random House, 2007.

Hemingway, Ernest. *Death in the Afternoon*. New York: Scribner, 2002.

———. *A Farewell to Arms*. New York: Scribner's Sons, 1929.

Hercus, John. *David*. 2nd ed. Chicago: InterVarsity, 1968.

———. *God Is God: Samson and Other Case Histories from the Book of Judges*. London: Hodder & Stoughton, 1971.

Hess, Richard S. *Joshua: An Introduction and Commentary*. Tyndale Old Testament Commentaries 6, edited by D. J. Wiseman. Downers Grove, IL: InterVarsity, 1996.

———. "Leviticus." In *The Expositor's Bible Commentary*, rev. ed., edited by Tremper Longman III and David E. Garland, 1:563–826.Grand Rapids: Zondervan, 2008.

Hill, Andrew E. *1 and 2 Chronicles*. The NIV Application Commentary. Grand Rapids: Zondervan, 2003.

House, Paul R. *1, 2 Kings*. New American Commentary 8, edited by E. Ray Clendenen. Nashville: Broadman & Holman, 1995.

Howard, David M., Jr. *Joshua*. New American Commentary 5, edited by E. Ray Clendenen. Nashville: Broadman & Holman, 1998.

Howell, Adam J., Benjamin J. Merkle, and Robert L. Plummer. *Hebrew For Life: Strategies for Learning, Retaining, and Reviving Biblical Hebrew*. Grand Rapids: Baker Academic, 2020.

Hubbard, Robert L., Jr. *The Book of Ruth*. New International Commentary on the Old Testament. Grand Rapids: Eerdmans, 1988.

———. *Joshua*. The NIV Application Commentary. Grand Rapids: Zondervan, 2009.

Jensen, Richard A. *Thinking in Story: Preaching in a Post-Literate Age*. Lima, OH: CSS, 1993.

The Jewish Bible. JPS Guide. Philadelphia: Jewish Publication Society, 2008.

Bibliography

Jobes, Karen H. *Esther*. The NIV Application Commentary. Grand Rapids: Zondervan, 1999.

Keillor, Garrison. *Lake Wobegon Days*. New York: Viking, 1985.

Keller, Timothy. *Making Sense of God: An Invitation to the Skeptical*. New York: Viking, 2016.

———. *Preaching: Communicating Faith in an Age of Skepticism*. New York: Viking, 2015.

———. *The Reason for God: Belief in an Age of Skepticism*. New York: Dutton, 2008.

Kim, Matthew D. *A Little Book for New Preachers*. Downers Grove, IL: IVP Academic, 2020.

———. *Preaching with Cultural Intelligence: Understanding the People Who Hear Our Sermons*. Grand Rapids: Baker Academic, 2017.

Klein, William W., Craig L. Blomberg, and Robert L. Hubbard Jr. *Introduction to Biblical Interpretation*. Dallas: Word, 1993.

Kort, Wesley A. *Story, Text, and Scripture: Literary Interests in Biblical Narrative*. University Park: Pennsylvania State University Press, 1988.

Krakauer, Jon. *Into Thin Air*. New York: Villard, 1997.

Kromminga, Carl G. "Remember Lot's Wife: Preaching Old Testament Narrative Texts." *Calvin Theological Journal* 13 (1983): 32–46.

Kruger, Michael J. "Are We Allowed to Use OT Figures as Moral Examples?" *Canon Fodder*, January 14, 2019. https://www.michaeljkruger.com/are-we-allowed-to-use-ot-figures-as-moral-examples/.

Kuruvilla, Abraham. "Christiconic View." In *Homiletics and Hermeneutics: Four Views on Preaching Today*, edited by Scott M. Gibson and Matthew D. Kim, 43–70. Grand Rapids: Baker Academic, 2018.

———. *Privilege the Text!: A Theological Hermeneutic of Preaching*. Chicago: Moody, 2013.

———. "Time to Kill the Big Idea? A Fresh Look at Preaching." *Journal of the Evangelical Theological Society* 61 (2018): 825–46.

Kutz, Karl V., and Rebekah L. Josberger. *Learning Biblical Hebrew: Reading for Comprehension—an Introductory Grammar*. Bellingham, WA: Lexham, 2018.

L'Amour, Louis. *Flint*. New York: Bantam Books, 1960.

Lane, William L. *The Gospel according to Mark*. New International Commentary on the New Testament. Grand Rapids: Eerdmans, 1974.

Langley, Kenneth. "Theocentric View." In *Homiletics and Hermeneutics: Four Views on Preaching Today*, edited by Scott M. Gibson and Matthew D. Kim, 81–106. Grand Rapids: Baker Academic, 2018.

Larsen, David L. *Telling the Old, Old Story: The Art of Narrative Preaching*. Wheaton: Crossway, 1995.

Leithart, Peter. *1 and 2 Chronicles*. Brazos Theological Commentary on the Bible. Grand Rapids: Brazos, 2019.

———. *1 and 2 Kings*. Brazos Theological Commentary on the Bible. Grand Rapids: Brazos, 2006.

Lewis, C. S. *The Weight of Glory: And Other Addresses*. San Francisco: HarperSanFrancisco, 2001.

Ligonier Ministries. "RC Sproul Interviews DA Carson on Biblical Exegesis." Orlando, FL. Uploaded March 10, 2011. Vimeo video, 25:27. https://vimeo.com/20890650.

Lister, J. Ryan. *The Presence of God: Its Place in the Storyline of Scripture and the Story of Our Lives*. Wheaton: Crossway, 2015.

Long, Burke O. *1 Kings with an Introduction to Narrative Literature*. The Forms of the Old Testament Literature 9, edited by Rolf Knierim and Gene M. Tucker. Grand Rapids: Eerdmans, 1984.

Long, Jesse C., Jr. "Text Story and Sermon Story in Dialogue: On Preaching Bible Narratives." *Preaching* 12 (January–February 1997): 19–23.

Long, Thomas G. *Preaching and the Literary Forms of the Bible*. Philadelphia: Fortress, 1989.

Longacre, Robert E. "Discourse Perspectives on the Hebrew Verb: Affirmation and Restatement." In Bodine, *Linguistics and Biblical Hebrew*, 177–89.

———. "*Weqatal* Forms in Biblical Hebrew Prose." In Bergen, *Biblical Hebrew and Discourse Linguistics*, 50–98.

Longman, Tremper, III. "Biblical Narrative." In *A Complete Literary Guide to the Bible*, edited by Leland Ryken and Tremper Longman III. Grand Rapids: Zondervan, 1993.

———. *Literary Approaches to Biblical Interpretation*. Grand Rapids: Zondervan, 1987.

———. *Old Testament Commentary Survey*. 5th ed. Grand Rapids: Baker Academic, 2013.

Lowry, Eugene L. *The Homiletical Plot: The Sermon as Narrative Art Form*. Atlanta: John Knox, 1980.

———. *The Sermon: Dancing the Edge of Mystery*. Nashville: Abingdon, 1997.

MacArthur, John, Jr. "Frequently Asked Questions about Expository Preaching." In *Rediscovering Expository Preaching*, edited by John MacArthur Jr., 334–49. Dallas: Word, 1992.

———. "An Introduction to Christ in the Old Testament." Sermon, February 19, 2012. https://www.gty.org/library/sermons-library/90-430/an-introduction-to-christ-in-the-old-testament.

Machen, J. Gresham. Afterword to *The Minister and His Greek New Testament*, by A. T. Robertson, 141–46. Port St. Lucie, FL: Solid Ground Christian Books, 2008.

Maclean, Norman. *A River Runs through It and Other Stories*. Chicago: University of Chicago Press, 1976.

Maier, Paul L. *The Flames of Rome*. New York: Doubleday, 1981. Reprint, New York: Signet, 1982.

———. *Pontius Pilate*. Wheaton: Living Books, 1983.

Mathewson, Steven D. "An Exegetical Study of Genesis 38." *Bibliotheca Sacra* 146 (October–December 1989): 373–92.

———. "Let the Big Idea Live! A Response to Abraham Kuruvilla." *The Journal of the Evangelical Homiletics Society* 19 (2019): 33–41.

———. "Prophetic Preaching from Old Testament Narrative Texts." In *Text Message: The Centrality of Scripture in Preaching*, ed. Ian Stackhouse and Oliver D. Crisp, 34–53. Eugene, OR: Pickwick, 2014.

———. "The Story of the Left-Handed Assassin and the Obese King: Judges 3:12–30." In *Models for Biblical Preaching*, edited by Haddon Robinson and Patricia Batten, 41–60. Grand Rapids: Baker Academic, 2014.

Matthews, P. H. *The Concise Oxford Dictionary of Linguistics*. 2nd ed. Oxford: Oxford University Press, 2007.

Mattingly, Terry. "Star Wars—the Only Parable in Town." *Scripps Howard News Service*. 2 June 1999.

Mawhinney, Bruce. *Preaching with Freshness*. Eugene, OR: Harvest House, 1991.

Mayhue, Richard L. "Rediscovering Expository Preaching." In *Rediscovering Expository Preaching*, edited by John MacArthur Jr., 3–21. Dallas: Word, 1992.

McDill, Wayne. *The 12 Essential Skills for Great Preaching*. Nashville: Broadman & Holman, 1999.

McDougall, Donald G. "Central Ideas, Outlines, and Titles." In *Rediscovering Expository Preaching*, edited by John MacArthur Jr., 225–41. Dallas: Word, 1992.

Merrill, Eugene H. *A Commentary on 1 & 2 Chronicles*. Kregel Exegetical Library. Grand Rapids: Kregel, 2015.

Michener, James. *The Source*. New York: Fawcett Crest, 1967.

Milgrom, Jacob. *Leviticus 1–16*. The Anchor Yale Bible Commentaries. New Haven: Yale University Press, 1998.

———. *Leviticus 17–22*. The Anchor Yale Bible Commentaries. New Haven: Yale University Press, 2000.

———. *Leviticus 23–27*. The Anchor Yale Bible Commentaries. New Haven: Yale University Press, 2001.

———. *Numbers*. The JPS Torah Commentary. Philadelphia: Jewish Publication Society, 2003.

Miller, Cynthia L. "Introducing Direct Discourse in Biblical Hebrew Narrative." In Bergen, *Biblical Hebrew and Discourse Linguistics*, 199–241.

———. *The Representation of Speech in Biblical Hebrew Narrative: A Linguistic Analysis*. Harvard Semitic Monographs 55, edited by Peter Machinist. Atlanta: Scholars Press, 1996.

Movshovitz, Dean. *Pixar Storytelling: Rules for Effective Storytelling Based on Pixar's Greatest Films*. Lexington: Bloop Animation, 2017.

Niccacci, Alviero. "Analysis of Biblical Narrative." In Bergen, *Biblical Hebrew and Discourse Linguistics*, 175–98.

———. "Basic Facts and Theory of the Biblical Hebrew Verb System in Prose." In *Narrative Syntax and the Hebrew Bible: Papers of the Tilburg Conference 1996*, ed. Ellen van Wolde. Biblical Interpretation Series 29. Leiden: Brill, 1997.

Noonan, Benjamin J. *Advances in the Study of Biblical Hebrew and Aramaic*. Grand Rapids: Zondervan Academic, 2020.

O'Neill, Lucas. *Preaching to Be Heard: Delivering Sermons That Command Attention*. Bellingham, WA: Lexham, 2019.

Parker, Simon B. *Stories in Scripture and Inscriptions: Comparative Studies on Narratives in Northwest Semitic Inscriptions and the Hebrew Bible*. Oxford: Oxford University Press, 1997.

Patrick, Dale, and Allen Scult. *Rhetoric and Biblical Interpretation*. Sheffield, UK: Almond, 1990.

Patton, Matthew H., Federeic Clarke Putnam, and Miles V. Van Pelt, *Basics of Hebrew Discourse: A Guide to Working with Hebrew Prose and Poetry*. Grand Rapids: Zondervan Academic, 2019.

Pennington, Jonathan T. *Reading the Gospels Wisely: A Narrative and Theological Introduction*. Grand Rapids: Baker Academic, 2012.

Peterson, Eugene. *Leap over a Wall: Earthy Spirituality for Everyday Christians*. New York: HarperCollins, 1997.

———. *Working the Angles: The Shape of Pastoral Integrity*. Grand Rapids: Eerdmans, 1987.

Petter, Donna, and Thomas Petter. *Ezra, Nehemiah*. The NIV Application Commentary. Grand Rapids: Zondervan, 2021.

Phillips, Elaine. "Esther." In *The Expositor's Bible Commentary*, rev. ed., edited by Tremper Longman III and David E. Garland, 4:569–673. Grand Rapids: Zondervan, 2010.

Polzin, Robert. *David and the Deuteronomist: A Literary Study of the Deuteronomic History, Part Three*. Indiana Studies in Biblical Literature. Bloomington: Indiana University Press, 1993.

———. *Moses and the Deuteronomist: A Literary Study of the Deuteronomic History, Part One*. Indiana Studies in Biblical Literature. New York: Seabury, 1980. Reprint, Bloomington: Indiana University Press, 1993.

———. *Samuel and the Deuteronomist: A Literary Study of the Deuteronomic History, Part Two*. Indiana Studies in Biblical Literature. San Francisco: Harper & Row, 1989. Reprint, Bloomington: Indiana University Press, 1993.

Postman, Neil. *Amusing Ourselves to Death*. New York: Penguin, 1985.

Pratico, Gary D., and Miles V. Van Pelt. *Basics of Biblical Hebrew Grammar*. 3rd ed. Grand Rapids: Zondervan Academic, 2019.

Pratt, Richard L., Jr. *He Gave Us Stories: The Bible Student's Guide to Interpreting Old Testament Narratives*. Brentwood, TN: Wolgemuth & Hyatt, 1990.

Price, Eric S. "Comparing Sidney Greidanus and Abraham Kuruvilla on Preaching Christ from the Old Testament." *Trinity Journal* 39 (Spring 2018): 69–93.

Provan, Iain W. *1 and 2 Kings*. Understanding the Bible Commentary Series. Grand Rapids: Baker Academic, 1995.

Rad, Gerhard von. *Genesis*. Translated by John H. Marks. London: SCM, 1961.

Rauber, D. F. "The Book of Ruth." In *Literary Interpretations of Biblical Narratives*, edited by Kenneth R. R. Gros Louis, 163–76. Nashville: Abingdon, 1974.

Reed, Rick. *The Heart of the Preacher: Preparing Your Soul to Proclaim the Word*. Bellingham, WA: Lexham, 2019.

Reid, Debra. *Esther*. Tyndale Old Testament Commentaries. Downers Grove, IL: IVP Academic, 2008.

Rhoads, David, and Donald Michie. *Mark as Story: An Introduction to the Narrative of a Gospel*. Philadelphia: Fortress, 1982.

Richter, Sandra L. *The Epic of Eden: A Christian Entry into the Old Testament*. Downers Grove, IL: IVP Academic, 2008.

Robar, Elizabeth. *The Verb and the Paragraph in Biblical Hebrew: A Cognitive-Linguistic Approach*. Leiden, Netherlands: Brill, 2015.

Robinson, Haddon W. *Biblical Preaching: The Development and Delivery of Expository Messages*. 3rd ed. Grand Rapids: Baker Academic, 2014.

———. "The Heresy of Application." In *The Art and Craft of Biblical Preaching*, edited by Craig Brian Larson and Haddon Robinson, 306–13. Grand Rapids: Zondervan, 2005.

Robinson, Haddon W., and Torrey W. Robinson. *It's All in How You Tell It: Preaching First-Person Expository Messages*. Grand Rapids: Baker Books, 2003.

Rocine, Bryan M. *Learning Biblical Hebrew: A New Approach Using Discourse Analysis*. Macon, GA: Smyth & Helwys, 2000.

Rofe, Alexander. *The Prophetical Stories: The Narratives about the Prophets in the Hebrew Bible, Their Literary Types and History*. Jerusalem: Magnes Press, Hebrew University, 1988.

Rooker, Mark F. *Leviticus*. New American Commentary 3a, edited by E. Ray Clendenen. Nashville: Broadman & Holman, 2000.

Ross, Allen. *Creation and Blessing: A Guide to the Study and Exposition of Genesis*. Grand Rapids: Baker, 1988.

Ryken, Leland. *How Bible Stories Work: A Guided Study of Narrative Literature*. Wooster, OH: Weaver Book Company, 2015.

———. *How to Read the Bible as Literature*. Grand Rapids: Zondervan, 1984.

———. *Words of Delight: A Literary Introduction to the Bible*. Grand Rapids: Baker, 1987.

Ryken, Leland, and Tremper Longman III. *A Complete Literary Guide to the Bible*. Grand Rapids: Zondervan, 1993.

Sailhamer, John H. "A Database Approach to the Analysis of Hebrew Narrative." *MAARAV: A Journal for the Study of the Northwest Semitic Languages and Literatures* 5–6 (Spring 1990): 319–35.

———. "Genesis." In *The Expositor's Bible Commentary*, rev. ed., edited by Tremper Longman III and David E. Garland, 1:21–331. Grand Rapids: Zondervan, 2008.

———. *Introduction to Old Testament Theology*. Grand Rapids: Zondervan, 1995.

———. *The Pentateuch as Narrative*. Grand Rapids: Zondervan, 1992.

Sandburg, Carl. *Complete Poems*. New York: Harcourt, Brace, 1950.

Silva, Moisés. *God, Language, and Scripture: Reading the Bible in the Light of General Linguistics*. Grand Rapids: Zondervan, 1990.

Simmons, Annette. *The Story Factor: Inspiration, Influence, and Persuasion through the Art of Storytelling*. Rev. ed. New York: Basic Books, 2006.

Ska, Jean Louis. *"Our Fathers Have Told Us": Introduction to the Analysis of Hebrew Narratives*. Roma: Editrice Pontificio Instituto Biblico, 1990.

Smith, James K. A. *Imagining the Kingdom: How Worship Works*. Grand Rapids: Baker Academic, 2013.

Stanley, Andy. *Irresistible: Reclaiming the New That Jesus Unleashed for the World*. Grand Rapids: Zondervan, 2018.

Steinbeck, John. *East of Eden*. New York: Viking, 1952.

Stek, John H. "The Bee and the Mountain Goat: A Literary Reading of Judges 4." In *A Tribute to Gleason Archer*, edited by Walter C. Kaiser Jr. and Ronald F. Youngblood, 53–86. Chicago: Moody, 1986.

Sternberg, Meir. *The Poetics of Biblical Narrative: Ideological Literature and the Drama of Reading*. Indiana Studies in Biblical Literature. Bloomington: Indiana University Press, 1985.

Strawn, Brent. *The Old Testament Is Dying: A Diagnosis and Recommended Treatment*. Grand Rapids: Baker Academic, 2017.

Stuart, Douglas K. *Exodus*. New American Commentary 2, edited by E. Ray Clendenen. Nashville: Broadman & Holman, 2006.

Sunukjian, Donald. "A Night in Persia." In *Biblical Sermons*, edited by Haddon W. Robinson, 69–88. Grand Rapids: Baker, 1989.

Talmon, Shemaryahu. "The Presentation of Synchroneity and Simultaneity in Biblical Narrative." In *Studies in Hebrew Narrative Art throughout the Ages*, Scripta Hierosolymitana 27, edited by Joseph Heinemann and Samuel Werses, 9–26. Jerusalem: Magnes Press, Hebrew University, 1978.

Thomas, T. L. "The Old Testament 'Folk Canon' and Christian Education." *Asbury Theological Journal* 42 (1987): 45–62.

Thompson, J. A. *1, 2 Chronicles*. New American Commentary 9, edited by E. Ray Clendenen. Nashville: Broadman & Holman, 1994.

Throntveit, Mark A. *Ezra-Nehemiah*. Interpretation: A Bible Commentary for Teaching and Preaching, edited by James L. Mays. Louisville: John Knox, 1992.

Tisby, Jamar. *The Color of Compromise: The Truth about the American Church's Complicity in Racism*. Grand Rapids: Zondervan Reflective, 2019.

Tsumura, David Toshio. *The First Book of Samuel*. New International Commentary on the Old Testament. Grand Rapids: Eerdmans, 2007.

———. *The Second Book of Samuel*. New International Commentary on the Old Testament. Grand Rapids: Eerdmans, 2019.

Turner, Laurence A. "Preaching Narrative: Plot." In *Reclaiming the Old Testament for Christian Preaching*, edited by Grenville J. R. Kent, Paul J. Kissling, and Laurence A. Turner, 13–29. Downers Grove, IL: IVP Academic, 2010.

van der Merwe, Christo H. J. "Discourse Linguistics and Biblical Hebrew Grammar." In Bergen, *Biblical Hebrew and Discourse Linguistics*, 13–49.

van der Merwe, Christo H. J., Jackie A. Naudé, and Jan H. Kroeze. *A Biblical Hebrew Reference Grammar*. 2nd ed. London: Bloomsbury T&T Clark, 2017.

Vanhoozer, Kevin J. *Hearers and Doers: A Pastor's Guide to Making Disciples through Scripture and Doctrine*. Bellingham, WA: Lexham, 2019.

———. *Is There a Meaning in This Text?* Grand Rapids: Zondervan, 1998.

van Wolde, Ellen. "The Verbless Clause and Its Textual Function." In *The Verbless Clause in Biblical Hebrew: Linguistic Approaches*, edited by Cynthia L. Miller, 321–36. Winona Lake, IN: Eisenbrauns, 1999.

Walsh, Jerome T. *Old Testament Narrative: A Guide to Interpretation*. Louisville: Westminster John Knox Press, 2009.

———. *Style and Structure in Biblical Hebrew Narrative*. Collegeville, MN: Liturgical, 2001.

Waltke, Bruce K., and Cathi J. Fredricks, *Genesis: A Commentary:* Grand Rapids: Zondervan, 2001.

Walton, Benjamin H. *Preaching Old Testament Narratives*. Grand Rapids: Kregel, 2016.

Walton, John H. *Old Testament Theology for Christians*. Downers Grove, IL: IVP Academic, 2017.

Wangerin, Walter, Jr. *The Book of God*. Grand Rapids: Zondervan, 1996.

Wardlaw, Don M. "Introduction: The Need for New Shapes." In *Preaching Biblically*, edited by Don M. Wardlaw, 11–25. Philadelphia: Westminster, 1983.

Webb, Barry G. *The Book of Judges*. New International Commentary on the Old Testament. Grand Rapids: Eerdmans, 2012.

Weitzman, Steven. *Song and Story in Biblical Narrative: The History of a Literary Convention in Ancient Israel*. Indiana Studies in Biblical Literature. Bloomington: Indiana University Press, 1997.

Wenham, Gordon J. *The Book of Leviticus*. New International Commentary on the Old Testament. Grand Rapids: Eerdmans, 1979.

———. *Genesis 1–15*. Word Biblical Commentary 1. Waco: Word, 1987.

———. *Genesis 16–50*. Word Biblical Commentary 2. Waco: Word, 1994.

———. *Numbers: An Introduction and Commentary*. Tyndale Old Testament Commentaries 4, edited by D. J. Wiseman. Downers Grove, IL: InterVarsity, 1981.

———. *Story as Torah: Reading Old Testament Narrative Ethically*. Grand Rapids: Baker Academic, 2000.

Wenig, Scott. "A Different Exegetical and Homiletical Approach to a Prominent Biblical Narrative: Interpreting and Preaching 2 Samuel 11–12." *The Journal of the Evangelical Homiletics Society* 10, no. 2 (September 2010): 7–26.

Wiersbe, Warren W. *Preaching and Teaching with Imagination: The Quest for Biblical Ministry*. Wheaton: Victor, 1994.

Williamson, H. G. M. *Ezra, Nehemiah*. Word Biblical Commentary 16. Waco: Word, 1985.

Winther-Nielsen, Nicolai. "The Miraculous Grammar of Joshua 3–4." In Bergen, *Biblical Hebrew and Discourse Linguistics*, 300–319.

Wolf, Herbert M. "Implications of Form Criticism for Old Testament Studies." *Bibliotheca Sacra* 127 (October 1970): 303–6.

Wolterstorff, Nicholas. *Divine Discourse: Philosophical Reflections on the Claim That God Speaks*. Cambridge: Cambridge University Press, 1995.

Wright, Christopher J. H. *Deuteronomy*. Understanding the Bible Commentary Series. Grand Rapids: Baker, 1996.

———. *How to Preach and Teach the Old Testament for All Its Worth*. Grand Rapids: Zondervan, 2016.

Wright, N. T. *The New Testament and the People of God*. Vol. 1 of *Christian Origins and the Question of God*. Minneapolis: Fortress, 1992.

Younger, K. Lawson, Jr. *Judges, Ruth*. The NIV Application Commentary. Grand Rapids: Zondervan, 2002.

Scripture Index

Old Testament

Genesis
2:16–17 51
2:20 78
2:20–23 78n9
2:23 77
3:1–3 51
8:21 56
11:1–9 60, 62
12–25 30
13 96, 100, 113, 119, 123, 124
15:1 31
17:1 31
17:19 72
18:12 72
18:13 52
18:33 31
19:1 31
20:1 31
21:1–7 72
21:9 73
22 22, 127
22:1 31
22:1–9 162
22:1–19 79
22:2 54, 54n59, 132, 162
22:8 77
22:9–10 54
24:63 57
25 78
25–27 46
27:11 70
27:41 56
28:12–13 57
29:25 57
37 67
37:28 51
37:29 205
38 42, 46, 49, 56, 67, 79, 84, 208–14
38:1–6 43
38:1–11 6, 44, 53, 54
38:7 56, 79
38:7–11 44, 44n8
38:7–24 44
38:9 56, 79, 197
38:10 214n56
38:11 79, 214
38:12 53n51, 54
38:12–23 54
38:12–24 44
38:12–30 54
38:14 79, 205n52, 214
38:15 79
38:16 79, 214
38:24 44, 54, 77, 215
38:25 197, 215
38:25–26 45
38:26 77
38:27 215
38:27–30 45
38:28 215
38:29 215
38:30 215
39 78, 84, 127
42:1–2 205n52
42:14 52
45:1–13 127
46:30 52
49:25 78n9
49:29–50:26 77

Exodus
3:1–12 127
15 31
15:22–27 144
15:22–17:7 32, 143
15:24 144
15:25–26 144
16:1–36 144
16:3 144
16:4 144
16:7–8 144
16:20–28 144
17:1–7 144
17:2 144
17:7 144
18:4 78n9
20:4–6 70
32:1 205n52

Leviticus
10:1–20 223
24:10–23 223

Numbers
3:9–10 70, 182
18:20–24 185

Deuteronomy
5:8 181, 190
5:8–10 70
5:19 184, 191
12:4–7 70, 181, 190
20:1–4 102, 103
20:10–15 185

Joshua

1   215–18
1:1–9   76
1:8   172
1:10–11   76, 218
1:12   218
1:12–15   76, 218
1:16–18   76, 218
2   166
3:14–17   162, 203, 204
3:17   204
6   152
6:2–5   162
6:5   50
6:20   50, 51
10   47
17:7–12   70
19:41–48   183
21:9–16   70, 182, 190

Judges

1:1–2:5   85
1:1–3:6   84
1:11–15   61
2:6–3:6   85
2:11–19   83n6
3–16   61
3:7–11   61
3:12–30   116, 118, 179
3:12–31   61
3:15–17   70, 116n20
3:20–23   200
3:24–25   57
3:28   116
4   30, 117, 136, 161
4:1–5:31   61
4:8   117
4:9   117
4:20   58
5   31
5:2   117n23
5:9   117n23
5:23   117n23
5:24–27   117n23
5:31   180
6:1–8:32   61
6:13   52
6:36–40   114
8:23   52
8:28–35   45
8:33–10:5   61
10:6–12:15   61
13–16   46, 133
13:1–16:31   61
17–18   42, 43, 44, 45, 46, 79, 84, 85, 96, 101, 118, 123, 124, 131, 179–91
17–21   84
17:1   43
17:1–4   63, 85, 190
17:1–13   62, 63, 141, 142, 190
17:1–18:17   142, 143, 190
17:2–18:10   44
17:4–5   70
17:5   63, 131, 181, 187, 190
17:6   63, 79, 123, 182, 190
17:7–9   182, 190
17:7–13   63
17:10–12   190
17:10–14   182
17:13   190
18:1   63, 79, 205
18:1–2   63, 183
18:1–3   191
18:1–10   62, 63, 141, 142, 190
18:2–6   63
18:3   183, 188
18:4–5   183
18:5–10   191
18:7–10   63
18:7–13   183
18:11   44
18:11–17   63, 142, 191
18:11–26   62, 63, 141
18:11–30   45
18:14   184, 188
18:18–21   63
18:18–26   45, 142, 191
18:18–31   142, 191
18:22–26   63, 185, 189
18:27–28   64, 185
18:27–30   142, 191
18:27–31   62, 63, 141
18:28–31   185
18:29   64
18:30   45, 64
18:31   45, 64, 85, 131, 142, 187, 191
19–21   85, 188
19:1   79
20:16   116n20
21:25   79

Ruth

1:1   83
1:20   72

1 Samuel

1:6–7   70
2:1–10   78
4–7   30
7:2   11
7:2–6   11
7:3–4   11
7:5–6   11
7:7   11
7:8–9   11
7:10–11   11
7:12   11
7:12–17   11
7:13   11
7:13–17   11
8–31   46
9   59
14:6   103
15   51
15:13–31   175
15:23   104
16   66, 153
16–31   30
16–2 Sam. 8   84
16:1–13   73, 102
16:14–23   102
17   21, 30, 66, 76, 89, 96, 102, 124
17:11   102
17:26   73, 102, 103
17:28   102
17:34–37   77, 102
17:36   103
17:45–47   77
17:46–47   102
17:47   103
17:48–49   200
24   78, 84
24–26   32
25   67, 84, 111
25:1   84
25:24–31   76
25:28–29   84
26   84

2 Samuel

6:20   57
8   47
9   51, 76
11–12   67, 79, 83, 94, 95, 97, 98, 115, 126, 131, 162
11:1–5   73
11:10   58
11:11   58, 77, 131

Scripture Index

11:14 201
11:27 80
12:1–7 46
12:9 95
12:10 95
12:11–12 95, 96
12:26–31 97
12:31 97
13–18 167, 170
14:1–23 46
15:24 57
18:1–19:8 133
18:24 57
18:33 133, 167, 170
19:1 51
19:3 51
19:5 51
19:7 51

1 Kings

1–2 67
3:1–15 83, 112
3:16–27 46, 47
3:16–28 83, 112
11:26–14:18 90
17–18 16
17:1–19:21 90
18 30
18:7 57
20:1–22:40 90
20:38–42 46
22–23 111

2 Kings

1:9 83
3:4–27 47
4:1–7 46
5 67n7, 153
5:27 59
6:24–30 46
6:24–7:20 47
8:1–6 46
13–14 47
18:13–19:37 47
23:10 159

Esther

2:23 43
3–4 44
5 44n10
5:1–9:19 45
9:20–10:3 46

Psalms

1:2 172
46:1 78n9
121:1–2 78n9

Proverbs

6:16 36
27:17 122

Jeremiah

13 135
13:1–11 135
18–19 135
27–28 135
34 135

Ezekiel

3:24–27 135
4:1–17 135
5:1–17 135
6:1 135
12:1–16 135
12:17–20 135
21:6 135
21:14 135
21:12 135
21:18–23 135
24:15–27 135
37:15–17 135

Daniel

4 33n10

Micah

6:1–8 190

New Testament

Matthew

1:1 110n12
1:23 109
5:17 118
6:10 20
12:39 114n17
16:4 114n17

Mark

1:15 20
8:11–12 114n17

Luke

2:4 110n12
2:11 110n12
16:31 114n17
24:25–27 19
24:27 25
24:44–47 19

Acts

2:38–41 25
7 12
13:32–41 110n12

Romans

1:3 110n12
8:29 20

1 Corinthians

1 7
2 7
10:1–13 26n63
10:6 17
15:1–3 25

2 Corinthians

12:7–10 128

Galatians

2:14 25
3:13–14 110

Ephesians

1:19–21 109

Colossians

3:1–11 6
3:5 119, 186

1 Thessalonians

1:9 124

2 Timothy

2:8 110n12
3:16 9
3:16–17 113

Titus

2:14 110

Hebrews

10:19–25 36
10:22–24 36n30
10:24 36n30
10:25 36n30
11:35–38 17

James

5:17–18 16, 17

1 Peter

1:18–19 110
3:18 187

2 Peter

1:21 20

1 John

5:21 119, 187

Revelation

19:11–21 110
21–22 109
22:16 110n12

Subject Index

Abigail, 76, 83–84
Abraham, 31, 54, 72, 77, 79, 84, 100
Absalom, 51
achievement sequences, 49
action (ACTS)
    archetypes, 46–49
    chiasmus, 59–61
    exegetical outline, 61–64
    plot shape, 42–46
    point of view, 55–59
    repetition, 50–52
    summary, 88
    time and pace (plot), 52–54
action sequences, 49
ACTS exegetical process
    about, 37–39, 41, 88
    See also action (ACTS); character (ACTS); setting (ACTS); talking (ACTS)
Adam, 77–78, 78n9
adjectives, 155–57
admiration, 47
adverbs, 155–57
Alcántara, Jared, 104, 119
alliteration, 11
Alter, Robert, 33, 38, 48, 49, 69, 75–76, 77–78, 89
Amit, Yairah, 35
analogy, 21
analytical outlines, 11–12

announcement sequences, 49
antagonists, 66
application, in sermons
    characters' actions and speech, 116–17
    ethical thrust of narrative, 118
    images, 160–61
    and listeners, 119
    and moralizing, 113–15
    and new covenant believers, 118–19
    where to include, 136
application images, 160–61
archetypes, 46–49
Aristotelian logic, 11
Arthurs, Jeffrey, 148, 173–74
Art of Biblical Narrative, The (Alter), xvi, 89, 222
attention, listener's, 166–68
Auerbach, Erich, 36
Aurandt, Paul, 130–31
Avishur, Yitzhak, 60

background information, 160
Barak, 71, 117, 117n22, 161
Bar-Efrat, Shimon, 34, 44n9, 51, 58, 69n19, 89
Bathsheba, 67
Beck, John, 83
behavior, character's, 70–71
Berlin, Adele, 55, 69–70, 90, 227
Biblical Preaching (Robinson), 12, 93

246

Subject Index

biblical theology, 109–10
big idea, the
  components of, 90–93
  and the depravity factor, 96
  developing, 93–94
  examples of, 96–104, 144–45
  in Genesis 13, 124
  in Judges 17–18, 189–90
  nailing down, 94–96
  packaging, 121–24
  and the purpose statement, 125
  quest for, 36–37
  and vision of God, a passage's, 95–96
Block, Daniel, 35, 224, 225
Boaz, 72
Book of God, The (Wangerin), 152–53
Borden, Paul, 94–95, 98, 132–33, 169, 174
Buechner, Frederick, 153
Buttrick, David, 140
Buttry, Daniel, 167

Calvin, John, 19, 20
captioned survey form, 11–12
Carson, D. A., 25–26, 26n63, 109
Chapell, Bryan, 5, 22, 137–38
character (ACTS)
  about, 65, 88
  behavior, 70–71
  and characterization, 68–69
  classifying, 66–68
  description, 69–70
  designations, 72–73
  names, 71–72
chiasmus, 59–61, 62
Chilion, 72
Chisholm, Robert, 82–83, 103, 225
Christiconic approach, 20
Christocentric view, 16, 19–23, 25
Christotelic view, 23. *See also* theocentric-Christocentric view
Chronicles commentaries, 226
Cinderella motif, 47
cold open, 166–67
Coles, Robert, 36
colloquial language, 154

comedy, 46, 47
commentaries and scholarly works, 87–90, 221–22
  Chronicles, 226
  Deuteronomy, 224
  Esther, 227
  Exodus, 223
  Ezra-Nehemiah, 226–27
  Genesis, 222–23
  Joshua, 224
  Judges, 224–25
  Kings, 226
  Leviticus, 223
  Numbers, 223–24
  Ruth, 225
  Samuel, 225–26
complement (big idea), 92–93
complication (plot), 43–44
concision, 157
conclusion (denouement)
  of a sermon, 168–70
  of a story, 45–46
concrete language, 155
conflict (plot), 43–44
contrast, 21
contrastive dialogue, 78
costuming, 173–74
Craddock, Fred, 10–11, 176–77
crime-and-punishment motif, 47
crisis (plot), 43–44, 63
Culley, Robert, 48, 49

David, 51, 57–59, 66–67, 76–77, 79–80, 83–84, 94–95, 96–99, 102–4, 110
  and John Hercus, books by, 151
deadeners, 157–58
death-rebirth motif, 47
Deborah, 71, 117
deconstruction, 32
deductive preaching, 128
Denver Journal, 221
depravity factor, 96, 116
Derrida, Jacques, 32
designations (characterization), 72–73
Deuel, David C., 9, 128

Deuteronomy commentaries, 224
dialogue, 75–78
Dickson, Charles, 8
description, 69–70
discourse analysis, 90, 195–97, 203–5
Dorsey, David A., 60, 61
dramatic irony, 57–58
dramatic monologue, 135
dress and props, 173–74
Dryden, J. De Waal, 8
Dutch Reformed church, 15–16

Ehud, 70, 116, 116n20
elder-serving-the-younger motif, 49
Elijah, 16, 17, 83
Elimelech, 71, 83
Er, 79
Esau, 70, 76, 78
Esther, 43, 44, 45, 46
Esther commentaries, 227
ethical thrust, 118
Evans, Mary, 35, 78, 117n22, 224
examples, New Testament's use of, 17
exegetical idea
  about, 94–96
  and application, 113–19
  and the Bible's storyline, 108–11
  and explanation, 111–12
  in Genesis 13, 124
  and the theological idea, moving to, 96–104
  and validation, 112–13
exegetical lecture, 6–7, 162–63
exegetical outline, 61–64
exegetical strategy
  and the ACTS process, 37–39, 41, 88
  and the big idea, 36–37, 90–104
  in dialogue, 77
  in Old Testament narratives, 32–34
  and the prophetic message, 34–36
exemplary approach, 16, 17, 18
exhortation, 19–20
Exodus commentaries, 223
explanation, in sermons, 111–12
explanatory images, 159–60

exposition, 42–43
expository preaching
  about, 5–7
  and homiletical method, 10–11
external focalization, 55–57
eye contact, 176–77
Ezekiel, 135
Ezra-Nehemiah commentaries, 226–27

factual information, 162–63
fall, the, 22
Fewell, Danna Nolan, 32, 50
Fields, Weston W., 48
first-person narratives, 134–36, 167–70
Flames of Rome, The (Maier), 150
flashback approach, 133, 166–67
focalization, 55–57
foils, 66
Fokkelman, J. P., 33, 51, 60, 62, 89, 103–4
Former Prophets, 35
Franklin, Jon, 138, 139–40, 155

Gehazi, 59
Genesis commentaries, 222–23
genre, 31
gestures, in sermons, 176
God Is God (Hercus), 151–52
gospel glasses, 22
Greidanus, Sidney, 7, 15–16, 17–18, 20–22, 128
Gunn, David M., 32, 50

Hagar, 73
Hall, Oakley, 158
Hannah, 70–71, 78
happiologists, 10
Harvey, Paul, 130–31, 169
heart, engaging the, 7
Heath, Chip and Dan, 121
Hebrew, 13, 90
  clause taxonomy, 197
  data, using the, 205–19
  direct speech, 201–3
  discourse analysis, 195–97, 203–5

Subject Index

discourse layout, 207–19
discourse markers, 204–5
getting up to speed, 194–95
marked text, 203–4
in narrative exegesis, 193–94
verbal forms and narrative sequence, 197–203
verb form identification, 206–7
Hebrew Bible, The (Alter), 222
Hercus, John, 151–52
heroic narrative, 47, 68
historical books, 34–35
historical-cultural research, 154–55
historical-cultural setting, 82–83
historiography, 9
Hoekstra, T., 17
Holland, 15–16
homiletical idea, 94

idea, big. *See* big idea, the
idolatry, 101, 118–19, 124
idols, 85
illusory conclusion, 44n9
illustrations, 7, 161–62, 189
images, in sermons, 159–61, 189
indicative-imperative structure, 20
inductive-deductive approach, 133–34
inductive preaching, 128–33, 189–90
initiation, 47
internal focalization, 55–57
introduction, sermon, 165–68
irony, 57–59, 71–72
Isaac, 54, 72, 77, 79
Ishmael, 73
It's All in How You Tell It (Robinson and Robinson), 179

Jacob, 70, 78
Jael, 71, 117
Jensen, Richard, 33
Jeremiah, 135
Jericho, 50–51
Jesus
 as fulfillment, 23
 pointing to, 24

Jordan River, 154–55
Joseph, 70, 84
Joshua commentaries, 224
journey motif, 47
Judah, 43, 44, 45, 49, 53–54, 67, 77, 79, 84
Judges 17–18, sample sermon, 179–91
Judges commentaries, 224–25

Keller, Tim, 6, 7, 23, 24
key word, 51
Kim, Matthew, 39–40, 119
Kings commentaries, 226
Kort, Wesley, 7–8, 34
Kruger, Michael, 26
Kuruvilla, Abraham, 20, 24

Lane, William, 40
Langley, Kenneth, 19–20
Latter Prophets, 35
Leap over a Wall (Peterson), 153–54, 225
Leviticus commentaries, 223
Lewis, C. S., 112
life change, 20
literary setting, 83–85
Literary Structure of the Old Testament, The (Dorsey), 61
longitudinal themes, 21
Lot, 31
Lowry, Eugene L., 131n8
Luther, Martin, 19, 20

Mackie, Tim, 61
Mahlon, 72
Maier, Paul, 150
manuscripts, sermon, 147–48
Marcionites, 10
Mattingly, Terry, 4
Mawhinney, Bruce, 39
Mayhue, Richard, 6, 7
McDougall, Donald, 139
meaning. *See* exegetical strategy
Micah, 43, 44, 45, 62–64, 70, 101, 131
Michener, James, 150–51, 160
Miller, Cynthia, 76

Mimesis (Auerbach), 36
minor characters, 66–67
Moab, 83
Models for Biblical Preaching (Robinson and Batten), 179
Modern Preacher and the Ancient Text, The (Greidanus), 18, 61
modifiers, 155–57
monologue, 168
moral principles, 36
motifs, 46, 47
movement
  during sermon, 174–75
  from ignorance to epiphany, 47

Nabal, 83–84
names, 71–72
Naomi, 72
narrated time, 52–54, 69n19
narration time, 52–54, 69n19
narrative
  importance of, 7–8
  meaning in, 32–34, 36–37
  and story form (sermon), 128
  subtlety of, 8
Narrative Art in the Bible (Bar-Efrat), 89
Narrative in the Hebrew Bible (Gunn and Fewell), 89, 90
narrator, 78–80
New Atheists, 10
New Testament, 21
nominal verbless clauses (Hebrew), 199–200
notes, sermon, 171–73
Numbers commentaries, 223–24

Old Testament
  and stories, 3–5
  in the New Testament, 21
  scope and length of, 10
Old Testament Commentary Survey (Longman), 221
Old Testament Is Dying, The (Strawn), 10
Old Testament Narrative, (Walsh), 89, 90
omniscience, 78–80
Onan, 79

O'Neill, Lucas, 25, 131
oral tradition, 50n30
"Our Fathers Have Told Us" (Ska), 89, 90
outlines
  exegetical, 61–64, 141–42
  sermon
    about, 137–38
    preparing, 141–45
    tips for, 138–41

pace of plot, 52–54
parallelism, 11
Parker, Simon B., 34, 46–47
passive voice, 157–58
pathetic plot, 47
Patrick, Dale, 33
pausing, 177
Peculiar Treasures (Buechner), 153
Peninnah, 70–71
Pentateuch, 35
persons, 31
persuasion, 7, 9
Peterson, Eugene, 8, 150, 153–54, 225
petitionary narratives, 46, 47–48
place, 31
plot
  motifs, 46–48
  shape of, 42–46
Poetics and Interpretation of Biblical Narrative (Berlin), 89, 90
Poetics of Biblical Narrative, The (Sternberg), 89, 90
point of view, 55–59
Pontius Pilate (Maier), 150
Potiphar, 84
pragmatics, 118
prayer, primacy of, 39–40
Preaching Christ from the Old Testament (Greidanus), 18
preaching idea, 94, 122–23
  in Genesis 13, 124
Preaching with Cultural Intelligence (Kim), 119
Preaching with Freshness (Mawhinney), 39
principles, lists of, 127–28

Subject Index

prohibition sequences, 49
promise fulfillment, 21
props, 173–74
prosperity gospel, 10
protagonists, 66
Provan, Iain, 9, 226
punishment sequences, 49
punitive plot, 47
purpose statement, 125–26

quest motif, 47
quotations, 162

rags-to-riches motif, 47
Reading Biblical Narrative (Fokkelman), 89
reasoning, inductive and deductive, 128–29
redemption, 22, 110
redemptive-historical approach, 16–17, 18. *See also* Christocentric view
redemptive-historical progression, 21
Reed, Rick, 39
rehearsal, 173
renominalizing, 51
repetition, 50–52
rescue motif, 47, 49
research, historical-cultural, 154–55
resolution, 44–45, 63–64
revelation story, 47
reward sequences, 49
Robinson, Haddon, 4, 5, 8, 12, 13, 30–31, 37, 93–94, 112, 137, 140, 147–48, 174
Ruth commentaries, 225
Ryken, Leland, 46, 47, 48, 67–68

Sailhamer, John, 34
Samuel commentaries, 225–26
Sarah, 72, 73
Saul, 84
Scult, Allen, 33
semantics, 118
semi-inductive approach, 134
sermon delivery
  dress and props, 173–74
  notes, 171–73
  on a stage, 174–75
  and voice, 175–77
sermon development
  about, 107–8
  and application, 136
  of conclusion, 168–70
  and factual information, 162–63
  and first-person narratives, 134–36
  flashback approach to, 133
  and illustrations, 161–62
  and images, 159–61
  inductive-deductive approach to, 133–34
  and inductive preaching, 128–33
  of introduction, 165–68
  Lowry's stages for, 131n8
  manuscript preparation, 147–48
  and outlining, 137–45
  and purpose, 125–26
  and quotations, 162
  Robinson's stages of, 12, 13
  semi-inductive approach to, 134
  and shaping, 127–28
  and storytelling, 148–59
  See also ACTS exegetical process; big idea, the
sermon sample, 179–91
  afterword, 188–90
  conclusion, 186–88, 190
  foreword to, 179–80
  introduction, 180–81, 188
  manuscript of, 180–88
  outline, 190–91
setting (ACTS)
  about, 81–82, 88
  historical-cultural, 82–83
  literary, 83–85
showing, 158–59
silence, 177
Simmons, Annette, 177
Sisera, 71
situational irony, 58, 59
Ska, Jean Louis, 38, 43, 44–45, 57–58, 71, 78, 90
Sola Scriptura (Greidanus), 16
Solomon, 83

Source, The (Michener), 150–51
specificity, 155
speech. *See* talking (ACTS)
Sproul, R. C., 4, 25–26, 26n63
Spurgeon, Charles Haddon, 21
stage, and the sermon, 174–75
Stanley, Andy, 9–10
Stedman, Ray, 174
Stek, John, 71
Sternberg, Meir, 34, 70, 90, 148
stories, 3–5, 7–10
  of military campaigns, 46–47
  of miraculous deliverance from a siege, 47
storyline, the Bible's, 108–11
storytelling, in sermons
  about, 148–50
  and creative descriptions, 150–54
  and historical-cultural research, 154–55
  and style conventions, 155–59
Strawn, Brent, 10
Streefkerk, N., 16
style conventions, 155–59
subject (big idea), 91–92
suffering-servant motif, 47
Sunukjian, Don, 128, 167–68, 174

talking (ACTS)
  dialogue, 75–78
  omniscience of narrator, 78–80
  summary, 88
Tamar, 43, 44, 45, 49, 53–54, 67, 77, 79, 84
temptation, the, 47
tension (plot), 43–44, 131–33
text selection, 29–32
theocentric-Christocentric view, 23–26
theocentric view, 19–20, 24–25
theological idea
  about, 94–96
  and the Bible's storyline, 108–11
  and exegetical idea, moving to, 96–104
  in Genesis 13, 124

third-person narration, 55
time and pace (plot), 31, 52–54, 69n19
timing, 177
Torah, 35
tragedy (motif), 46, 47
Trinity, and preaching, 20
type scenes, 46, 48–49
typology, 21

units of thought, 30–31
Uriah, 58–59, 67, 76–77, 79–80

Vanhoozer, Kevin, 25, 32
verbal irony, 57–58
vision of God in a passage, 95–96, 116
voice projection and sermon delivery, 175–77

Walsh, Jerome T., 90
Walton, Benjamin, 97, 99
Walton, John, 23, 109n8
Wangerin, Walter, Jr., 152–53
Wardlaw, Don, 10
war of destruction, 85
wayehi (Hebrew), 201
wayyiqtol verbs (Hebrew), 198
Wenham, Gordon J., 35, 222, 223
Wenig, Scott, 97, 99
weqatal verb forms (Hebrew), 200
"Why It Pays to Avoid Idolatry" (sermon, Mathewson), 179–91
Wiersbe, Warren, 12, 138
wisdom agendas, 8
Wolterstorff, Nicholas, 32, 34
Wright, Christopher, 23–24
Wright, N. T., 8, 109

x + *qatal* (Hebrew), 199

zero focalization, 56–57